VLADIMIR DE PACHMANN

Vladimir de Pachmann

A Piano Virtuoso's Life and Art

MARK MITCHELL

INDIANA
University Press

Bloomington & Indianapolis

This book is a publication of

Indiana University Press
601 North Morton Street
Bloomington, IN 47404-3797 USA

http://iupress.indiana.edu

Telephone orders   800-842-6796
Fax orders   812-855-7931
Orders by e-mail   iuporder@indiana.edu

MANUFACTURED IN THE UNITED STATES OF AMERICA

Library of Congress Cataloging-in-Publication Data

Mitchell, Mark (Mark Lindsey)
Vladimir de Pachmann : a piano virtuoso's life and art / Mark Mitchell
p. cm.
Includes discography (p.).
Includes bibliographical references (p.) and index.
ISBN 0-253-34169-8 (alk. paper)
1. Pachmann, Vladimir de, 1848–1933. 2. Pianists—Biography. I. Title.
ML417.P17 M58 2002
786.2'092—dc21

2002004040

1   2   3   4   5   07   06   05   04   03   02

For
Dad, Graham, and Larry

Dana Gioia, "An Elegy for Vladimir de Pachmann"
—*Odessa, 1848–Rome, 1933*

"How absurd," cried the pianist de Pachmann to reporters from the *Minneapolis Dispatch*,
   "that
my talents or the talents of a Liszt were confined to so small a planet as the earth. How much
more we could have done given the dimensions of a fixed star." He began a prelude quietly,
   then
stopped. "Once Chopin could play this well. Now only me."

When he brought his socks into the concert hall and dedicated that night's music to them, or
relearned his repertoire at sixty-nine using only the fourth and fifth fingers of one hand, the
critics thought his madness was theatrical, but the less learned members of his audience, to
whom he talked while playing, knew the truth.

Porters and impresarios told of coming on him, alone in a hotel suite, his back curved like a
monkey's, dancing and screeching in front of a dressing mirror, or giving concerts for the velvet
furniture in his room, knocking it together afterwards for applause. "Dear Friends," he
   whispered
to it, "such love deserves an encore."

Now relegated to three short paragraphs in *Grove's Dictionary of Music* and one out-of-stock
recording of Chopin, he reappears only by schedule in a few selections broadcast on his
   birthday,
music produced by rolls on a mechanical piano where no fingers touch the keys as each piece
goes to its predictable finale.

CONTENTS

ILLUSTRATIONS

ACKNOWLEDGMENTS

For their help in the researching and writing of this book, I would like to thank the following: E. Carl Abbott, Caine Alder, Klaus-Peter Altekruse (Secretariat Pierre Boulez, IRCAM), Marco Anelli, Jeffrey Ankrom, Jin Auh (Wylie Agency), Kevin Bazzana, Gregor Benko, Kathleen M. van Bergen (St. Louis Symphony Orchestra), Barbara Berliner (New York Public Library), Michael Carroll, Steve Cork (British Library), Paul Cox (National Portrait Gallery, London), Brian Dean, David Dubal, Robert Dumm, Christopher Fifield, Gino Francesconi (Carnegie Hall Archives), Dr. Ingrid Fuchs (Gesellschaft der Musikfreunde, Vienna), Dana Gioia, Richard Glasser (Chicago Police Department), Gary Graffman, Jake Harris, Michael Hofmann, Stephen Hough, Allan Clive Jones, Frances and Howard Kiernan, James Kilvington (National Portrait Gallery), Kevin LaVine (Library of Congress, Washington, D.C.), Ellen K. Lee (corresponding secretary, Helena Modjeska Foundation), Annick Legros (Editions Durand, Paris), Francesco Libetta, Jean Lipman-Blumen, Claudia Locatelli, Donald Manildi (International Piano Archives at Maryland), Yve Menzies, Diane Mitchell, Bryce Morrison, William Murray, Ivan Nabokov, Nigel Nettheim, Elaine Durham Otto, Davide Pallottelli, Sergio Pallottelli, Terence Pepper (National Portrait Gallery), Barbara Perkel (Boston Symphony Orchestra), Sam Perryman (Library of Congress), David Plotkin (Corbis), Janet Rabinowitch (Indiana University Press), Joseph Rezits (professor emeritus, Indiana University School of Music), Charles Rosen, Charlene Ryan, Gayle Sherwood (Indiana University Press), Josef Škvorecký, Henry Z. Steinway, Edith Templeton, Michel Tournier, Frank Villella (Chicago Symphony Orchestra), James D. Walbert, Alan Walker, Rich Wandel (New York Philharmonic), Carol Lynn Ward-Bamford (Library of Congress), Edmund White, and Heide Winwood (Bösendorfer, Vienna). Thanks are due also to the numerous respondents to my author's queries in *Gramophone,* the *New York Review of Books,* and the *New York Times Book Review,* for providing encouragement and leads.

Lastly, I owe a special debt of gratitude to four friends whose assistance went far beyond the call of duty; indeed, it is hard to imagine that the book could have been written without them: Colin Armfield, Allan Evans, Steven Heliotes, and David Leavitt.

VLADIMIR DE PACHMANN

Introduction:
A Citizen of the World

ethos anthropoi daimon
—Heraclitus (fragment 54)

At the end of 1899, a young journalist named Willa Cather attended a recital, in Pittsburgh, by the pianist Vladimir de Pachmann. With her was an unnamed Pachmann pupil who, before the concert began, gave the future novelist some idea of what to expect:

> "But then," remarked the Pachmann pupil, "he is vain of everything; he is the vainest man I ever knew, and when I was with him I was almost as vain of him as he was of himself. One falls under the enchantment of the man, and Pachmannism becomes a mystic cult, an intellectual religion, a new sort of theosophy. His pupils usually copy his walk, his gestures. I think I used even to wish I had his nose and his little slits of Tartar eyes. But listen!"

Cather listened. Pachmann began, she wrote in a review published in the *Courier* (30 December), with Weber's sonata in A-flat—"wishing, I suppose, to give a certificate of his general musicianship and his complete dominion over his instrument before he began to 'specialize.'" He then moved on to Chopin. "He does not deign to play a number as you have heard it before," Cather observed. "He has a technique full of tricks and wonderful feats of skill, full of tantalizing pauses and willful subordinations and smothered notes cut short so suddenly that he seems to have drawn them back into his fingers again." By the time Pachmann had arrived at the third prelude, Cather's companion, the former pupil, had "utterly collapsed" and was murmuring, "The tone—the singing tone!" No one else had ever been able to produce a tone like that, he assured her. Then he told "a funny story of this quaint Russian egotist."

> When he was in Pittsburgh on his last American tour, he was playing the Chopin Valse Brilliante, opus 34, to a crowd of musicians in a wholesale

music store here. He played even better than usual, and when he had finished, he looked up and said with a sigh and a gesture of ineffable regret, "Ah, who will play like that when Pachmann is no more!" There were actually tears in his eyes, for he was overcome with the sense of the great loss which the world must someday suffer.

If this anecdote tells us anything, it is that Vladimir de Pachmann moved himself as much as his admirers. Excessive self-praise had always been an important facet of his comedy, just as comedy, even vaudeville, had always been an important facet of his concerts. At a Pachmann recital, in addition to a swoon-inducing performance of the third prelude of Chopin, you might find yourself witnessing the sort of scene that W. N. P. Barbellion described in *The Journal of a Disappointed Man:*

> As usual [Pachmann] kept us waiting for 10 minutes. Then a short, fat, middle-aged man strolled casually on to the platform and everyone clapped violently—so it was Pachmann. . . . He beamed on us and then shrugged his shoulders and went on shrugging them until his eye caught the music stool, which seemed to fill him with amazement. He stalked it carefully, held out one hand to it caressingly, and finding all was well, went two steps backwards, clasping his hands before him and always gazing at the little stool in mute admiration, his eyes sparkling with pleasure, like Mr. Pickwick's on the discovery of the archæological treasure.[1] He approached once more, bent down and ever so gently moved it about 7/8ths of an inch nearer the piano. He then gave it a final pat with his right hand and sat down.[2] (234–35)

At a Pachmann recital, you might see the pianist pantomime. If it was summer, he would pretend to mop his brow; if it was winter, he would shake his fingers to suggest that they were too cold to allow him to play. "Bravo, de Pachmann," or "C'est joli," he would say if his playing pleased him; "Cochonnerie, cochonnerie!" if he felt that he had "played like a pig." (On those occasions when he hit a false note, he would say that it was the piano's fault.) He often apostrophized his audience, greeting members whose faces he recognized or reading his mail aloud. "When some ladies at one of his concerts in London ostentatiously followed his performance with the score," one journalist wrote, "he stopped playing and shouted into the hall with frigid politeness: 'Will the ladies in the fourth row stop turning the pages of their music books? They brought the music to see if I will make any mistakes, but I make no mistakes, I am Pachmann.' He then added: 'In any case, the ladies have the wrong edition, I play from a different one.'" (As in the *Inferno,* they read no more that day.) Once in Milwaukee, when a man in the audience whispered to his wife, "Isn't it beautiful?"

Pachmann stopped playing and admonished, "If you can't be quiet, get out!" On another occasion, the presence of a woman in the front row cooling herself with an enormous fan drove him to distraction. "Madame, I am playing in 3/4," he is to have said, "and you are fanning in 6/8!"

The object of his running commentary was not always to amuse, however. He also tried to educate his audience about the music he was playing by describing the technical construction of a piece, or the significance of a figuration, even as he performed it. Because he customarily delivered his remarks in a patois of European languages, this commentary often went over the heads to which it was directed. Nor did he disdain poetic imagery if he thought this might help to evoke a composition for his listeners. As he concluded Schumann's *Prophet Bird,* a favorite encore, he would lift his hand into the air and say, "Ze bird has flied away." Or he would say as he played Weber's *Perpetuum mobile:* "Imagine a necklace of diamonds, glistening like water in the sunlight. I cut the golden string. See the diamonds fall— showers of them; they dazzle the eyes." According to a column called "Mephisto's Musings" (*Musical America,* 20 April 1912), "He lectured to them while he played, ordered one latecomer to 'sit down' in so peremptory a fashion that the unfortunate woman almost sank through the floor in her embarrassment, told about the way in which Weber wore his hair, and explained just why certain passages in Chopin were hard to perform." By calling attention to "beautiful passages," a Boston critic noted in 1923, Pachmann "creates an atmosphere of intimacy which very few artists ever achieve in a large concert room." The exigencies of being a "concert pianist" obliged him to play in "large concert rooms," of course, but his ideal was the Schubertiade.

Encores were central to his programs. One anecdote shows his masterful ability to "work" his public. After playing a Chopin recital at the Berlin Singakademie (destroyed during the Second World War), he acquitted himself of about fifteen encores. At the back of the stage were about this number of rows of steps where a chorus could be deployed. Upon concluding each encore, Pachmann would walk up to the corresponding step and wave an immaculate handkerchief at the audience, who caught on to the game and did their part to see him attain the top step.[3] On other occasions, having played a complement of encores, Pachmann would wave a handkerchief at the audience to indicate that he was taking his leave of it. "If any one else did this," J. Cuthbert Hadden wrote in *Modern Musicians,* "it would be ridiculous. Done by Pachmann, it was most graceful."

There was sometimes a touch of the séance to his concerts. Playing Chopin, he might gaze into the ether, then whisper, "Did you see? Did you see? Chopin was here." The intensity of his pianissimo, which came to be called a "Pachmannissimo," often drove his audiences into a state of anxiety that would release itself, at the recital's conclusion, as urgent applause. Then his fans would line up backstage for his autograph. He called them his "friends," and as with his real friends, he often tested them. Indiscriminate applause enraged him. If they clapped for what he considered a cochonnerie or before he came to the end of a piece, he would chastise them for being ignorant. By the same token, if someone he was close to criticized him even slightly, he would feel that he had been betrayed and go on the defensive. "Of all artists," the recording engineer Fred Gaisberg wrote in *The Music Goes Round,* "Pachmann had the greatest need of an audience to inspire him" (193).

What his listeners took from him depended on what they wanted from him. In Chicago, a female admirer might present him with the gloves she had split by applauding too loudly; in London, a would-be aesthete, at concert's end, might wax about the morbidity of his Chopin; in New York, a dry wit might see in his onstage behavior the starting point for a humorous essay. For Pachmann, the line between public and private was far less distinct than it is for most people. Thus he could behave onstage as if he were in his bedroom, and just as easily in his bedroom as if he were onstage. As a result he made good copy for journalists eager to record his latest antic, yet he left almost nothing in the way of a record of a personal life: no diaries, no journals, no date books, a handful of letters; less than a paucity of the very documents upon which biographers customarily rely. What we have is a superabundance of reviews, profiles, recollections, responses, and anecdotes, nearly all of them with variants, from which to tease out the shape and substance of his life. Pachmann himself left a key when he wrote, "When people laugh, they become more human."[4] That he survives for us at all is thanks entirely to his recordings and to the hundreds of men and women who wrote down their impressions of him, and if I often quote from their observations extensively, it is because paraphrase robs such documents of their most crucial quality—voice.

Of all the pianists of the generation born between 1840 and 1860, Pachmann has experienced the most precipitous decline in posthumous reputation. Yet during his years before the public (1882–1929), he was often regarded as one of the four or five greatest pianists in the world, and—thanks in part to his studies with Vera Kologrivoff Rubio, Chopin's last assistant—as *the* greatest exponent of the music of Chopin. Indeed, in the scene in Max Beerbohm's novel *Zuleika Dobson* where the shades of Chopin and George Sand listen in on a performance of Chopin's *Funeral March,* Chopin describes the playing as "Plus fin que Pachmann!" (99) then waves his arms wildly and dances à la Pachmann. Pachmann also attracted the notice of Cather, Raymond Chandler (who wrote in a letter to Hardwick Moseley that he thought the Chopin *Barcarolle* "[was] never played really well since de Pachmann"), Israfel, Vladimir Nabokov,[5] the poet and essayist Arthur Symons, and Alice B. Toklas. The obituary of the pianist from the *Times* (9 January 1933) read, in part:

> While Pachmann's reputation was one of extravagance, the artist had a passion for economy. There must be nothing wasted in piano-playing. Latterly the eccentrician might often obliterate the artist, perhaps through three-quarters or more of a recital programme. The careful listener and watcher would, however, be rewarded by a few moments, perhaps a single *étude* or prelude of Chopin, which could only be described by the word *perfect*. Ten minutes of such playing of Chopin, in which everything needful to be said was said through a touch on the keys of pearl-like smoothness, a control which was without a hint of strain, a naturalness in expression which made all the intellectualists seem mere fumblers—this was the reward of the patient listener and the revelation of the supreme artist in Pachmann.

If Pachmann is remembered today, it is typically as what critic James Gibbons Huneker called "Chopinzee"—the pianist being, like Chopin himself (Felix Mendelssohn called him "Chopinetto"), a small man, as well as famous for his "monkeyshines." He was labeled a clown for all this, but in fact the clown may be a sincere artist: one remembers Buster Keaton, Grock,[6] Victor Borge,[7] and Chico Marx.[8] (Marx's one-finger piano playing in *A Night at the Opera* suggests that he would have had no difficulty playing the pizzicato from Delibes's *Sylvie*.) Comic genius and musicianship are not, a priori, at odds. Chopin himself was, by all accounts, a superb mimic and caricaturist, as Liszt and others found out, sometimes to their discomfort. After improvising for his friends for an hour or two, Henry Finck writes in an essay on the composer, Chopin "would suddenly rouse them from their reveries by a *glissando*—sliding his fingers from one end of the keyboard to the other" (53).

Nor was Pachmann the only pianist of his day to have behaved unusually in concert.[9] There was Liszt's Hungarian pupil Jószef Weisz, of whom Alma Mahler wrote in a passage quoted by Zoltan Roman in *Gustav Mahler's American Years:* "[He] had a square, bald skull, with the merest tuft in the middle, and brown eyes wedged in slits, which could only mean either insanity or genius. He was the greatest pianist Mahler, according to his own account, had ever heard" (336). Alfredo Casella wrote in *Music in My Time*, "Because of his continual jests, his assurance, and his mania for talking to the public, [Francis Planté] somewhat resembled Vladimir de Pachmann, and like him, excelled in the miniature" (64). What distinguished Pachmann was that, in the view of a Boston critic, "Usually the quality of [his] playing rises in proportion to his display of his 'eccentricities'" (*Boston Transcript*, 11 December 1911).

Pachmann's remarkable force of personality, his magnetism and charm, do not by themselves explain the extraordinary esteem in which other musicians held him, however. Through his playing he seduced his "intellectual" colleagues—Wilhelm Backhaus and Casella as well as Ferruccio Busoni and Leopold Godowsky—no less than those who, one might say, thought with their hearts and felt with their minds—as did Pachmann himself. That is to say, Pachmann did not play as if the musical argument precluded the wooing of the instrument. A critic for the *Chicago Morning News* (26 November 1890) praised him for beginning Chopin's *Berceuse* "in the usual tone and gradually hushing it to sleep—a decidedly captivating maneuver in the presentation of the time-honored lullaby." Edward Steuermann (*The Not Quite Innocent Bystander*) wrote:

> I confess that years ago hearing the old Chopin interpreter de Pachmann made a strong impression on me; the manner in which he never departed from the basic mood, passing subtly over phrases which today have become lachrymose and hypersensitive, and permitting them to remain no more than premonitions, all this appeared to me to be compositionally more appropriate to this work. The lesson: with all clarity of detail the basic concept must not be destroyed. Despite the intoxication of color which our modern nerves long for, one must remember that it is for the most part one voice, in this art, which speaks to us, no, sings to us; the voice must not stray so far that from a lyric poem comes forth a drama. (122–23)

Arthur Symons had hymned this same quality in Pachmann's playing half a century earlier in the *Saturday Review* (11 July 1908): "The pianoforte was once a ship with sails, beautiful in the wind; it is now a steamer, with loud propellers and blinding smoke. And it is not only the Busonis and the Mark Hambourgs who sacrifice beauty to noise, but every great executant, with the single exception of Pachmann."

Although he never wanted for detractors, more pianists (and musicians generally) appreciated Pachmann than were appreciated by him. After Liszt, Godowsky alone was a god to him. Although his actual judgments varied according to the extent that he wished to be politic, he generally felt that Busoni was "Too hard. Too cold. Too heavy." Teresa Carreño "plays like a man, when she plays in the manner that she knows is right; but she does not always do that"; Eugen D'Albert (Carreño's third husband) was a good pianist "at one time"; Wanda Landowska was splendid, even though he thought it a pity that she played "that guitar"—that is, her Pleyel harpsichord—instead of a good piano; Planté was overrated; Edouard Risler without sufficient grace and poetry; Clara Schumann—whom he heard play her husband's music—"awful!" His attitude toward Paderewski was charged with ambivalence. He was more inclined to be generous to younger pianists—to Walter Gieseking (for his pianissimi), or to the young Jose Iturbi (for his Mozart playing)—although these younger colleagues were not always grateful for his patronage. On 20 January 1891, Louise Wolff, wife of the Berlin impresario Hermann Wolff, noted in her diary a meeting between Pachmann and the child prodigy Josef Hofmann, later quoted by her daughter, Edith Stargardt-Wolff.

> After lunch, Josef was called upon to play for the great Vladimir, I think it was Rameau's "Variations." Pachmann was very surprised by the boy's "good fingering," and agreed to play to him in return, first some Chopin, then Mendelssohn's "Rondo capriccioso," prestissimo, and with all the finesse and charm of which he is capable. Whereupon our little Josef seats himself with utter self-possession at the piano, says: "Moi, je joue ça comme ça" and plays the same piece just as fast, possibly with a little less subtlety, but still with astonishing command. We were all dumbstruck, especially Pachmann. At first, he may even have felt a tad envious, and gave the boy a little lecture on some points of his interpretation, which the rascal listened to respectfully enough, only to tell us, quite calmly, when he joined us later: "Je le trouve mieux comme moi je le joue, c'est plus expressif." (47)

Still, even with his juniors, Pachmann could be remarkably ungenerous. Carleton Smith offers two illustrations of this in "Gods of the Keyboard" (*Esquire*):

> De Pachmann frequently appeared in public with Godowsky, though he disliked being seen with any pianist. The two were eating in a continental restaurant when Ossip Gabrilowitsch approached. Mr. Godowsky said, "Of course you know Mr. Gabrilowitsch," to which de Pachmann answered, "Yes, yes, of course—the violinist." Godowsky corrected him, "Why, no! He's a pianist—you know that!"
> All the time, de Pachmann was tugging at Godowsky's coat to get his attention. When he could, he said, "Of course I know it, but I don't want him to think that I know he's a pianist!"[10]

On another occasion, Pachmann declined to accompany Godowsky to the debut of the young Backhaus at the Royal Albert Hall, explaining, "If I go I'll make him celebrated at once."
Godowsky replied, "But he's a nice looking fellow."
"Well, then, I'll take a chance," Pachmann said.

This anecdote shows, among other things, that Godowsky was aware of Pachmann's fondness for men.

A third illustration is offered by the Debussy specialist (and Carreño pupil) George Copeland in his unpublished autobiography:

> Years ago, in London, there was a young man who essayed to be a Chopin specialist, and his management thought it would be exciting and would give the young man a good deal of publicity if they could get Mr. de Pachmann to come to the debut and approve. They managed, and he went. Every time the boy played something and there was any applause, de Pachmann made himself conspicuous by raising his hands quite high over his head and applauding. This continued until the boy was getting practically an ovation, for everyone was of course following the lead of de Pachmann. At the end of the concert, as often happens, lots of the audience moved down to the stage demanding encores. De Pachmann made a frightful scene, pushing people right and left, and climbed up onto the stage and grabbed the boy. And then there was pandemonium and the boy thought he was made. Then de Pachmann turned to the audience and silenced them, and then he said to the boy, "Now, you go down and sit in one of those chairs there, and I will play your program the way it should be played!"
> He was amusing in one way, but very cruel.

While anecdotes about Pachmann's odd behavior have never wanted for telling, were it not for the revival of interest in the "golden age" of piano playing—and in Romantic music that was once anathema (Alkan, Berlioz, Liszt, Richard Strauss, Verdi)—his *artistic* legacy might well have been obscured. "The concert world of today may have lost some of the more questionable fits of caprice exhibited by the great virtuosos of the past," Kenneth Hamilton writes. "Vladimir de Pachmann's spectacular rallentando at the end of Chopin's C# minor Waltz [1907] sounds as if the audience might die of old age before he gets to the final note—but in consequence it has also made a sacrifice of interest, spontaneity, and sheer panache" (74).

When asked to choose a cherished recording from each decade of the twentieth century, two of the contributors to the *International Piano Quarterly* (Winter 2000) named ones by Pachmann: Michael Glover the aforesaid waltz; Charles Hopkins the nocturne 15/1 from 1911.[11] News to be glad of—yet what a contrast to the years when he could routinely fill the Albert Hall and provoke from critics on both sides of the Atlantic the wildest expressions of praise. As one put it, his career was a "long series of resounding triumphs won before audiences from Tiflis to Tacoma, and from Sebastopol to San Francisco."

Although Pachmann's supreme fame was as a Chopin interpreter—more specifically, as an interpreter of Chopin's smallest works—he bristled at this characterization, which he considered both limiting and inaccurate. When he did play all-Chopin recitals, at least one large work was included on the program. Yet Pachmann, like Chopin, was not one to be seduced by scale for its own sake. (It is important to note that Chopin was not *unequal* to scale; the B minor piano sonata and fourth ballade testify to this.) "The psychology of the sonata form is false," Finck writes.

> Men and women do not feel happy for ten minutes as in the opening allegro of a sonata, then melancholy for another ten minutes, as in the following adagio, then frisky, as in the scherzo, and finally, fiery and impetuous for ten minutes as in the finale. The movements of our minds are seldom so systematic as this. Sad and happy thoughts and moods chase one another incessantly and irregularly, as they do in the compositions of Chopin, which, therefore, are much truer echoes of our modern romantic feelings than the stiff and formal classical sonatas. And thus it is that Chopin's habitual neglect of the sonata form, instead of being a defect, reveals his rare artistic subtlety and grandeur. (42–43)

Nor did Pachmann subscribe to the emasculating view of the composer that Edward Blickstein (in an unpublished manuscript) and Edward Said (in "Performance as an Extreme Occasion," an essay in *Musical Elaborations*) would later put forward. Instead, he understood the compelling role of tension, occasionally even of sadism, in Chopin's music. As early as 1890, he was recognized to be "the first virtuoso of any great note to discover an unsuspected range and variety in a composer who has heretofore been given over to the tearful interpretations of pianists who believe Chopin to be a synonym for effeminacy and melancholy" (*Chicago Morning News*, 26 November). Two generations later, Sacheverell Sitwell wrote in his biography of Liszt: "In all the lesser Chopin the drawing-room atmosphere, the satin and the flounces, became too apparent when [Busoni] played. It was when Busoni played Chopin, and not when Pachmann played, that one realized the truth of Legouvé's remark that Chopin was the natural son of Weber and a Duchess" (318).

How *did* Pachmann play Chopin? In the first place, he gave evidence of a close acquaintance with the music of Chopin's idols: Bach, Scarlatti, and Mozart. Further, he was familiar with the differences among the first editions of Chopin's music (English, French, German) as well as of the variants the composer had written into the scores of his students (a few of whom—Karol Mikuli and Thomas Tellefsen among them—published their own editions of Chopin's music). That is to say, he knew of the many alternatives sanctioned by Chopin, and played them in a spirit almost of improvisation: From one to another, the notes may be different and at the same time completely faithful to the music. This is not to say that *all* of the notes Pachmann played were written by Chopin, of course. For instance, he elaborated the D-flat nocturne, in concert as well as in the recording studio. (His G & T recording of the "Minute waltz," with its interpolated scale in the right hand, is a divine illustration of where his pursuit of felicity could take him.) Nor did he always play Chopin's notes exactly as Chopin had written them; he often gave the F-sharp impromptu with a forte ending. But no pianist born in the nineteenth century played Chopin "straight." According to Joseffy, Tausig played the last rising scale of the ballade opus 23 in double thirds; Moiseiwitsch made alterations in the fourth ballade; Rachmaninov's dynamics in the *Funeral March* were not at all what Chopin indicated, nor did he refrain from touching up the waltzes; Koczalski's recording of the nocturne 9/2, based on the variants Chopin himself had penciled into Mikuli's score, showed how Mannerist the composer could be in his use of ornamentation. The editions of Alfred Cortot, Ignaz Friedman, and Arthur Friedheim were not more pure. (In the introduction to his edition of the études, Friedheim relates that when Liszt played the first of the *Trois nouvelle études,* "he usually went back from the 11th measure before the end to the corresponding place in the 22nd measure from the beginning, and repeated this entire part, bringing out the contours still more sharply and incisively.") Arguably—in fact, probably—the playing of the pianists born in the nineteenth century—also, for the most part, in the early twentieth century—is more "authentic" than that which struggles after a final text. Music, like choreography, depends upon interpretation, and Pachmann made the world hear Chopin's music in a way that no other pianist had managed: paradoxically, by making it sound as if he were not "interpreting" at all. It is, indeed, what distinguishes his playing rather than what his playing had in common with that of his compeers that is compelling. Among the Liszt pupils, Joseffy and the old Rosenthal—and to a lesser extent Sauer—perhaps came closest to him.[12] After Pachmann, Cortot's Chopin playing is hysterical (listen to the one, and then to the other, play Chopin's D-flat major waltz); Horowitz playing "L'Adieu" waltz is like a bulldozer trying to pick a daisy (as Jack Pfeiffer, his producer at RCA, once remarked to me). In the waltzes, those most elusive of Chopin's works, Pachmann, like Arrau after him, married a respect for their origins in the dance to the expression of an almost spiritual meditation upon them.

Even as Chopin was the composer with whose music Pachmann was most closely identified, however—just as Bolet was most closely associated with Liszt, Gould with Bach, Kempff and Schnabel with Beethoven, and Michelangeli with Debussy—he asserted time and again, and also proved, that his musical affinities were far more catholic. "It is curious how the audiences of various times and climes differ in their tastes and preferences," he once said (*Musician,* May 1908).

> Americans have set me down as a man who found his musical affinity in Chopin. I love him, of course, as I do all the great composers, but what would my American friends say if I told them that in Vienna I am hailed as a masterful interpreter of Beethoven; in France, as an authority on the early classics, Bach, Haydn, Scarlatti, and Mozart; and in the Scandinavian countries as a player con amore of Schubert and Schumann. But would not surprise turn to absolute amazement when I add that in my younger days I was everywhere considered an ideal exponent of Liszt, and received the most rapturous praise for my performance of such tours de force as the rhapsodies, and the Rigoletto and Don Juan fantasies?

This is an exaggeration, yet it is not false. In addition to Chopin, during his long career Pachmann played solo works by C. P. E. Bach, J. S. Bach, Barnett, Beethoven, Bülow, Brahms, Clementi, Cowen, Cramer (Aldo Mantia heard him play the first five studies in concert, in Rome), Dvořák, Field, Godard, Godowsky,[13] Grieg, Händel, Haydn, Henselt, Tom Hood, Hummel, Walter Imboden, Lamberg, Leideritz, Liszt, Mendelssohn, Moscheles, Moszkowski, Mozart, Marguerite de Pachmann, Poldini, Raff, Rubinstein, Scarlatti, Schubert, Schumann, Sgambati, Taubert, Tchaikovsky, Weber, and Van Westerhout, as well as his own transcriptions and improvisations, and transcriptions by Godowsky, Henselt, Liszt, Saint-Saëns (but nothing original by him, interestingly enough), and Tausig. Notwithstanding his reputation as a miniaturist, he also played numerous large-scale works by several of these composers: of J. S. Bach, the *Chromatic Fantasie and Fugue* and the *Italian* concerto; of Beethoven, half of the piano sonatas (opps. 53, 54, 57, 78, 101, 110, and 111 among them); of Brahms, the scherzo in E-flat minor; of Grieg, the *Ballade en forme de variations;* of Liszt, *Après une lecture de Dante,* ballade no. 2, *Harmonies du soir,* a handful of the rhapsodies, and piano sonata in B minor; of Mendelssohn, the *Fantasie* in F-sharp minor and *Variations sérieuses;* of Mozart, the piano sonata K. 331; of Schumann, *Carnaval, Davidsbündlertänze, Études symphoniques, Fantasie, Faschingsschwank aus Wien,* F-sharp minor and G minor piano sonatas, and Toccata; of Tchaikovsky, the piano sonata in G major (how marvelous the scherzo must have been!); of Weber (whom he regarded as "the healthiest of musicians"), the piano sonatas nos. 2, 3, and 4.[14]

Throughout his life Pachmann played chamber music—during the 1880s, Beethoven's "Archduke" trio with Joachim and Alfredo Piatti, and violin and piano sonatas with Madame Norman-Neruda[15]—and, of course, concertos: Beethoven's third (using Liszt's cadenzas), fourth and fifth, both of Chopin's as well as the *Andante spianato* and *Grande Polonaise* with orchestral accompaniment, Henselt's, Hummel's in B minor, Liszt's first, both of Mendelssohn's, Mozart's in A major (K. 488), C major (according to Mantia; K. 467 or 503?), and D minor (using Beethoven's cadenzas), and Rubinstein's in D minor.

That said, to feel an obligation to illustrate the range of Pachmann's musical performances is faintly embarrassing, not to say unjust. His reputation as a "miniaturist" owes to the fact that he recorded no large-scale works —nothing longer than Chopin's ballade no. 3. And yet how many pianists who recorded before 1927—the year Pachmann made his last visit to the studio—took on large-scale works? The time limit of a 78—little more than four minutes—militated against them; nor was it possible to edit them. In the event Chopin's B-flat minor piano sonata was not recorded until 1930 (by Rachmaninov), the Liszt sonata until 1932 (by Horowitz). Why, then, is Pachmann a scapegoat? He actually played more music than some of his equally illustrious colleagues; also more music than later pianists such as Arturo Benedetti Michelangeli and Martha Argerich, who has caught herself up in a neurotic double-bind: She will only record music that she has played in concert, but she will not give recitals.

Pachmann was—musically and in all other ways—a citizen of the world.[16]

ONE

Becoming de Pachmann

The year 1848 was the most tumultuous of the nineteenth century: In January, a popular rebellion in Sicily swept through the Kingdom of Naples; in February, Louis-Philippe ("The Citizen King") abdicated in France and the Second Republic was proclaimed; in March, uprisings in Vienna forced Prince Klemens von Metternich, who had helped to form the alliance that defeated Napoleon, into exile. Hungary separated from Austria (the emperor of Austria was also the Apostolic King of Hungary), three months later, the "June Days" revolt was brutally suppressed in Paris; in December, Ferdinand abdicated in Austria, to be succeeded by Franz Joseph, and Louis Napoleon was elected president of France (in 1852, he declared himself Emperor Napoleon III). And on 15 July (27 July new style), in the Black Sea city of Odessa,[1] a new subject was born to Czar Nicholas I: Vladimir Vikent'evic Pachmann, the thirteenth and final child of his parents.

That a great musician was born in this year was most apposite. "The nineteenth century is the century of the Rhapsody, as it is the century of nationalities," Vladimir Jankélévitch wrote in *Liszt: Rhapsodie et Improvisation*. "The principle of nationalities and 'the principle of the rhapsody' are almost synchronous, the one presiding over the disintegration of the Habsburg monarchy and the linguistic emancipation of subjugated nations, the other the breaking up of the monolithism of a symphonic tradition mandated since time immemorial by the Vienna Conservatory" (25). Liszt, for Jankélévitch, was the century's preeminent rhapsodist. Liszt was also to be Pachmann's pole star.

In the *Encyclopædia Britannica* of 1852, Odessa is described as "a town of European Russia, in the government of Kherson, [standing] on the northwestern shore of the Black Sea, 90 miles W.S.W. of Kherson, and 390 N. of Constantinople." Founded in 1794, the town was placed under the stewardship of the Duc de Richelieu, who oversaw its rise to prosperity. By 1804, the population had grown to 15,000, and Odessa was a thriving commercial center. According to the *Britannica*:

The town is regularly built; the streets are wide and straight; and the houses are for the most part built of stone, and two stories in height. The streets are, however, but partially paved. Odessa is defended by a strong citadel on the N.E., which has a double ditch and also several outworks; and there are batteries on the moles and on the shore between them. Among the public edifices, the most conspicuous is the cathedral, a large and elegant pile. There are a number of other churches for the Greek worship; and the Jews, Roman Catholics, and German Lutherans have their respective places of worship. A college has been established, with a museum and botanic garden. The admiralty, hospital, exchange, and theatre (where plays, in the Russian and Greek languages, and Italian operas are performed) are fine buildings. The town has several schools, a lazaretto, barracks, and the governor's house, containing the public offices. Along the quay runs a boulevard, lined with handsome houses, and adorned with a statue of Richelieu. Most of the water is brackish; and to provide the necessary element in purity, an aqueduct has been constructed at great expense, which conveys it from a distance of nearly 20 miles. The climate is healthy, though the summer is intensely hot. Winter is short, but severe, the sea being more or less frozen for about two months.

The entry goes on to describe the inhabitants of Odessa as being "of very mixed races," chiefly "Russians, Greeks, and Jews."

German handicraftsmen are also to be found amongst them in considerable numbers; whilst the more extensive mercantile houses are composed of Italians, English, French, or Armenians. In no spot perhaps in Europe are there so great a number of languages spoken as on the exchange of Odessa. The admixture of oriental dresses, manners, and languages presents a very novel and lively picture; and the bazaars contain all the productions of the East, from Persian shawls down to rose-pastilles. Pop. (1850) 71,392.

Pachmann's father, Vincent, was a professor of Roman law at the Lyceum in Odessa (there was then no university in the city) as well as a musical adept. Indeed, he was a cellist of some ability and the author of a treatise on harmony. His origins are obscure. Pachmann told Francesco Pallottelli (his manager and partner, as well as the author of a short biography of him) that his father had been born and educated in Prague of a family from Aix-la-Chapelle. The fact that he emigrated to Odessa, which was one of the few Russian cities hospitable to Jews, has also led to supposition that he was Jewish. (In 1927, Gdal Saleski included Pachmann in *Famous Musicians of a Wandering Race;* revised and republished in 1949 as *Famous Musicians of Jewish Origin.* James Gibbons Huneker wrote to Pitts Sanborn, one-time music critic of the *New York Globe,* that Pachmann's father was, in fact, a cantor.) The fact that Vincent brought up his children in the Russian Orthodox Church is not to be taken as proof that he was *not* Jewish, however. Although the post–Crimean war period during which Pachmann came of age was the period of Russia's Great (to some extent liberalizing) Reforms, Vincent was skeptical of the possibility of permanent social change, and on the resonant question of religion adhered to the Church of the state. Vincent's skepticism was to be vindicated when Alexander III ascended to the throne, for his rule was a harsh, repressive one under which Jews particularly were persecuted. Nicolas Slonimsky, a nephew of the pianist Isabelle Vengerova, told Joseph Rezits that, although his aunt was Jewish, "she had to be baptized, because at that time in the 19th century, the choice was either to adopt the orthodox religion and get all the rights (except the right to be an officer of the army) or else be confined to [the] so-called bale of residence, which meant Minsk and Odessa" (Rezits 44).

Anastasia, Pachmann's mother, apparently was a Turkish countess. At the age of six she had been taken prisoner by the Russians during their war against the Turks and, as Pallottelli writes, "received by a wealthy countess who after a time placed her in the 'Institute of Noble Ladies'" (12). It was here that she took music lessons from Vincent, whom she married when she was fourteen. (He was twenty-four.) Nine of their thirteen children, five boys and four girls, reached maturity. When Vladımır was born, Anastasia was in her mid-forties. Nonetheless, she nursed him herself—"a circumstance," Pallottelli wrote, "to which [Pachmann] has ever attributed the soundness of his constitution" (15). Although she died when Pachmann was quite young, whereupon he was cared for by Elizabeth, his favorite sister, there is no evidence to suggest that her death was hastened by financial hardship. On the contrary, the Pachmanns were sound members of the middle class in this mercantile city. Three of Vladimir's brothers were officers (not soldiers) in the army. One of them, Gregory, became violent when he drank and terrified Vladimir, who would hide under the stairs to keep out of his way. "My heart still trembles when I remember the sound of his boots on the stairs," Pachmann told Pallottelli, adding in Italian, "Paura, paura" ("Fear, fear"). His brother Simon, on the other hand, was both an intellectual and an excellent violinist who enjoyed a long and brilliant career as teacher, jurist, professor (at the university in St. Petersburg), senator of the Russian Empire, and private counselor to Alexander III—a career possible, in that time and in that place, only for a Christian. (Pallottelli noted that a famous portrait of Simon, wearing all the orders and decorations Russia could bestow, hung in Paris.)

Within the family, the name Pachmann was said to derive from that of an ancient Frankish family called "Pachomme" that had been ennobled in the reign of Charlemagne. (This name, in turn, derived from "Pachome," the founder of the first monastic rule in the Coptic language.) References to Vincent and Simon in Russian sources give their name as simply "Pachmann," however, so it is probable that the particule (sometimes "de" and sometimes "von") originated with Vladimir. The *Musical Review* (13 January 1883) noted: "As a Russian pianist [Pachmann] is no more entitled to the German than to the French prefix; but as Gospodin ["sir" or "gentleman"] is rather a mouthful, and moreover cannot properly be used by all Russian subjects, it will be preferable to speak of the artist as Mr. Pachmann."

To a man who invents himself, such details are of little account. Pachmann himself indicated as much when he said, "My father is a Rabbi, my mother a Turkey, *and I am a pianist.*"

Although from his infancy Pachmann showed a sensitivity to music, it was not until he was six that his father set him to study the violin. He progressed so swiftly that soon he was able to participate in the family's musicales: Vincent would play the cello, one of the daughters the piano, and Vladimir (and/or Simon) the violin. During the Great War, when he was giving recitals with Eugene Ysaÿe to benefit the English Red Cross, Pachmann once took up his violin (at that time a 1740 Guarneri del Gesù) and played upon it. "Beautiful instrument," he told Ysaÿe, "but no good for ze velvet fingertips."

At the age of ten, however, Pachmann manifested a preference for the piano over the violin. "In my early pianistic training," he told an interviewer from the *Étude* (December 1923), "my father was too much concerned in teaching me music to take any time with the niceties of touch or technic. Of hand position I knew nothing. My texts at the beginning were the ordinary instruction books. If I remember rightly, they were those of Müller or Adams." Further: "My father was a critic but not a pianist. He merely advised me but could not show me how. I studied everything that came my way. How long did I practice? It would be easier to find out how long I didn't. I was at work at it all the time. Good health permitted me to work enormously. I felt that either you play or you don't."

The boy studied Bach (when Vladimir turned twelve, Simon made him a birthday present of the *Well-Tempered Clavier*), Beethoven, Chopin, and "the then popular Thalberg." Pallottelli:

> One day when barely twelve whilst playing Handel's double fugue in C minor[2] [E minor—*mi minore*—in the Italian text],[3] he attracted the attention of a passing gentleman, a doct. Morgan who became interested in knowing the name of the able performer of the difficult piece, and who was greatly astonished in learning that this perfect pianist was the youthful Vladimir. At eighteen he had already given public proofs of the talented skill which had gained the universal admiration of Odessa. Many

among his chief admirers being aware of Vladimir's longing to pursue his musical studies, which the scanty resources of his father, laden with the support of a numerous family could not gratify, decided to raise a collection, to which many of the aristocracy contributed, by which means sufficient funds were raised to enable Vladimir to enter the Vienna Conservatory of Music. (16)

To repay the investment in him, Pachmann often played at the music parties of the city's aristocracy, and it was at one such party, he later claimed, that he met one Madame Slepouchkine, the memory of whom—or the myth of whom—would haunt his life. According to Pallottelli, she was "a former lady friend of [Pachmann's] sister's, married to a Russian general, a Madame Slepouchkine . . . the true personification of the spirit of contradiction" (31); of what the English call "topsy-turvydom."

> As an instance [Pachmann] affirms that on a cold day she would assert that the weather was mild and put on summer attire, whereas when it was bright and sunny she would complain of the cold and don her furs!! Again when Madame Slepouchkine was invited to dinner by Miss de Pachmann she used to try to eat her soup with a fork saying that it was delicious, and whenever after dinner Vladimir as a joke would play some light piece, she would applaud it as the wonderful work of Beethoven, but when the young artist really played some classic piece, she would not hesitate to call it a graceful waltz!
>
> De Pachmann further relates that when this extraordinary creature went to church, she would carry a pack of cards or some irreligious work instead of her missal. Again, still by his account, when he went with his sister to call on this eccentric lady she would receive them with profuse compliments, but at the same time turning towards her maid would remark: "What a bore these people are to make me waste my time!" De Pachmann adds that in spite of her eccentricities Madame Slepouchkine was highly good-natured, a circumstance to which she probably owed her distressed condition at her death.
>
> I cannot myself vouch for the actual existence of this strange being, but I can certify that whoever has known de Pachmann, even for a short time, is familiar with the name of Madame Slepouchkine, to whom he constantly refers, displaying much fervent imagination in the recital of anecdotes concerning this lady. Whenever it chances to rain he is almost invariably wont to exclaim, "If Madame Slepouchkine were here she would say that we must take advantage of the fine weather to go out." (31–32)

All of his life, whenever Pachmann was obliged to behave in a manner contrary to what he felt, he would say, "Today I am Madame Slepouchkine."

References to Madame Slepouchkine recur in the Pachmann literature. In an excerpt from his diary published in *Gramophone* (October 1943), Fred Gaisberg recalled suppers he attended after Pachmann's concerts at London's Queen's Hall: "Here the standing joke was the empty place consecrated to a mythical Madame Kaplatsky [*sic*; perhaps he was conflating her with the Theosophist Madame Blavatsky], to whom we were all formally introduced, to whom toasts were drunk and all disputes referred for 'her' decision. Whether or not she ever existed I don't know, but we got a lot of fun out of the hoax."

Because Vincent Pachmann regarded Viennese training as fundamental for a musician, he sent his son to the Hapsburg capital in 1867 to study at the Konservatorium der Gesellschaft der Musikfreunde, then located in a building known as "Zum roten Igel" ("The Red Hedgehog") at 12 Tuchlauben. (This was more or less across the street from the White Stork Pharmacy and around the corner from the famous restaurant Zum Schwarzen Kameel—The Black Camel—where Beethoven often ate.) Pachmann took lodgings with the Luksch family. At that time Vienna was being rebuilt, Emperor Franz Joseph having decreed the demolition of the old city walls and, in their place, the construction of the horseshoe-shaped Ringstrasse, lined with monumental buildings that constituted a résumé of architectural styles, among them the stock exchange, the university, the Burgtheater, the city hall, the parliament, the Imperial museums, and the opera house. (The cityscapes of Paris and Florence were also being redrawn.) This same year Johann Strauss II composed the waltz that would become the city's anthem: *An der schönen blauen Donau*. If change was the watchword of the city, however, it was not the watchword of the conservatory; for nearly a generation it had been under the directorship of Josef Hellmesberger, who was valuable to the city's musical life as both pedagogue and performing musician (outstanding violinist, founder of the Hellmesberger Quartet, and conductor). One of his protégés, Joseph Dachs—a pupil of Czerny (himself a pupil of Beethoven), Anton Halm,[4] and Simon Sechter[5]—became Pachmann's piano teacher. Dachs, who had come to the conservatory as professor in 1850, at the age of twenty-five, maintained a fine pianistic career of his own. He appeared as soloist in the Gesellschaft concerts under Herbeck, Dessoff, and Hellmesberger and was regarded as a pioneer for his performances of Schumann's music—an influence that was felt not only by Pachmann but by two of Dachs's other pupils, Anton Rubinstein and the composer Hugo Wolf.

Speaking through the persona of "Old Fogy," Huneker later wrote that he had known Pachmann "when he studied many years ago in Vienna with Dachs. This same Dachs turned out some finished pupils [in London,

Benno Schönberger, who had 'a touch of gold and a style almost as jeweled as Pachmann's—but more virile'; in Chicago, Anthony Stankowitch], though his reputation, curiously enough, never equalled that of the over-puffed Leschetizky, or [Julius] Epstein, or Anton Door,[6] all teachers in the Austrian capital" (71). Pachmann himself gave varying accounts of his audition for Dachs, in all of which the pianist is audacious, the teacher both impressed and nonplussed by him. "When I went to Dachs for my two lessons a week he assigned me two [Bach] fugues for the first one," he recalled (in 1923).

> When I came I asked what key he would like to hear them played in. He thought this was a joke and named a difficult key. But after I had played them he called in the director of the conservatory and had him listen. Then I told him that I could play any of the fugues in any key and they were both amazed. I cite this merely to show the student who is struggling along without a high-priced teacher that even the authorities of a great conservatory can be astonished by what real love for playing and hard work can produce. Of course, I played the fugues from memory. After this I played for them the Chopin Sonata in B minor and they saw that a very different course would have to be devised for me. Many of the graduates of the conservatory, with all the advantages of years of study under great experts, could not have done as much as I did virtually alone.

This (for Pachmann) measured account is from an interview on the topic "Should Piano Playing Undergo a Radical Reform?" (*Étude*, December 1923, 819–20). In fact, the story itself had undergone a number of radical reforms over the years, at the hands of both journalists and the pianist. Pachmann suggested to an interviewer from the same publication that he had memorized the *Well-Tempered Clavier* in a matter of days. "Dachs was not acquainted with my method of study," Pachmann explained. "He did not know that I had mastered the art of concentration so that I could obliterate every suggestion of any other thought from my mind except that upon which I was working" (*Étude*, October 1911, 657).

> At the following lesson I went with my book under my arm. I requested him to name a fugue. He did, and I placed the closed book on the rack before me. After I had finished playing he was dumbfounded. He said, "You come to me to take lessons. You already know the great fugues and I have taught you nothing." Thinking that I would find Chopin more difficult to memorize, he suggested that I learn two of the études. I came at the following lesson with the entire twenty-four memorized. Who could withstand the alluring charm of the Chopin études? Who could resist the temptation to learn them all when they are once commenced?

(The closed yet conspicuously displayed book is a lovely bit of scene setting. Yet it seems strange that Pachmann had not played any of Chopin's studies until then.)[7]

During the scholastic year of 1867–68, Pachmann was one of twenty-six pupils in Dachs's class. The following year he studied counterpoint with Anton Bruckner, the result of which was that Pachmann wrote a piano concerto in F minor; this has apparently been lost, and no record of its performance, even in a student concert, has been found. This was Bruckner's first year at the conservatory. For many years the organist at the Cathedral of Linz, he had been named professor in preference to Johannes Brahms, which only intensified the enmity that Brahms felt for this "poor crazy person whom the priests of St. Florian have on their consciences" (Swafford 499).

In 1869, Pachmann took part in three students' concerts: on 13 April, he played Liszt's E-flat concerto; on 24 July, a movement from Ludwig Lackner's trio for piano, violin, and cello with Wilhelm Junck (violin) and Theodor Stransky; and, four days later, Rubinstein's D minor piano concerto. Among the twenty-two pupils in Dachs's class that year, the outstanding ones were Pachmann, Julie Engel, Ernestine Goldmann, Marie Hager, Sigmund Hupka, Laura Kahrer-Rappoldi, Emilie Riegele, Emil Schwarzkopf, and Betti Tranquilini. (Arnold Bárdás, Kalliwoda, Marie Kupka, Rosa Márton, and Guido von Török were a level below them.)[8] But Pachmann learned as well from the virtuosi who played in the "Imperial City": Brahms, Josef Joachim, Hans von Bülow (Pachmann was amused by his astringent personality, but most people were not; much of his behavior was thought to be premeditated), Sophie Menter, and Anton Rubinstein.[9]

At the end of the school year, Pachmann was one of three students awarded the conservatory's silver medal (there was no gold medal); the others were Kahrer and Junck, who studied with Hellmesberger. Ere long Pachmann would discover that this medal meant very little in forming him into the artist he wished to be. He had acquired an excellent technique in Vienna but no artistic identity. Old Fogy: "So let us call Pachmann a survival of an older school, a charming school. Touch was the shibboleth of that school, not tone; and technic was often achieved at the expense of more spiritual qualities" (72). As if symbolically, the old conservatory closed in 1869.

Upon finishing his studies Pachmann returned to Odessa. During the next two years he gave lessons and played concerts there, as F. Forster Buffen wrote in *Musical Celebrities,* "under the general support of the aristocracy of that city, combined with the powerful influence of the Strogenhoff family" (56). He also gave successful performances in Kherson and Kiev, among other cities, and resolved to make his debut in St. Petersburg.

Thanks to Maximilien von Leuttenberg, whose intimate friend Pachmann had become, he presently heard Carl Tausig, Liszt's great pupil (his master described him as "all bronze and diamonds"), who was on his final tour of Russia. Tausig's playing was, in the truest and grandest sense, a revelation to Pachmann.[10] Indeed, it so overwhelmed the young pianist that he abandoned plans for a debut in St. Petersburg, choosing instead to retire for a period in order to consolidate his technique and his musical ideas. (Tausig died the following year, of typhoid fever, at thirty.)

Much speculation surrounds the next eight years (1870–78) in Pachmann's life, years during which, to all intents and purposes, he disappeared. (He told one journalist that he spent his "retirement" in a monastery, but this was probably a caprice.) "Like Wanda Landowska," Blickstein later wrote, "[Pachmann] was jealous of his own skill and eager to preserve an illusion of necromancy in his art." During his long life, he himself rarely spoke of how he worked during this period except to say he played certain pieces as many as 10,000 times. (According to Buffen, Pachmann devoted himself to the études of Tausig, Bülow, and Liszt, and to Tausig's edition of J. S. Bach's fugues.)

In 1878, Vincent Pachmann died. In a 1980 interview with Allan Evans, Aldo Mantia, a student of Pachmann's in Rome during the late 1920s, compared the pianist's feelings for his father (antipathy mingled with devotion) with those of Mozart for *his* father. Thus Pachmann could never abide the sound of the cello, his father's instrument. (When, later, his managers got hold of this intelligence, they used it to bring the pianist into line when he threatened not to play; they would tell him that a cellist was waiting to take his place.) In fact, there are several similarities between W. A. Mozart and Vladimir de Pachmann (including a scatological bent)—and no less between Leopold Mozart and Vincent Pachmann.

In the wake of his father's death, Pachmann went to Leipzig to give some recitals and to play under Carl Reinecke with the Gewandhaus orchestra. From the city of Mendelssohn, he then traveled to Berlin, where he gave a recital at the Architectural Hall that was favorably reviewed. His playing was still not what he wanted it to be, however, and he retired for two further years of study—a period during which, according to Evans, he went to Florence and worked with Vera Kologrivoff Rubio (1816–1880), who had been one of Chopin's last assistants.[11] "The preparation and style she imparted to Pachmann," Evans writes, "enabled him to return to performing" (www.arbiterrecords.com/museum/pachmann.html).

Once he emerged from this second exile, as the *Herald-Tribune* obituary of the pianist deftly put it (8 January 1933), "from that time on De Pachmann failed to find fault with De Pachmann's playing."

TWO

Building the Myth

S igns of the ambivalent attitude that Pachmann would later show toward
public performance were evident in a somewhat mythologized account
of his debut in Vienna under the sponsorship of Sophie Menter's impresario, Waldmann. According to this account, Pachmann was so apprehen-
sive about performing for an audience that he twice canceled his debut
recital, each time almost at the last minute, claiming illness. Finally, Waldmann arranged for a doctor to be present backstage. When Pachmann complained, once again, of being too unwell to perform, the doctor told him
that such a response was typical of great artists. This did the trick, and on
Monday, 16 January 1882, at 7:30 P.M., "Woldemar v. Pachmann" (note
the particule) gave a sensational concert in the Bösendorfersaal, which was
then located in the former riding school of Prince Liechtenstein, at 6 Her-
rengasse.[1] His program included Beethoven's piano sonata opus 101, Schumann's *Novellette* 21/4, Liszt's *Bénédiction de Dieu dans la solitude*, Weber's
Episodischer Gedanke, and Chopin's polonaise opus 44, fourth scherzo, and
études 25/6 and 10. According to the *Presse* (22 January), Pachmann's playing of each work drew forth a "wahrhafter frenetisher Beifall" (a "truly fre-
netic round of applause"). The étude in thirds, in fact, had to be given
twice.

This was the real beginning of his professional career. The concert,
which was also reviewed in *Neue Welt* (21 January) and *Neue Freie Presse* (24
January), led to an engagement with the Vienna Philharmonic later in the
year that impressed even the corrosive Viennese critic Eduard Hanslick
(*Neue Freie Presse*). Further recitals followed, after one of which Pachmann
played eight encores. Not since Chopin himself had visited Vienna, many
of the older folk said, had such exquisite performances of his music been
heard in the city. (Vienna, it must be said, had welcomed Chopin unre-
servedly only during his first visit, in August 1829; his second stay, from
November 1830 until July 1831, was only a qualified success.)

Thence to Paris, where *Le Ménestrel* trumpeted Pachmann's arrival. He made his debut—a recital of works by Beethoven, Weber, Schumann, Mendelssohn, Chopin, and Liszt—at the Salle Érard; on 2 April 1882 *Le Ménestrel* applauded the "pianiste de bonne école" above all for the way he played Chopin's étude in G-sharp minor, Liszt's transcription of a Mendelssohn romance, and Schumann's *Études symphoniques.* He also performed at one of Saint-Saëns's "Mondays" whereupon the composer is reputed to have told him, "I have some technique myself, also a touch; but you are simply *épatant!*" Arthur Friedheim, a Liszt pupil who happened to be present at the musicale and would recall it years later in *Life and Liszt,* told Saint-Saëns afterwards: "If de Pachmann would apply energy to his dynamic range, instead of the exact opposite, he would probably be *the* pianist after Liszt" (134).

Pachmann made many friends in the French capital. At one of Carlotta Patti's soirées, he met the prodigies Jeanne and Louise Douste de Fortis (the dedicatees of Leopold Godowsky's *Märchen*). The Scottish conductor and composer Frederic Cowen, who had known Pachmann in Vienna, was also in town. He wrote in *My Art and My Friends,* his autobiography, that Pachmann was "even then full of those quaint little personal ways and mannerisms which have always delighted his audiences almost as much as his great pianistic gifts, and which made him, then as now, a very entertaining person in private life" (116). He thought Pachmann's playing of Chopin's étude in double thirds "the most perfect thing of the kind I ever listened to."

Pachmann's contribution to a gilded musical party hosted by one M. Campbell Clarke was also reported in *Le Ménestrel.* Here, "the young and already celebrated pianist" played pieces by Liszt, Chopin, and Adolf von Henselt; in addition, Mlle. Castellan and M. Paul Viardot played the violin, the American soprano Emma Thursby "delighted her listeners with her marvelous fluency," and M. Delle Sedie, "the most accomplished Italian baritone of our age," sang the *Largo al factotum* from *Il Barbiere di Siviglia.* Among the notables in the audience were General Fleury, the illustrator Gustave Doré, and Carolus-Duran (pseudonym of Charles Durand, French portraitist), "who sang a French romance with perfect taste; the portraitist par excellence of the *high life* [English in the original] is as good a musician as he is a painter."

Pachmann's final scheduled performance in Paris was of Chopin's F minor concerto, at one of the Concerts Pasdeloup. This was so enthusiastically received that even Henri-Georges-Stephan-Adolphe Opper de Blowitz, the correspondent for the *Times* (described by Colette in her novel *Claudine in Paris* as "Blowitz of the gorilla face"),[2] devoted a few words to it in his column. Presently the conductor Wilhelm Ganz wrote to Pachmann (in care of Messrs. Érard in Paris) and invited him to play in London.

For his debut at the Ganz Orchestral Concerts at St. James's Hall, on 20 May 1882, Pachmann again played Chopin's F minor concerto—and not, as was reported in the 1907 *Grove,* Beethoven's E-flat concerto. Francis Hueffer[3] wrote in the *Times* for 23 May:

> His touch is of the utmost delicacy; the subtlest gradations of time and strength are to him as natural as they were to the composer when he wrote; there is, indeed, about his playing that charm of dreamy poetry of which those speak with enthusiasm who heard Chopin himself. Nothing more perfect in its way could, indeed, be imagined than the slow movement of the concerto as rendered by M. de Pachmann.[4]

On this occasion, the *Musical Times* (1 June) reported, Pachmann also played solos by Haydn, Field, and Liszt. Afterwards, by way of thanks, and as was the custom of the day, he inscribed a musical quotation to Ganz on 8 July: "Au provoqueur de mon premier Triumph à Londres au Dirigent par excellence Mr. Wilhelm Ganz" (Ganz 151).[5] It did not hurt that the audience at this concert included the future King Edward VII, who took an immediate liking to Pachmann and presented him with a box of Havana cigars. By the end of his life, Pachmann had played for and befriended nearly every crowned head in Europe, as well as the shah of Persia.[6] Nor had he lost his taste for Havana cigars.

Because some of the English papers had suggested that Pachmann's talents could be judged objectively only once he was heard in music of a different stamp than Chopin's, Ganz chose Beethoven's G major concerto for the pianist's second appearance in London on 17 June. ("We must, of course, hear him in a leading pianoforte classic before venturing to give a precise estimate of his powers," the *Musical Times* of 1 June 1882 had opined.) At that time, Chopin was widely regarded as what Field had called "a talent of the sick chamber," and the sphere in which he had moved in Paris was a little notorious—louche artists such as Liszt and George Sand, and aristocracy such as the Princess Cristina Belgioioso, being among its lights.[7]

The princess, who figures in Mario Praz's famous work on decadence, *La carne, la morte, e il diavolo nella letteratura romantica,* was a most extraordinary woman. In 1848, the Austrian police had discovered the corpse of her secretary and lover, the revolutionary Gaetano Stelzi, in her palace; the corpse had been preserved with balsam. Marie, the countess d'Agoult, Liszt's mistress, described her as "pale, thin, bony, eyes flaming" (Praz 117)—a ghostly effect—while her bedroom was worthy of Huysmans, "its white hangings setting off a *lit de parade* covered in matte silver, the whole resembling a virgin's catafalque. A turbaned negro, who slept in the antechamber, introduced an element of melodrama into this ingenuous atmosphere" (Praz 118). The famous "duel" between Liszt and Thalberg took place in the princess's salon in 1837. She also commissioned the *Hexaméron.*[8]

The response to Pachmann's playing that day established a precedent for criticism of his interpretations of Beethoven's works: namely, the belief that his luminous playing was somehow unequal to, or even did an injustice to, received conceptions of the philosophical (and physical) weight that Beethoven's music was supposed to bear. "Music in England at the time just before Paderewski appeared [1890] had been reduced to a state of desperate dullness through the predominant influence of the heavy German style of interpretation," Mark Hambourg wrote in *From Piano to Forte*. "It was almost impossible to make any headway in England without the hallmark of Leipzig,[9] Dresden, or Berlin stamped on one's credentials, and the general preponderance of sacred music had damped progressive spirit, either in musical composition or executive ability" (37). Yet during his own student days in Vienna, Pachmann's father had seen Haydn's funeral, lived in the same house as Weber, and become familiar with Beethoven. Pachmann made the most of the one degree of separation between himself and Beethoven, explaining that his interpretations of Beethoven's music—the "Moonlight" sonata,[10] for instance—were founded on instructions that had come to him, through the person of his father, from the composer himself. Who is to say that they did not?

Still, the prevailing critical line, especially in England, was that Pachmann was not up to Beethoven. The following are three representative early reviews from the *Musical Times:*

1 July 1883

> M. de Pachmann came to us as an apostle of Chopin, and his supremacy in the music of the Franco-Polish composer was frankly acknowledged. We have now had opportunities of judging him in the works of other masters, and it must be averred that his success or failure has been in proportion to the Chopinesque spirit of the music he has played. At the last Recital, on the 9th ult., at St. James's Hall, he selected Beethoven's Sonata in A, Op. 101, and the result was extremely unsatisfactory. The *tempo rubato* is not required in Beethoven's music, and unfortunately the masculine breadth of style which really is needed was not forthcoming. In its place we had exaggerated *nuances* and a dreamy sentimentality of style ill befitting the Bonn master's utterances. M. de Pachmann made ample amends for whatever shortcomings were apparent in this instance by his exquisite interpretation of a selection of Chopin's compositions, including five of the Études, which were given to absolute perfection.

1 March 1886

> That M. de Pachmann is unsurpassable in certain departments of pianoforte playing is as incontrovertible as his desire to gain equal recogni-

tion in others is natural, and to a certain extent laudable. In his program of the 2nd ult. only three composers were included—namely, Beethoven, Chopin, and Henselt. The greatest of all masters was represented by his thirty-two Variations in C minor and his Sonata Appassionata. The rendering of the former did not call for adverse criticism, but the first and last movements of the latter were disfigured by effeminate tricks of style and a lack of masculine breadth and vigour which the master-works of Beethoven demand. In the remainder of the programme M. de Pachmann was thoroughly at home, and some of the Chopin selections were rendered with irresistible charm, notably the Nocturne in G (Op. 37, No. 2) and the Polonaise in F-sharp minor (Op. 44) [sic].

1 November 1892

M. de Pachmann, who played [Beethoven's C minor concerto] from notes, rendered the opening movement in a robuster, or, perhaps we should say, a more energetic style than we have hitherto been accustomed to from him. But the impression conveyed was rather of a conscious straining after enhanced sonority than of the legitimate exercise of the player's energies. The *Cadenza* introduced at the close of the movement was that by Liszt, and was played with extraordinary fluency. But M. de Pachmann spoilt everything by what followed. The opening movement of the Concerto is in C minor. The *Largo* is in E major, and the sequence of keys apparently jarred on the nerves of the susceptible virtuoso, for he must needs preface the slow movement with a modulatory improvisation of his own, an act of inartistic impertinence for which he deserved to be hissed. What was good enough for Beethoven should be good enough for M. de Pachmann. We don't want the sweetness of violets enhanced by libations of Ess. bouquet [a perfume made for Queen Victoria]. For the rest, M. de Pachmann played the *Largo* with an entire lack of simplicity and extravagant use of the *tempo rubato*. The crispness and daintiness of his touch were displayed to great advantage in the concluding Rondo. But, as a whole, the performance was artificial, affected, and irreverent.

For these critics, Pachmann was not the man for Beethoven—or, rather, he was not *enough* of a man for Beethoven. Yet what they so deftly failed to acknowledge was that Beethoven and Chopin were not the opposites they would have had them be. The Adagio con molta espressione of Beethoven's piano sonata opus 22, for instance, is practically a nocturne, while Beethoven's inclusion of a funeral march in his piano sonata opus 26 may have given Chopin permission, in effect, to do the same. Moreover, both composers owed a debt to Weber. In Paris, in the 1820s, Weber's piano sonatas were considered the most important works in the piano repertoire. Wilhelm von Lenz, in fact, wrote in *The Great Piano Virtuosos of Our Time from*

Personal Acquaintance that he had first called upon Liszt in 1828 because he had seen a concert notice —"gigantic black letters on a bright yellow ground (*la couleur distinguée* of those days, in Paris)" (7)—for a performance by Liszt of Beethoven's E-flat piano concerto. For Lenz, "Beethoven was then (and not only in Paris) Paracelsus personified, in the concert-room" (6), meaning that any performance of his music was exceptional. Of his piano sonatas, according to Lenz, only three were played: opus 26, the "Moonlight," and the "Appassionata." (Artur Schnabel recalled that during his student years in Vienna, just before the turn of the twentieth century, he was ignorant not only of the "Hammerklavier" sonata and the *Diabelli Variations* but of Mozart's piano concertos. Beethoven's fourth concerto "was generally labelled, among musicians, as the 'ladies' concerto. Hardly any of the great pianists ever played it.") Indeed, it remained for Liszt—who would play Chopin's works in a manner their composer himself wanted to steal from him—to make Beethoven comprehensible.

Pachmann, as an advocate of Beethoven and Chopin, was a musical paradox, and the Victorian mind did not like paradoxes—as Wilde's career showed. The Victorians found the implications of the word *and* disturbing, preferring infinitely the certainties implicit in the word *or*. Ambiguities, to them, were immoral.

His performance of Beethoven's fourth concerto under Ganz's auspices was not his only contribution to the program; according to Ganz, he also "played some Chopin most beautifully. I had also arranged to play a duet with him, on two pianos—variations on the Gypsy March from Weber's [incidental music to Pius Alexander Wolff's] *Preciosa,* arranged by Mendelssohn and Moscheles,[11] which pleased immensely, and we were both recalled" (152). This concert was significant for another reason: It was Ganz's final "Orchestral Concert," an institution that for almost a decade had done much to improve London's musical life.

For Pachmann, however, the signal event of this (second) sojourn in England was his meeting with the woman who was to become not only his principal pupil but also his wife. Although he would have other pupils, among them Allan Bier, Richard Capell (one lesson), Moissaye Boguslawski, Aldo Mantia,[12] Virgilio Pallottelli, and a Miss Stillwell, whom he was reputed to have ordered to lie on the floor under the piano in order to observe his pedaling, he would have no other wife.

Annie Louise Margaret "Maggie" Okey[13] was the first-born daughter of William and Anna Maria (née King) Okey. (William had been born in Lambeth, England, in 1836 and married Anna Maria on 4 January 1864.) Although eight children were to be born to them, three died in infancy—one with the extraordinary name of Oceana Duthie (b. and d. 1869).

Those who lived into adulthood, in addition to Maggie, were William Frederick, Harry Wagstaff, Caroline Louise Pattie, and Olivia Violet.

Considering the amount of ink devoted to Pachmann, astonishingly little has been written about Maggie. The most reliable account of her early life was published in Buffen's *Musical Celebrities,* which I quote because the unavailability of documents that would either confirm or refute it precludes my presenting a paraphrase of it as unimpeachable fact.

> Marguerite de Pachmann, *née* Maggie Oakey, was born in [Pipeclay Diggings,] Mudgee,[14] New South Wales [Australia], on the 15th of December, 1864.[15] Although she actually began to learn the notes on the piano at the age of two, she only received her first lessons from the organist at St. Leonards [a suburb of Sydney] in 1869. About this date her family migrated to the Mother Country, and at seven years of age the young artiste having played with great success at an entertainment given at the Queen's Concert Rooms, Hanover Square, it was decided to give her the advantage of a thorough musical education, and she accordingly entered the London Academy of Music and remained there several years, studying the piano under the late Dr. Henry Wylde, and harmony and composition with Ferdinand Praeger. Upon leaving the Academy she played first at the Crystal Palace, then at the Covent Garden Promenade Concerts, subsequently undertaking several provincial tours, which were attended with considerable success.[16] (61)

An article entitled "The Fairy-tale Career of Maggie Oakey," published in the *Sydney Daily Mirror* (11 October 1961) nine years after her death, fleshes out some of the details of the pianist's childhood and musical studies. According to the unnamed author, by the time Maggie was five, her "startled" St. Leonards music teacher had admitted that he could not do the child's talent justice: "Protesting against her ability being buried in Mudgee, he urged she be taken to one of the best city teachers before she developed faulty techniques." Presently her parents arranged the best tuition available in Sydney for her, and in the early 1870s her mother took her to London to study. At her first appearance at the Queen's Concert Rooms, "No notice was taken of the child pianist from Australia until she was halfway through her first number. Then the gossip and the rattle of the teacups died."

Unfortunately, as this biography goes on, it becomes more and more inaccurate, sending Maggie to study at the Royal College of Music and marrying her, after her divorce from Pachmann, to a "sedate Parisian doctor who preferred his wife to restrict her music to the drawing room." In fact, Maggie married Fernand-Gustave-Gaston Labori, the lawyer who would be one of Captain Alfred Dreyfus's defenders, and she had four children with him. Although her musical career took a different direction after her marriage, it in no way diminished: She composed—her largest works being an opera[17] and a piano concerto[18]—and later founded a piano school in Paris.

In souvenirs occasioned by Pachmann's death and published in *Candide* (31 August 1933), Maggie explains that she first heard of Pachmann when her father read Blowitz's article aloud to her at the breakfast table. She first heard him play when the pianist substituted for an indisposed Caroline Montigny-Remaury in a Philharmonic concert at St. James's Hall, playing Chopin's F minor concerto. "The enthusiasm of the public and of the orchestra musicians was indescribable," Maggie wrote. "As for me, I was completely discouraged." Just as Pachmann, upon hearing Carl Tausig, felt the disparity between his accomplishments and his vision, so Maggie felt after hearing Pachmann. "I had never heard the piano *sing* like that," she continued, and wrote to the pianist to ask if he might give her lessons. She received no reply, however, and continued to study and to give concerts, "with a sense that I was truly *bien médiocre,* and that the artists I heard were also *bien médiocres.*"

Presently, the manufacturer of the piano that Maggie played sought to persuade Pachmann to use his instrument as well. Pachmann tested the piano and liked it, but had some doubts about how its sound would carry in a large concert hall. As it happened, Maggie was giving a recital at St. James's Hall the next day, and Pachmann attended in order to judge the performance of the instrument. Yet it was the performance of the pianist that made the stronger impression on him, and afterwards he went to see Maggie in the green room.

"He advanced toward me," she recalled, "and in front of all my friends . . . he said to me (in French, for he was Russian and did not know English): 'Mademoiselle, you know nothing, nothing, nothing! but' (happily there was a *but*) 'you have the divine sensibility of touch and the necessary musical intelligence. Do you want to be my *only pupil*?'" If she accepted, he told her, she would have to start all over again from the beginning, and for four years withdraw from the concert stage; she would also have to promise never to share his method with anyone else. Without hesitating, Maggie said yes. "My parents and my friends treated me as if I were crazy, but I knew what I stood to learn from him."

Lessons began at the end of the 1881–82 musical season, when Maggie was seventeen. When Robert Dumm interviewed him in 1979, Pachmann and Maggie's son Lionel said these lessons were initiated in Italy but eventually moved across the continent because his mother accompanied Pachmann on his tours. (Her *Rêverie du lac* was composed at the beginning of her studies with Pachmann, when they—like Liszt and Marie, the countess d'Agoult, half a century before them—were sojourning on Lake Como.)

The majority of the lessons, however, took place in Berlin, which despite its provincialism was the principal "piano city" in Europe: In addition to the virtuosi who resided in Berlin, there were several music schools (among them the Hochschule für Musik, Klindworth-Scharwenka Conservatory, and Stern Conservatory), as well as the office of the impresarios Hermann and Louise Wolff. Nonetheless, then as now, Berlin's reputation as a musical capital was based almost entirely upon the foreign musicians who studied and played there.

The poet Jules Laforgue, who went to Berlin in 1881 as French reader to the empress Augusta, wrote a remarkable book about the city, *Berlin, la cour et la ville* (published in 1922). This book, perhaps better than any other, shows the actual life of the city in the 1880s, a life oddly uncongenial to music.

In the Berlin that Laforgue described, everything revolved around the court and the splendid presence of the military: "Berlin lives and breathes in a slight state of siege" (61). There was only one café (Café Bauer, at the corner of Friedrichstrasse and Unter den Linden). Water and bookstores were scarce (there was no bath even in the royal palace), titles and decorations abundant. A coffin store in a rich quarter displayed in its window

> metal coffins, catafalques, models draped in crêpe, urns for ashes after cremation. There are those in the poor districts with their coffins stacked in the open air and their touching signs: complete selection of coffins, whole-sale prices; coffins of polished oak from 30 francs; coffins for adults, from 15 francs; for children, from 1 franc, 50. (174)

There were also many prostitutes—or, as they were called, *demi-mondaines,* "for Berlin tact has reduced Dumas' word to this level" (159). "In the winter it's frightful. Fortunately the lantern of the hot sausage-vendor shines in the distance. The ladies help themselves and eat, leaning over the gutter so as not to soil themselves" (159). The city also had an extensive homosexual population, its members ranging from so-called *Lustknaben*—young male prostitutes—to highly placed politicians and aristocrats. Two notable cruising points for male homosexuals were the exotic postcard shop at the Panopticum and the chestnut grove at the Singakademie (Large 97).

The centrality of the court meant that the intellectual tenor of the city was diminished. The soldierly emperor Wilhelm I had no interest in art, literature, or music, but owned the Opera and the Royal Theater. "Before putting up a poster," Laforgue wrote, "they consult the sovereign" (51–52). Even those musical institutions not subject to the emperor's authority reflected, to some degree, his personality. "The finest orchestra in Berlin, the Philharmonic [founded in 1882 by dissidents from the orchestra directed by Benjamin Bilse], plays before a hall of beer drinkers. On certain days, as

visible as possible, there is a sign reading, 'Today fricasee of partridge'"
(196).

Some years after the fact, in an interview with A. M. Diehl (*Musician,*
May 1908), Pachmann recounted his own musical dealings with the emperor (who, after 1888, would have been the equally inartistic Wilhelm II,
the antithesis of his cousin, the Crown Prince Rudolph von Habsburg). Although Wilhelm figured "as the composer of several songs," he was not, in
Pachmann's view, "an essentially musical monarch, and his peculiar attitude
toward the tonal art is indicated by his published opinions concerning the
works of Wagner and Richard Strauss."

> The emperor prefers folk songs to all other forms of music, which is in it-
> self not a reprehensible taste, but is an extremely simple one for the ruler
> of the land that has produced such contrapuntal and symphonic giants as
> Bach, Beethoven, and Brahms, not to mention others only a trifle less fa-
> mous. When I played at Potsdam the emperor presented me with his *Song
> to Aegir* and remarked: "In the words of an eighteenth-century humorist,
> you must be careful how you criticize this, for there is no telling who really
> writes the music of a king." The potentate roared at the joke on himself,
> but it is easy to imagine my embarrassment.

Wilhelm I's empress, Maria Luise Katharina Augusta of Saxe-Weimar-
Eisenach, was "of Russian origin, brought up at Weimar, in the company
of Goethe, reared in the admiration of the great French century" (87). For
Wilhelm, she was ever "a special being, of another race, whose superior
nervous makeup would not admit of any interference, and even her anti-
Germanic tastes and manners must be respected" (87–88). (She attended
every performance of Bizet's *Carmen* in Berlin before she fell at Babelsberg,
a royal palace in Potsdam, and had to be confined to a wheelchair.) In spite
of her intellectual propensities, however, the empress made no attempt to
reform the cultural life of the city. She and the emperor lived in separate
apartments.

In Berlin, Pachmann gave Maggie a lesson every day. Perhaps because he
was jealous of his art and resented those who would lay down the conditions of their learning only slightly less than those who disdained labor, he
discouraged his pupils, even Maggie, from speaking much about how he
taught them. Nonetheless, Maggie shared some of her memories with their
son, Lionel, who shared them with several interviewers. As a teacher, Pachmann was unreliable and would often cancel lessons at the last minute,
claiming to have a headache or to have to prepare for a concert. Other
lessons lasted past midnight. He also taught his pupils to sit low. Old Fogy:
"All the pianists I have heard with a beautiful tone—Thalberg, Henselt, Liszt,
Tausig, Heller—yes, Stephen of the pretty studies—Rubinstein, Joseffy,

Paderewski, Pachmann, and Essipoff, sat *low* before the keyboard" (67). Pachmann placed particular emphasis on hand position, exhorting Maggie, "Never forget the dignity of the hands." Vengerova, another Dachs pupil, also believed in (and taught) a beautiful appearance of the hands: "The listener's ear should first be seduced through the eye, and thus be rendered more impressionable" (Rezits 106). For six months Maggie was allowed to play nothing but Cramer studies supplemented by exercises that Pachmann invented for her and that were intended to improve the lay of her hands on the keys; indeed, he refused to teach her a single composition until she had mastered them.

Maggie accompanied Pachmann to Vienna, where he had been invited by Franz Joseph to play Mozart's D minor piano concerto with the Philharmonic—his first appearance in the Musikverein—on November 26. (This concerto was the same one that Dachs had played in the city, Liszt conducting, in commemoration of the centennial of Mozart's birth.)[19] Here she came to a crisis that says much about her personality. Although Pachmann had forbidden her to practice more than five hours a day at the piano, she disobeyed him; soon she developed pain in her wrists, and a doctor had to be called. The doctor, to whom she confessed having practiced eleven hours a day, found cysts in her wrists and ordered her to leave off playing at once. His recommended treatment was extraordinary. She was to wear a bracelet of live ants. (This was not as loony as it sounds; the ant bites would have drained the fluid-filled cysts, or ganglia.) After a few days, the cysts disappeared and the pain subsided.

In Vienna, Pachmann and Maggie were introduced to Theodor Leschetizky, one of the three most important piano teachers working at that time. (The others were Liszt and Nikolai Rubinstein.) As teachers, he and Liszt could not have been more dissimilar. Liszt, with the philosopher, said, "Do not seek to follow in the master's footsteps; seek what he sought"—that is to say, he had no method, no system. Leschetizky, on the other hand, taught by precept and with unexpected humor. After he heard Harold Bauer perform Chopin's C-sharp minor étude in a recital, he told him, "You played it so fast that it sounded as if it were in D minor!" Not surprisingly, Leschetizky praised Pachmann's teaching, while complimenting his pupil for her accounting of some Cramer studies.

At various times during his career Pachmann "wrote" articles and gave "interviews" of a vaguely pedagogical nature that do a little to fill in these lacunae. In "The Pianism of de Pachmann" (*Musician,* September 1907), he revealed some of his "state secrets." He believed that "all lies in the fingering" and, accordingly, worked assiduously to achieve a unique tone quality and legato in the performance of Chopin's music.[20] "I do not use the first finger in playing passages where a delicate effect is needed," he explained. "The first finger is too heavy—too harsh. I use the middle finger instead. Then I get the quality of tone that I want."

Let me show you how I trill. Bend the first finger until it is the length of the thumb, that they may be even. Then trill almost on the nail. There you have a Chopin trill.

In playing octaves I find a much better effect gained by the use of the thumb and little finger than by alternating the third and fourth fingers on the top notes in the Liszt style of playing.

There you have some of my Chopin secrets—touch and tone quality, octaves, and the trill.

There is yet another thing. In playing passages marked for both hands, with the top note to be struck by the left hand crossing the right, a much better effect is made by taking with the left hand the lowest note marked for the right. This makes it possible for the top note to be struck by the right, a crossing of the hands being avoided.

In a piece entitled "How to Play Chopin" published in the October 1908 issues of *Strand Magazine* and the *Étude*, Pachmann offered some remarks on the Chopin preludes that are noteworthy for both their poetic content and their interpretive insight.

The first of them is in a style that reminds one very forcibly of Schumann. To play it is very refreshing, like a draught of cool spring water on a hot day, but the second is, I think, somewhat poor, and I remember that Liszt himself once told me he thought it a little weak. The third, though it has not a very high meaning, is a delightful little prelude. The melody is so smooth that it reminds me of oil floating upon water, while a sort of zither accompaniment is running. The fourth, though more poetical than the second, would have been more attractive if written in the shape of a song for a lady's voice accompanied by a little harmonium. The fifth is one that is so difficult to properly interpret that one of the great pianists of the day once stated that he studied it for years before he ventured to play it in public. No. 6 could very well be played by a cello and violin, but it is possible on the piano to get more effect than could be got with the cello itself. A little curiosity is to be found in this prelude at the end of the fifth bar from the finish, when there comes a sort of trumpet call announcing the conclusion. The seventh is gay, the eighth an exercise, the ninth makes me think of returning after a funeral, and in the tenth Chopin seems to me to point at and imitate his master, Hummel.

No. 11 is a fine prelude. There is melody all the time, and at this point in the preludes we begin to get genuine Chopinism. But it should not be played *vivace!* It should be *allegro moderato.* Liszt thought this prelude was nonsense if played *vivace.* In the 12th prelude, again, there is a mistake very commonly made as to the matter of its playing. Besides being a great *tour de force,* this prelude is also exceedingly poetical. Now, if it is played *presto,* all the beautiful poetical meaning is lost, and it becomes a *tour de force* only. If it is played *poco presto,* however, not only does it remain a *tour de force,* but all the poetry in it can be brought out.

I do not like the 13th prelude. The 14th is all fun from beginning to end—a regular volcano of gaiety! The 15th is my favourite. It is the longest of the preludes, and reminds one of an impromptu. The 16th is my great favourite! It is *la plus grande tour de force* in Chopin. It is the most difficult of all the preludes technically, possibly excepting the 19th. In this case *presto* is not enough. It should be played *prestissimo,* or, better still, *vivacissimo.* No. 17 was the favourite of Mme. Schumann and Rubinstein. It is very majestic, and in it Chopin introduces harmonies not previously found in other composers. The 18th is really a cadenza. In it Chopin never repeats himself. From beginning to end it is brilliant and interesting. No. 19 is another one I am very fond of, but I think it the most difficult thing in the world to play.

The 20th prelude is a very beautiful one, but with the 21st I find fault—musical fault. I am quite sure that when he started to write this he meant to make it a ballade for the orchestra. Apparently he failed to hit upon any second or third motive for succeeding movements, so he included it in the preludes. It is obviously written for first violin and two cellos, and it is not piano music at all. It is most poetical, I grant, but, emphatically, it was not meant for the piano. This is no decision arrived at in a hurry, I assure you. I thought over this matter for thirty years before I dared to express this opinion!

In the 22nd prelude Chopin created energetic modern octave play. It was the first prelude of its kind in the world. In the 23rd prelude pretty well all editions indicate short *legato* passages. Chopin never played such passages. He sometimes introduced a long *legato* passage, but never short ones of a few notes only. In the 24th the amateur would do well to remember that the whole beauty of this prelude is generally spoilt by the left-hand notes being banged. They should be *masqué* the whole time and should never be allowed to drown the right hand.[21]

From all this, one gains a sense of what Pachmann was telling Maggie during the long afternoons and evenings of their lessons.

The *Musical Review* (13 January 1883) reported: "Mr. Pachmann has left London for Paris, where he will play Chopin's E minor Concerto under Pasdeloup's auspices. He will afterwards go to St. Petersburg and return to us in the spring." A clutch of French reviews of Pachmann's playing at this time evidences the ever higher regard in which he was held in Paris. *National* (23 January): "This virtuoso . . . interpreted Chopin as well as Chopin himself." *Gaulois* (28 January): "M. de Pachmann . . . deserves to be placed beside Liszt and Rubinstein." *Moniteur Universel* (5 February):

"The lion of the musical season." *Liberté* (5 March): "He interprets like a second creator of the work."

As promised, Pachmann returned to England in the spring, and on 1 June 1883 one of the most perceptive and essential reviews of Pachmann's playing appeared in the *Musical Times:*

> Emulous of Von Bülow, Rubinstein, Sophie Menter, and other pianists of high rank, M. de Pachmann is now engaged upon a short series of Recitals, in which he alone suffices to maintain interest and give pleasure. The performances, so far, have been highly successful, a large audience attending on each occasion and applauding the Russian artist with great cordiality. At the first Recital (5th ult.) M. de Pachmann limited himself to the works of Chopin, whose music he plays with such remarkable taste, finish, and distinction. It is understood that he does not care to be known as the interpreter of one master, but if by some happy combination of circumstances, a pianist is better fitted to render Chopin's music than any other, the public cannot be blamed for preferring to hear him in that capacity, and, after all, a performer *par excellence* of the Polish master's work holds a very enviable position. He must be a master of his instrument and a man endowed with subtle appreciation and the finest sensibility. . . .
>
> The second Recital, given on the 22nd ult., was scarcely less well attended than the first, albeit M. de Pachmann's program included very little of Chopin. That little, however, comprised the Sonata with the Funeral March and the well-known Valse in A-flat, which the artist gave with special brilliancy, to the delight of all who heard him. Other selections were taken from Bach, Schubert, Mendelssohn, Beethoven, Moscheles, &c. In these M. de Pachmann fell short of the uniform success gained on the previous occasion, not that his skill was inadequate, but that his temperament was, perhaps, at variance with their spirit. The Russian pianist is by no means a cold, intellectual performer, like Von Bülow, who plays all masters equally well. He executes as he feels, and his sympathy, or the want of it, necessarily affects his execution. Nevertheless, it is always pleasurable and interesting to hear so gifted an artist play, and to this fact the audience abundantly testified.

He executes as he feels. It could not have been said more elegantly, and yet Pachmann was not the special case the writer seems to make of him. The greatest musicians *always* execute as they feel. (Notwithstanding the critic's testimony, it is understood that Bülow was, in fact, a one-sided performer—and on a side that was not Pachmann's.) Incidentally, this review reminds us that the piano recital as we know it—the one "invented" in 1840 by Liszt, in London, when he played alone—had not at that time become tradition. The usual concert program was still an assemblage.

Later that month the *Musical Review* (9 June) offered rare praise of Pachmann's playing of Beethoven's music (fourth concerto and 32 Variations in C minor) at a Crystal Palace concert, which he programmed in reply to those who pegged him as a Chopin player: "The performance of both works was very fine, the interpretation of the Concerto being particularly noteworthy for the scrupulous reverence with which every indication of the composer's intentions was observed, without at all detracting from the individuality of the performer's reading of the work." The critic objected only to the cadenzas (Bülow's, possibly?), which were "unfortunately not at all composed in the spirit of Beethoven; they might have been extracted from some of the most inflated compositions of Rubinstein, where they would have been more in keeping than in a Beethoven Concerto."

Lionel de Pachmann grew up hearing that Liszt was present at Pachmann's debut in Budapest—not merely present, in fact, but an actor in the drama. Upon the conclusion of Pachmann's performance of a Chopin sonata, Liszt is said to have risen and told the audience, "Those who have never heard Chopin before are hearing him this evening"—a tribute Pachmann answered, depending upon the source, with a performance of Liszt's D-flat étude (*Un sospiro*) or Liszt's arrangement of Mendelssohn's *Auf Flügeln des Gesanges*. Liszt himself then played his arrangement of one of Chopin's *Chants polonais* for Pachmann.

Very possibly this story is an exaggeration, or even a fiction. In fact, Alan Walker, Liszt's finest biographer, writes to me that his own notes are silent about any meetings between the two men other than the ones described in volume 3 of his biography of Liszt.[22] (The occasion of Pachmann's Budapest debut is not among these meetings, nor is there evidence that Pachmann followed Liszt to Weimar. There was always much *va-et-vient* at the Altenburg, however, and so it is not impossible that Pachmann actually was there for a brief period.) Regardless of where he first heard Liszt play, however, Pachmann was unprepared for the experience. As Pachmann later said, Liszt was "more than a musician, more than a composer, and more than a poet—he was all three, and then the story was not half told."

The most essentially truthful, as well as the most amusing, of Pachmann's many Liszt stories is the one written by Archie Bell (a critic in Cleveland) reprinted in Adella Prentiss Hughes's *Music Is My Life*. Bell had asked Pachmann to describe the greatest compliment he had ever received for his playing:

> One night it happened that three of us who had more or less reputations as pianists had the opportunity to play before Liszt at Rome. Anton Rubin-

stein was at the heyday of his popularity and had never played better in all
his life. The first man played a thundering affair called *The Awakening of
the Lions,* which he thought was certain to please the great musical lion.
After he had finished, Liszt asked what he called the selection. "*The Awakening of the Lions,*" answered the pianist proudly. "It sounded like *The Awakening of the Donkeys,*" said Liszt, and of course everyone either laughed
outright or was shocked. Rubinstein played, and played beautifully. And
afterward Liszt said: "Yes, tra-la-la-bang, quite pretty." Then it came my
turn. I played an étude by Chopin, and afterward the greatest genius the
world has ever known came up to me and embraced me before the audience. "Play that again," he begged, and I did so. "Play it the third time," he
said, and I again did as he asked. Liszt stood there and raised his hands
over me and said merely: "Divine." That, perhaps, was the greatest compliment I ever received. (150)

The myth of inheritance that Liszt created for himself was to have received a "kiss of consecration" from Beethoven; Pachmann's, as we have
seen, was to have been anointed by the greatest pianist of the nineteenth
century. Yet the veracity of these myths is finally less significant than the degree to which they define each artist's ideals, his aspirations, his values.
(Every great artist must have a myth, or mythology; if he does not create it
himself, it is created for him.) In other words, an artist must be judged not
for inventing himself but for the quality of his invention. Wilde, in "The
Decay of Lying," exalts the lie that is art, and most of Pachmann's really
were art. (One of the few times he went too far was when he claimed that
he, Liszt, Rubinstein, Bülow, and Tausig had played in the salon of a London peeress on the same occasion. This was impossible: Liszt visited England only in 1824, 1825, 1827, 1840, 1841, and 1886; Tausig was born in
November 1841 and died in July 1871.)

Few were the pianists of the nineteenth century who were able to resist
the personal greatness and artistic magnanimity of Liszt; few, too, the pianists who could resist his music, which lies so comfortably beneath the
hand. The spell of Liszt was only slightly less on pianists of the twentieth
century nourished by the tradition of the nineteenth: Arrau, Bolet, Fioren-
tino, Horowitz, Nyiregyhazi, Richter, and Sofronitsky. By the beginning of
the twenty-first century, however, Liszt's music was being rejected wholesale
by such notables as Piotr Anderszewski, Radu Lupu, and András Schiff;
more sadly, the pianists who did play it rarely came close to attaining its
ideal. For Pachmann, a pianist who did not aspire to Liszt was inconceivable.

On Monday, 14 January 1884, both Pachmann and Maggie took the
stage at St. James's Hall. According to the *Musical Times* (1 February 1884):

Some curiosity attached to the appearance of Miss Maggie Okey, a young pianist, formerly of the London Academy of Music, but now receiving the benefit of tuition from M. de Pachmann. She played the sixth study of Henselt, "Danklied nach Sturm," and Nos. 6, 8, and 10 of Chopin's Études, Op. 25. In all of these she displayed very neat mechanism and a sympathetic touch, but not much power. Her reception by the audience was flattering in the extreme. The study in thirds of Chopin (No. 6) had to be repeated, and at the end of her selection she was again encored, when she gave Schumann's "Vogel als Prophet." Later in the evening Miss Maggie Okey joined her preceptor in Chopin's Rondo in C, for two pianofortes, Op. 73, one of the posthumous publications, and an early composition, despite its high opus number.

Now that she was studying with Pachmann, Maggie's playing was described in the same terms as his own—sympathetic, but lacking in power—an implicit criticism aimed less at her sex (many women pianists of the day elicited compliments for the scale of their playing) than at her "preceptor."

Pachmann married his pupil on 30 April 1884. She was nineteen years old and bore such a strong resemblance to the actress Lillie Langtry that admirers called her "the Lillie Langtry of the piano."

A copy of the marriage certificate obtained from the General Register Office (London) gives Pachmann's address as 78 Hamilton Terrace[23] and the bride's as 162 Portsdown Road, off the Finchley Road, in Golders Green. (That Margaret was changed to Marguerite speaks to what Arthur Loesser, in *Men, Women, and Pianos,* called the "ancient established English equation of performing instrumentalist with foreignness." Anglo-Saxon pianists commonly took up Slavic-sounding names—Lucy Hickenlooper, for instance, became "Olga Samaroff," while Josef Levine imbued his surname with distinction simply by changing its spelling to Lhévinne.) The marriage—an Anglican service, in deference to the bride—was solemnized in the Parish Church of St. Mark's (Hamilton Terrace, St. John's Wood) in the presence of Maggie's parents and Waldmann. As it happens, though, there was a second ceremony in the Russian Church in Maida Vale, which Cowen attended. "I believe I was the only one of his colleagues who was present at his wedding," he wrote, "and took part in the curious ceremony of the Greek Church which appertains to these occasions" (116). The reception took place at the Hotel Ronveau, the proprietress of which Pachmann already counted as a friend.

The month before (on 17 March), in the tiny town of Campodonico in central Italy, a son had been born to Salvatore Pallottelli and Annunziata Tulli. Twenty-one years later, Francesco Pallottelli would become the most significant figure in Pachmann's life.

THREE

M. and Mme. de Pachmann

Although nothing like a complete record or schedule of the concerts of the early years of their marriage survives, an analysis of press clippings, programs, reviews, and oft-repeated anecdotes, together with information gleaned from interviews with Lionel de Pachmann and Francesco Pallottelli, allows us to piece together part of the sequence. The couple took their honeymoon in Switzerland in 1884; then, almost imperceptibly, the holiday gave way to the desultory life of the virtuoso on tour. We learn that on a train Pachmann got into a fight with a fellow passenger about whether a window ought to be left opened or closed; the dispute grew so heated that Maggie had to intervene. Then, in Kraków, while backstage preparing for a concert, Pachmann was approached by a young man wanting his opinion of some music he had composed. Pachmann looked over the manuscript, complimented the youth on his beautiful handwriting and the fine quality of the paper he had used, and handed it back, saying, "It is a pity to waste this fine paper on such music." The young man left in a rage. When Maggie reproached her husband for his cruelty, he sent someone after the youth—but he had gone. Later they would learn that his name was Ignace Jan Paderewski.[1]

In one of his last interviews, Paderewski identified the work he had shown to Pachmann as the ubiquitous minuet in G, a piece that began as part of his unpublished suite opus 1 (1879) and eventually made its way into print as part of his published opus 1: *Zwei Klavierstücke* (ca. 1886). The international fame of the minuet was no more proof of its musical worth than that attending Rachmaninov's prelude in C-sharp minor, of course, but fame it had—and, having that, Pachmann's failure to divine its destiny was sweet to Paderewski.

Paderewski's eminence as a Chopin interpreter would eventually approach Pachmann's, and this led to their performances being compared—which did nothing to mitigate the enmity-mingled-with-respect each man felt for the other. Philip Hale preferred the older pianist as a Chopin player

("Mr. de Pachmann has the finer sense of proportion"); so, too, did W. S. B. Mathews (*Music*, vol. 17):

> Aside from this deplorable poverty in molecular nuance, Mr. Paderewski has positive faults; or, rather, one great fault which vitiates his whole art. He pounds the piano most brutally; crowds even the noble Steinway piano, upon which he played, until its tone far passes beyond the domain of music. He adds to the pounding the animal trait of kicking the pedal, in order to add the noise of the whole frame of dampers falling upon the wires to the over-forced tone-volume; he put in a middle note or two in his sforzando octaves in the bass. This is work for the gallery—and for a very bad gallery at that.

While admitting that "Mr. de Pachmann is certainly distinguished for a very fine sense of rhythm, which Paderewski would be much benefited by having," Mathews did have one cavil about Pachmann:

> In one sense De Pachmann belongs to the modern world; he is a specialist. One thing he does better than any other person. It is to play Chopin. The consequence is that when one hears him, one carries away a distinct impression, despite defects in the larger and more serious moments. When one had heard Paderewski one remembers to have seen him; one recalls the dim light, the "lucrative hair," as Hale calls it, and the sentiment of the cantilena. One also remembers the pounding; and if one is young enough or hysterical enough, one can even remember this as a phase of art. But not otherwise.

In St. Petersburg, Pachmann and Maggie stopped at the Hotel Europe, on the Nevsky Prospect. Comfort and cleanliness were not what most travelers were accustomed to finding in nineteenth-century Russia. At the Hotel Europe, however, one was less likely to encounter bedbugs or the infamous St. Petersburg flea. There they saw Sophie Menter,[2] who taught at the conservatory, and they were visited each day by Henselt, whom Pachmann knew from Vienna. Henselt was a musician greatly esteemed by his colleagues: Schumann had dedicated his *Novelletten* to him, while Liszt, upon hearing him play Weber's *Polacca* in E, had remarked, "J'aurais pu me donner ces pattes de velours, si j'avais voulu!" (147)—"I could have [his] velvet paws, if I had wished." Henselt was one of the four pianists to whom Lenz paid tribute in *The Great Piano Virtuosos of Our Time* (the others being Liszt, Chopin, and Tausig). Pachmann, who adored Henselt's études, was at this point beginning to gain a reputation as an inspired interpreter of them, particularly *Si oiseau j'étais, à toi je volerais* (a study in double notes that calls upon the pianist to play "con leggerezza quasi zeffiroso"; sometimes called the

Vöglein-Etüde).[3] If we bear in mind Lenz's assessment of it, Pachmann's affinity with Henselt's music was not only natural but inevitable:

> Romanticism is a distinctly German propensity which is most promi-
> nently developed in Henselt. Even when the artist develops a lighter vein,
> proffers a modest drawing-room piece (Liebeslied, Fontaine), and the or-
> dinary listener discerns sentimentality, refined sensibility—there too, and
> in the smallest possible compass, is Henselt romantic in the same sense in
> which Weber is romantic in *Der Freischütz*, where even Ännchen's simple
> songs are flooded with moonlight for every one that has taste to appreciate
> them. (125)

Lenz's recognition that Romanticism was a German propensity locates Pachmann in a tradition that music history has tended to revise in order to exclude him. The critical disapprobation he received as a Beethoven inter-preter was taken, on many occasions, as an opportunity to run down his ability to play any major work by a German composer. And while one may argue that Weber and Henselt did not approach the achievements of Bach and Mozart, or Beethoven and Schubert, their place in the German musical tradition—particularly Weber's for the operas *Euryanthe, Der Freischütz*, and *Oberon*, the *Konzerstück*, the piano sonatas, and the clarinet sonata   is indisputable. Lenz, however, did not regard Henselt's achievement as being in any way less important, or even less revolutionary, than Beethoven's. On the contrary, for him, Henselt's music (for which Hummel was the starting point) ushered in a "new era":

> The era of lyric personality, subjective dramatic intention, plastic execu-
> tion, bearing internal evidence of a real human right to be. This tendency,
> this new *salon*-literature, had its origin in the good old school and be-
> longed, from a technical standpoint, to a straight guild; now, however, it
> had nothing more to do with schools and pedants, with pattern and rou-
> tine, but turned its doctrinary ideas to account for humanity, in audience
> and adepts. (130)

If Henselt's advocacy of the "real human right to be" no longer seems orig-inal to us, that is in the nature of things. Liszt's day as a composer came long after he was dead. And perhaps our reverence for Mozart is beyond the bounds of reason. In short, the musical values of every age have an innate integrity, whether or not other ages approve, or even understand, them.

Incidentally, Lenz recorded a personal mannerism of Henselt's that Pachmann found endearing:

> Wherever his enthusiasm seizes him, when he soars towards his ideal, he
> doubles the singing melody that quite fills his heart, by humming it him-

self! The artist's voice is anything but lovely, and injures the effect, as he knows right well when he is told that he has been singing again, for he himself does not know it, or suspect it! *Never,* never have I heard such a magical *cantilena* flow from the pianoforte, as in those moments when Henselt's voice joined his playing! (127)

While in St. Petersburg, Pachmann also spent time with his brother Simon, through whom he was able to secure an invitation to play for Alexander III. The czarina gifted him with an Etruscan arabesque vase, yet it was the jewels worn to his concert by the czar that made the greater impression on the pianist and that prompted him to begin collecting precious stones himself.

Next came Scandinavia, where in December Pachmann played two glorious concerts in Finland, the first a recital, the second an orchestral concert in which he performed Mozart's D minor and Chopin's F minor concertos, as well as solo works by J. S. Bach, Henselt, Brahms, Liszt, and Raff. A recital in Copenhagen in the spring of 1885 (April) so moved Christian IX that he invited both Pachmann and Maggie, who was then visibly pregnant, to perform at court. The queen of Denmark took a great liking to Maggie, sending "for her to spend the morning in playing with her duets upon two pianos, and many were the beautiful presents bestowed by Her Majesty upon Madame de Pachmann as souvenirs of the Queen's appreciation of her artistic performances" (Buffen 63). Concerts in Norway and Sweden also met with popular and critical approbation. Word of Pachmann's success in Scandinavia traveled through the royal grapevine, and presently the Danish-born czarina, a sister of both the Princess of Wales and Queen Louise of Denmark, invited him to play, once again, in St. Petersburg. It was here that Maggie gave birth to a son, Victor, whom they seem to have left behind when they went to Odessa to visit Pachmann's sister, Elizabeth. While they were away, the infant died. Not surprisingly, Maggie decided at this point that she wanted to return to England and to her family. This was Pachmann's last documented visit to his native Russia.

Back in England, he and Maggie stayed with her parents in Hampton, where he could sometimes be seen in the garden, polishing the few precious stones he had so far collected. On such a day, the violinist Daisy Kennedy later wrote, he threw the jewels into the air to watch them flash in the sunlight.[4] He knew better than anyone what they had cost, yet his delight in them was the delight of a child.

On 10 December 1885, Pachmann made his second appearance with the Hallé Orchestra, playing Mozart's D minor concerto and solo works by Raff, Chopin, and Henselt. On 14 December, he was once again at St.

James's Hall, playing a program of Weber, Raff, Barnett, Liszt, Henselt, Schumann, and Chopin. It was at this concert that Pachmann made one of his first onstage outbursts. "Some amusement was caused in the Hall by the demonstrative way in which M. de Pachmann expressed his annoyance at the disturbance caused by late-comers," the *Musical Times* reported.

> We can sympathise with a sensitive artist under the circumstances; but it must be remembered that many persons come from long distances to St. James's Hall, and those who are dependent upon public conveyances cannot be certain of arriving in time. The best solution of the difficulty is to allow a short pause after every piece, in order to enable those who have been delayed to take their seats quietly.

Allowing for a short pause after every piece, as the critic proposed, may be thoroughly disturbing to the pianist's own rhythm or run counter to the sense he is making of his program: Musicians do not have pause buttons. Pachmann differed from the overwhelming majority of his colleagues on this front only in that he chose to voice his pique.

The fact that the couple was now settled in England (and that they had just lost a child) in no way meant a diminution of Pachmann's concertizing. On the contrary, he was playing as much as ever. In *Brother Musicians*, the reminiscences of her brothers Edward and Walter, Constance Bache described a concert in January 1886 "at the house of Miss Emerson, to help raise funds for the projected Liszt scholarship." The program included a Beethoven piano trio, played by Pachmann, Otto Peiniger, and Edward Howell,[5] as well as songs of Beethoven and Dvořák, sung (and the latter also accompanied) by William Shakespeare and solos for violoncello, violin, and piano; "amongst the latter," Bache wrote, "may be singled out M. de Pachmann's masterly rendering of one of Liszt's rhapsodies" (283).

In March, Pachmann played two concertos: one by Mozart (K. 488?) and Chopin's F minor. The *Musical Times* (1 April 1886) reported that his performance of the Chopin "displayed his now familiar virtuosity of touch, and, let us add, of gesticulation," until, near the end of the work, he suffered a memory lapse—an incident that prompted him to play from the notes on numerous subsequent occasions. Pachmann's solo contributions to the program were a nocturne by J. F. Barnett ("of a mild Chopinesque character"), Raff's *La Fileuse,* and Mendelssohn's *Rondo capriccioso* ("a piece which serves to show his peculiar qualities at their very best"). Mozart's "charming concerto," according to the *Monthly Musical Record* (1 April 1886), was played "with taste, especially the adagio, and a considerable degree of 'antic gesture,' which might have been left at home. Profiting by former mental lapses, he had the copy in front of him this time, though he did not seem often to refer to it."

In April, Liszt visited London, for the first time in forty-five years, to attend a performance of his oratorio *The Legend of Saint Elizabeth*, a work which Henry Wylde, Maggie's teacher, had introduced to England in 1870. During the seventeen days he stayed in England, Liszt was presented with a number of honors and tributes. He dined with the actor Henry Irving at the Beefsteak Club, visited Queen Victoria at Windsor Castle, and was received by Cardinal Manning. On 8 April, Walter Bache gave a private-invitation party for him at the Grosvenor Gallery, with many illustrious guests among the four hundred attending: Robert Browning, musicologist George Grove, Sir Charles Hallé, Joseph Joachim, the painters Lord Leighton and Alma Tadema, Pachmann, Lord and Lady Walter Scott, and Arthur Sullivan.

The next day, at the last of the so-called Smoking Concerts of the Royal Amateur Orchestral Society, hosted by the Prince of Wales, Pachmann played piano solos by Henselt and Liszt for the master. Later, he and Maggie visited Liszt at Sydenham, and Liszt, ever captivated by beautiful women, asked Maggie to play for him. (She essayed Chopin's étude 25/8.) This was the last time they would see Liszt, for he would die on 31 July at Bayreuth, having gone there to attend performances of *Parsifal* and *Tristan*.

In May, hot on Liszt's heels, Anton Rubinstein played, and from memory, his epic historical recitals in the English capital—he had given them in Vienna in November and December 1885—in anticipation of which Pachmann concluded his own London season with a recital at St. James's Hall. As the *Musical Times* (1 June 1886) put it, "While the sun is shining, even stars of the first magnitude cannot be seen, and it would have been unfortunate had the popular favour in which M. de Pachmann is held been permitted to decline even temporarily." Pachmann and Maggie attended Rubinstein's concerts, at which two Becker grand pianos were put on the stage in case one should go out of tune or he should break a string (or strings). When, after the Schumann recital, the couple went backstage to congratulate Rubinstein, he showed them his hands, which were bleeding. No wonder: His program had consisted of not only the *Fantasie* but also the *Kreisleriana, Études symphoniques,* F-sharp minor sonata, four of the *Fantasiestücke, Vogel als Prophet* from *Waldszenen, Romanze* 32/3, and *Carnaval.* Nor had blood prevented him from performing the *Traumes Wirren* as an encore. "Never shall I forget the feeling he stirred in me with the opening phrases of Schumann's *Fantasie* which opened the concert," Maggie later told Lionel. "The gradations of his tone in that divine phrase were so marvelous that I felt my throat swell with emotion." Of course, Pachmann himself admired Rubinstein's tone, which he later compared to Enrico Caruso's. (Pachmann maintained that from an aesthetic standpoint, tone was more important than technique, although technique—flawless technique—was fundamental; more precisely, technique without tone was irrelevant.)

Harold Bauer was also present at this recital and wrote of it in *His Book.* He remembered Rubinstein's playing of Schumann's *Études symphoniques* "solely because he failed to turn into the major key at the point indicated on the very last page, and played the major chord only once instead of twice. Was it a lapse of memory, or did he purposely make the change? I shall never know, but the effect is so fine that I have always played it that way." He also remembered Rubinstein's "impatient gesture as he dashed away a small flower thrown by an admirer, which lodged on the top of his head" (19).

In "A Fairy-Tale Untold—Rubinstein—A Last Look," an essay he collected in *Long-Haired Iopas,* Edward Prime-Stevenson observed:

> Rubinstein often did not trouble to leave the platform during all intervals of a recital. He had a queer, informal habit of merely quitting the pianoforte, and thence retiring up-stage, and standing there, frequently with his back to the auditorium; perhaps gazing at a pyramid of chairs piled before him, or staring around at the blank wall, occasionally rubbing his hands briskly on a spacious handkerchief; as if such [a] cavalier way of resting thought and muscles, and of cooling off, after one of his tremendous examples of sonority, would serve well enough, though in indifference to formality and to his hearers' avid eyes. It was very funny, as it comes back to memory now; a contrast to the elaborately social conduct, the repeated exits and entrances, the suggestions of toilet-changes, usual by pianists of recent years. (284)

Another son, Adrian, was born to Pachmann and Maggie on 19 August 1886.

At the beginning of 1887, the couple were in Berlin, where Maggie played three solos—a Henselt étude, Beethoven's *Rondo à capriccio,* and Chopin's *Andante spianato* and *Grande Polonaise*—in a concert of the Berlin Philharmonic conducted by Klindworth on 21 January. (Pachmann had made his debut with the Philharmonic on 6 January, playing Chopin's F minor concerto and solo works by Raff and Henselt.) After this concert, F. Forster Buffen wrote, "The Princess Royal went to Marguerite in the artists' room and invited her to the Palace, this being the first time this honor was conferred on an English artiste" (63).

On 11 January 1887, Louise Wolff wrote in her diary:

> Went last night to hear Vladimir von Pachmann in concert, his fourth public appearance here in Berlin, artistically a rousing success, but the hall

almost empty. Silly old world, turning out for fame and fashion, but never the time or money for true artistic delight. Pachmann is a phenomenon— an absolutely faultless technique, but as a means to an end, never empty virtuosity. His playing is characterized by its crystal clarity. He has the sweetest, most charming tone imaginable, his playing is like a sea of beauty. There are those who would say a few reefs would make the sea more interesting—but who's to say that the rocks wouldn't rather wreck the poetry of his tone. I believe Pachmann is the most gifted pianist of the present day, his unerring technique, his easy mastery of the greatest technical obstacles, are the fruit of dogged application through long, hard years of practice. Pachmann told me that when he was already the finished article, a performer with great successes already to his name, he withdrew from society for eight years to study, beginning with humble finger exercises. That takes energy. Now: what does such an energetic man look like? A man? No, a manikin, a little dwarfish fellow, what you'd imagine "Dwarf Mime" to look like, a ridiculous megalomaniac, a little monster of delusion and vanity—it's even hard not to laugh when he's playing, such are his antics. Get him talking about himself, and see the way his face clears, the whole creature puffs itself up, he talks like the lover of his beloved, or the priest of the godhead. Phrases like "I play divinely," "no one plays as well as I do," "my miraculous playing," simply trip off his lips—one no longer notices after a while. But it is too funny to picture him—his wife describes it—standing in front of the mirror after a concert, petting himself, or smacking his own face, if he's played badly.

The whole being is a caricature, an impossibility, not an individual but a divinely inspired automaton. And yet this machine, this automaton has managed to acquire the most charming and delightful wife, an English girl, from such a fine family. Maggie also plays and composes, and she's linked herself to him "like a third," as someone very wittily observed the other day. (116)

That year, Maggie also gave her first public recital since beginning her studies with Pachmann at the Salle Érard. It was an estimable success, not only with the critics and the public but with her husband. When, after the concert, one of the directors of the hall complimented her "marvelous" playing, Pachmann shouted, "Marvelous? She plays *genius-ly.* You don't know anything about music." Maggie was, indeed, becoming recognized as a leading light among women pianists.

She gave birth to a third son, Leonide (Lionel), on 28 August.

With two children, and no longer wanting to impose on Maggie's sister, the Pachmanns decided to settle in Paris, which was in any case a better base than London from which to depart for European tours. They returned frequently to England, however. "Madame de Pachmann had a large and sympathetic audience at her recital of music by Brahms (F minor sonata opus 5), Schubert (impromptu in G opus 90, no. 3),[6] Chopin (étude in G-sharp minor and *Andante spianato*), Henselt (*Si oiseau j'étais*), and herself at the Princes' Hall, on Monday, the 6th ult.," the *Musical Times* allowed (1 March 1888): "It may be said at once that Madame de Pachmann is a very charming executant within certain limits, her touch being peculiarly musical and absolutely devoid of hardness, while her execution of rapid passages is very true and even." The critic made special note of the two works of Maggie's own composition, *Thème et variations* (G minor) and *Rêverie du lac:* "The second is only an elegant trifle,[7] but the former is written with a large amount of musicianly skill, and left a very favourable impression." Once again, however, criticism of Maggie's playing repeats that made continuously against Pachmann's. "Power and passion, however, are wanting, and we fancy she will always be heard to the fullest advantage in a room of moderate size, and in music suited to her style and idiosyncrasy."

On 13 June 1888, Pachmann shared the stage with Hans Richter in a testimonial concert for Ambrose Austin, the retiring manager of St. James's Hall. The hall, in which Pachmann would play many times, had an interesting history, as Robert Elkin wrote in *The Old Concert Rooms of London:*

> In 1856 it was announced that a company was being formed for the construction of a new hall for concerts and public meetings, on a site between Air Street, Vine Street, Regent Street, and Piccadilly. The company was called the St. James's Hall Company, and a large proportion of the capital was subscribed by Tom Chappell, then head of the famous publishing firm of that name. The erection of the building was made difficult by the discovery of a quicksand on the site, which had to be saturated, at great expense, with concrete so as to make a secure foundation. The hall was ultimately opened in March 1858 with a concert, in aid of the Middlesex Hospital, in the presence of the Prince Consort. (149)

When St. James's Hall was demolished in 1905, Elkin notes:

> The eminent critic J. A. Fuller-Maitland was unmoved; "there was an element of danger," he wrote, "from the presence of the kitchens and the Christy Minstrels' hall below, and in spite of the beautiful acoustics of the great hall[8] and its wonderful artistic associations, it was not wholly a misfortune when it was determined to pull it down and use the site for a hotel." It was not comfortable either; Sir George Henschel wrote, after its destruction, of the "uncomfortable, long, narrow, green-upholstered benches (pale-green horse-hair), with the numbers of the seats tied over the straight backs with bright pink tape, like office files." Yet to him it was "dear old St. James's Hall." (155)

The Piccadilly Hotel itself went the way of all things. Fittingly, Tower Records Piccadilly now stands upon the quicksand from which St. James's Hall once rose.

On 1 July 1888, the *Musical Times* published a review of a concert by Maggie at Princes' Hall, which was distinguished by the premiere of her sonata for violin and piano (in the performance of which she was assisted by Richard Gompertz).[9] "Though the work is in four movements it is more remarkable for condensation than elaboration of the thematic material," the critic wrote, adding, somewhat archly, "To say that she appears to have been principally influenced by Schumann and Brahms is tantamount to placing on record that the composer has taken the best of the modern masters as her models."

Two months later, the same publication announced the publication of Maggie's *Thème et variations,* which had been brought out by Novello, Ewer and Co. "The theme is simple, and the variations, eight in number, are carried out in a style which is at once indicative of the correct taste and the musicianship of the composer," judged the critic for the *Musical Times* (1 September 1888). "It is a sterling, though unpretentious work, and may be recommended as an excellent addition to the *répertoire* for the piano-forte."

Pachmann's onstage mannerisms, in the meanwhile, were attracting more and more attention—even that of the astringent George Bernard Shaw, who complained in the *Star* (19 August 1889): "M. Vladimir de Pachmann gave his well-known pantomimic performance, with accompaniments by Chopin, a composer whose music I could listen to M. de Pachmann playing for ever if the works were first carefully removed from the pianoforte." Bauer, who happened to be sitting next to Shaw (as he had been at Rubinstein's Schumann recital in London), admitted in *His Book* that he was "deeply shocked" when Shaw said "monkey" under his breath: he himself cherished the pianist as a genius to whom "everything was permissible" (18). As for Maggie, she agreed with Shaw. Although she recognized the psychology behind her husband's evolving onstage behavior—that in this way Pachmann put himself at ease—she, too, found it irritating, particularly when they played together.[10] Mark Hambourg summed up the situation in *The Eighth Octave* with an observation that would be repeated by friend and foe alike throughout Pachmann's career:

> Unfortunately, [his] mannerisms of talking to his audiences made him appear a mountebank which he certainly was not. He was a serious musician but highly eccentric, and this eccentricity detracted from his art in the eyes of many musicians who would otherwise have admired his playing as it deserved. But that there was method in his madness is certain, for he

once told my father that when he talked to the public his concerts were full, and when he did not they were empty! (53)

On 20 February 1890, Pachmann and Maggie gave a recital at St. James's Hall that consisted of solos for each of them and duets for either piano four hands or two pianos; the latter works were Schumann's Andante and variations in B-flat, opus 46, Henselt's *Si oiseau j'étais,* a scherzo (op. 87) by Saint-Saëns, and a Beethoven fugue in D (a transcription, published in 1827, of a piece composed for string quintet in 1817). The critic for the *Musical Times* (1 March 1890) gave higher marks to Maggie: "We have recently spoken in high terms of Madame de Pachmann's poetical and highly refined performance of Schubert's beautiful Sonata in G (Op. 78),"[11] he wrote, "and need only state that she repeated it on this occasion with even greater success. She was equally commendable in Mendelssohn's *Variations sérieuses,* and trifles by Chopin." Pachmann's own Mendelssohn playing— the *Fantasie* in F-sharp minor—"could not be greatly admired," even if in smaller pieces by Schumann and Chopin "his light delicate style was displayed to greater advantage." The review concluded with an announcement that "On the 3rd inst." Pachmann would "give a Recital consisting entirely of [Chopin's] music, this being his last appearance previous to the American tour of the gifted artistic pair." The review of the latter recital in the *Musical Times* (1 April 1890) noted:

> Unfortunately it was the coldest day of the winter, and although the pianist arrived in good time, his fingers were too numbed to permit him to play. The audience being ignorant of the cause of the delay waxed impatient, but when Mr. de Pachmann at length ascended the platform and explained in pantomime his temporary disablement, they encouraged him by a round of applause. There was no falling off whatever in the manner of his interpreting the works of [Chopin], and as by common consent he realises their poetic significance more fully than any other pianist, it is obvious that the listeners enjoyed a great treat and at the same time gained a valuable lesson.

The generous attitude of this piece, in which Pachmann's tendency to "pantomime" is regarded as an amusing aberration, is actually more typical of the audience response to his concerts than Shaw's dismissal. Indeed, as a rule, Pachmann's behavior endeared him to listeners, augmenting his popularity.

It seemed inevitable that America should be the next step. Later, the impresario Frederick A. Schwab told a representative of the *American Musician* (12 April 1890) how he had come to engage Pachmann for an American tour:

When I visited Europe last summer, as I have done every year or two since 1866, I had no more thought of engaging M. de Pachmann than I have now of signing a contract with General Boulanger. I had heard of the virtuoso, of course, but we have had so many pianists in America that I had grave doubts as to the possibility of any new comer's creating an excitement. M. de Pachmann gave a Chopin recital in London the day before I left London, however, so I thought it judicious to go and hear him, at any rate. I went, intending to remain ten minutes—and I staid an hour and a half. That same night I wrote to him and asked him to confer with me on the subject of an American *tournée,* and simultaneously, I wrote to Chickering & Sons. I met M. and Mme. de Pachmann a few days later in Paris, where, by the way, they have one of the prettiest *intérieurs* imaginable, not the least adornment of which are two lovely children—and you know the rest.

Significantly, Schwab observed, "It required no end of eloquence and imaginative imagery to induce M. de Pachmann to cross the Atlantic, for he suffers terribly from sea-sickness [unkind souls called him "Mal de Mer" de Pachmann], and both Mme. de Pachmann and I were afraid to put him aboard a Liverpool steamship for fear he would jump off in Queenstown Harbor."[12] Indeed, Schwab doubted whether "any offer, however liberal, will induce him to cross the Atlantic again."

For Pachmann, this was to be the first of many crossings.

FOUR

"My Wife, Madame Labori"

B y the time Pachmann made his first American tour, accompanied by
Maggie, the tradition of a piano manufacturer sponsoring the concerts
of foreign-born virtuosi was well established. Steinway had already brought
Anton Rubinstein, and Chickering had sponsored Hans von Bülow. Additionally, some manufacturers built concert halls, of which the largest, Chickering Hall in New York, at Fifth Avenue and Eighteenth Street, had about
two thousand seats —much larger than the Salles Érard and Pleyel in Paris,
Bechstein Hall in London, or even Steinway Hall in New York. (Chickering
built a hall in Boston as well.) The sponsorship arrangement was beneficial
to both the firm and the pianist. Pianists had the advantage of access to the
firm's American contacts, while the firm gained from the prestige that a virtuoso lent to its name. Yet Bülow's tour, at least, had not gone happily, either
for him or for Chickering, notwithstanding Bülow having given the American premiere of Tchaikovsky's first piano concerto in his debut in Boston.
In *Men, Women, and Pianos*, Arthur Loesser recalled:

> At a rehearsal with an orchestra [in Baltimore] he spied the large gilt-let-
> tered sign saying "Chickering" that had been hung on the side of his
> piano, facing the audience. He took it off, threw it on the floor, looked at
> it malevolently, and said furiously for all to hear: "I am not a traveling ad-
> vertisement!" Presently, in an intermission, he picked up the offending
> piece of wood, hooked it on the tail end of the piano, and proceeded to
> give it a poke with his foot. Kicking his patron and collaborator Chicker-
> ing in the behind, publicly, was not likely to gain him friends, even among
> disinterested parties. (532)

The tour was aborted after Bülow had played only 139 concerts of the
scheduled 172. Thus did Chickering recruit Pachmann to play its piano in
the New World.

Although Pachmann was happy with the Chickering piano itself, like
Bülow, he was unhappy to discover, upon arriving in one midwestern town,

that the firm's local agent had hung an enormous advertisement for the company on his piano. When he walked onstage and saw the sign, he tore it from the instrument à la Bülow and jumped on it until it had broken. Only then did he sit down and begin to play. Pachmann wrote to Frank Chickering himself, the company's president, explaining that the sign had made him feel like an employee instead of an artist. Chickering good-naturedly replied that he was glad that Pachmann had jumped only on the sign. (When Mr. Chickering died the following year, Pachmann—who appreciated his goodwill—played the *Funeral March* from Beethoven's piano sonata opus 26 in his memory.)

Although Rubinstein had played an enormous Chopin recital as part of his farewell to America,[1] Pachmann's Chopin *cyclus* (three recitals each in New York and Boston) was the first of its kind to be performed there, and it caused a sensation—notwithstanding the pianist initially having been received, as Americo Gori wrote for the *American Musician* (12 April), "with indifference, almost with coldness." This *cyclus* was impresario Frederick A. Schwab's idea. As he explained: "We had had so many pianists this season that it was necessary to make some special feature of Mr. De Pachmann's debut."

The only major Chopin works not included on these programs—although Pachmann would play them on other occasions—were the fourth ballade and the *Polonaise-fantasie* (which Liszt, according to his pupil August Göllerich, judged unpianistic). In fact, several of the notable works in Pachmann's Chopin repertoire were less commonly played then than now—meaning that while he did not have the field of their performance exclusively to himself, he had nonetheless the distinction of being a pioneer. Among these works were the second and fourth ballades, F-sharp and G-flat impromptus, E-flat minor ("Siberian") and F-sharp minor polonaises, rondo opus 16, fourth scherzo, and the *Allegro de Concert*.[2] Had Pachmann's interpretations of these works, however, not been compelling, on occasion amounting even to revelation, his pioneerism would have been of little account. Apropos Pachmann's performance of the *Allegro de Concert*, for instance, E. Prout (*Athenaeum*, 21 January 1888) wrote: "That which seemed dry and involved became under his fingers instinct with beauty and feeling; the musicians and amateurs present listened as if spellbound, and opinion was unanimous that the performance was nothing short of an artistic creation. For the sake of the composer, if not for his own reputation, the pianist should repeat it, not once, but many times." The *Musical Times* (1 April 1890) seconded the opinion: "Mr. de Pachmann is the only pianist who renders the [*Allegro de Concert*] interesting. As generally interpreted, it appears one of the least inspired of Chopin's efforts."

Presently, on 11 April (Friday evening), Pachmann and Maggie each played a concerto as well as solos in a "Grand Concert with Orchestra" conducted by F. Van der Stucken in Chickering Hall. Pachmann, Gori wrote in the *American Musician* (19 April), "revealed himself in a new light by his magnificent delivery of the Chopin [F minor] concerto":

> [H]e displayed [power and authority] in a triumphant manner in the passages of the concerto where they were required; at the same time M. de Pachmann did not neglect the *cantabile* parts, but gave them with that full singing quality of tone, that poetic feeling and perfect finish which distinguished his solo playing and which he found occasion to exemplify later in the evening, in the selections by Schumann [*Romanze* 32/3] and Raff [*La Fileuse*], and particularly in Mme. de Pachmann's "Rêverie," a charming little *pièce de genre* which was successful for both the composer and for the executant.

"The advent of Mme. de Pachmann (*née* Maggie Okey) was awaited with considerable interest," Gori reflected, "as public curiosity had been excited by the accounts of her beauty and talents, which had preceded her arrival in America."

> Mme. de Pachmann is undoubtedly a pretty woman; her face is aristocratic in outline, extremely pleasing in expression, and is crowned with a diadem of wavy locks, gathered in a knot at the back of her head, which is poised on a slender and graceful neck; her figure is lithe and *elancée*, her carriage is elegant, her attitude and movements at the piano unaffectedly charming.
> Mme. de Pachmann's playing corresponds to her personal appearance; it is grace and elegance personified; it is brilliant and dainty, without exaggerations in style or manner; it is accurate and conscientious, without being pedantic in the least.

Despite his gallant effort to sound praiseworthy, however, Gori was clearly more impressed by Maggie's beauty than by her talents: "Her performance of the Liszt concerto [E-flat], though not very powerful, was correct in execution and intelligent in conception; it was not distinguished by remarkable originality, but was, nevertheless, pleasing, owing to the taste and feeling with which each measure was imbued." As for her solo numbers (Henselt's *Danklied nach Sturm* and Weber's *Rondo brillante*), Gori wrote:

> Mme. de Pachmann displayed an uncommonly reliable *technique* and a delicacy of expression which were highly artistic; her style has many qualities which betray the results of her talented husband's teachings and example, modified, of course, by her womanly temperament—not possessing his force and breadth, she compensated for their absence by an earnestness of purpose and an unmistakable sincerity, which met with hearty appreciation.

Nor was Gori the only critic to be underwhelmed by Maggie's playing. While the writer for the *Musical Courier* (16 April 1890) confessed to being enamored of her "most soulful and intense eyes," he also lamented, "If she would only get a little of their intensity as far as the keyboard!" At the end of this concert Pachmann and Maggie played Saint-Saëns's scherzo for two pianos, a performance Gori admired for its "perfect *ensemble* in color and execution"—although not for its value as a work of art.[3]

On 17 April, Maggie participated in a private concert of the Rubinstein Club at Chickering Hall; on 28 April, she gave a Chopin recital at the same venue; and on 30 April, she made her Boston recital debut.[4] Additionally, she and Pachmann would sometimes give "two-piano" recitals, although these were not usually "two-piano" in the sense that we understand today (that is, a work written for two pianos): then, it meant "played in alternation." One such concert was given at Philadelphia's Academy of Music on 13 May: [Mr.] Beethoven: 32 Variations in C minor; [Mrs.] Chopin: *Andante spianato* and *Grande Polonaise;* [Mr.] Chopin: nocturne, *Allegro de Concert*, études 10/11 and 12, and waltz 64/2; [Mrs.] Liszt: *Au bord d'une source*, *Waldesrauschen*, and *Galop russe;* and [Mr.] Chopin: impromptu opus 29, *Berceuse*, mazurka 41/1, and *Tarantella*.

Two days later, at Chickering Hall, they played this program: [Mr.] Chopin: ballade opus 38, *Fantasie-impromptu*, and scherzo opus 31; [Mrs.] Henselt's *Danklied nach Sturm* and *Si oiseau j'étais*, and Rubinstein's *Galop* (*Le Bal*); [Mr.] Chopin: nocturne 37/2, études 10/3 and 25/1, mazurka 56/2, and waltz 34/3; [Mrs.] Liszt's *Au bord d'une source*, Schubert's impromptu no. 4 (opus unspecified), and Raff's *Rigaudon;* and [Mr.] Chopin: nocturne 55/1 and polonaise opus 53.

The couple then made a "farewell appearance" ("farewell" meaning good-bye to a particular city) on 17 May at Chickering Hall: [Mr.] Chopin: *Fantasie* and *Allegro de Concert;* [Mrs.] Mendelssohn's *Variations sérieuses* and Rubinstein's *Barcarolle* in G major and *Galop;* [Mr.] Chopin: nocturne 37/2, études 10/3 and 25/1, mazurka 56/2, and waltz 34/3 ("The above five numbers for the first time," the program indicates); [Mrs.] Liszt's *Waldesrauschen* and Raff's *Rigaudon;* and [Mr.] Chopin: ballade opus 38, impromptu opus 29, and scherzo opus 31.

A common feature of these concerts—almost never heard today—was unison playing. Here the idea was for the two pianists to select a celebrated solo and to play it synchronously, as Pachmann and Maggie did in London with *Si oiseau j'étais*. Among the works the couple specialized in performing this way was Mendelssohn's *Spinnerlied*. In their private lives, however, they were not nearly so much in unison, and too often Pachmann publicized his frustrations, jealousies, and resentments at concerts. If for some reason he did not feel like playing, he might step onto the stage and announce without warning that Maggie would be performing in his stead—a change of personnel that pleased neither his wife nor his audience. Or he would call out, "Charmante! Magnifique!" from his seat while she performed, with the result that he received the attention that should have been hers. On one occasion, according to James Gibbons Huneker (*Steeplejack* 168), he actually hissed her playing of a Henselt étude: "Oscar Hammerstein, I remember, had hissed a performer in his Manhattan Opera House, but for a husband to hiss his wife in public we must go to the pages of *Artists' Wives,* by Alphonse Daudet." (In "A Couple of Singers," a story from *Artists' Wives,* the tenor husband—covetous of his soprano wife's glory—hires a cabal to hiss her.) Perhaps because constant travel deprived him of the stability he required in order to maintain his equilibrium, Pachmann's behavior usually degenerated as a tour progressed. In this case, in the weeks before Maggie returned to England he took to flying into a rage at the slightest provocation, once losing control so completely that he threatened to "kill everyone" and had to be locked in a cupboard.

His temper was legendary. A story about him that would circulate widely took place at Lüchow's restaurant in New York, not far from the Prince George Hotel on East Twenty-seventh Street, where he stayed until his last American tour. As Josef Škvorecký tells it in his novel *Dvořák in Love,* Huneker was dining with pianist Rafael Joseffy, when Pachmann appeared.

> "Oh dear, it's Chopinzee!" [Huneker] whispered. They looked around. A small man with wild eyes had walked into the café and was looking around cockily. He caught sight of the massive Huneker crouched behind his tankard. The little man crouched too, but it was more like the stance of a wrestler about to lunge. He stretched out an extraordinarily long arm pointed straight at Huneker. "Aha!" he cried. Everyone stopped and looked around. Huneker huddled down almost out of sight. "I see you, don't try to hide. So, the great music critic Mr. Huneker says de Pachmann plays his Chopin effeminately, does he? De Pachmann is the fairy of the piano whose Bach is worse than his bite? De Pachmann isn't what he once was, isn't that what you wrote, Huneker?" The man stormed over to a piano at the side of the restaurant. "Now you listen to this, Huneker. This is just for you. Listen carefully." He sat down and began to play, while the others stared at each other uncomprehendingly. The man's body wove strangely about but his eyes were fastened firmly on Huneker. What he played made little sense. It might have been Chopin, performed with a torrent of feeling and theatrical virtuosity—but if so it was a strange, unfamiliar Chopin. As he played, he talked in a loud voice: "Huneker, I'm playing you a very difficult composition—and I hope I'm playing it well." Several chords, and then: "Listen to my left hand. Pianissimo! Is it good?

No? Yes! Ha-ha-ha! Liszt played it faster, but—ha-ha-ha!—Rubinstein was slower." An acrobatic flourish in the left hand, then the right, the piercing eyes never once looking at the keyboard but stabbing Huneker's face, which had now broken out in a sweat. The critic shuddered. "Ha-ha, Huneker! There used to be two great pianists in the world: Liszt and de Pachmann—and now, Liszt is dead. Joseffy tried to play it, Huneker, but it's far beyond his abilities, ha-ha! But I, Vladimir de Pachmann—the greatest interpreter of Chopin in the world—oh yes, I know how, Huneker." . . .

. . . A final, lightning arpeggio, and the little man stood up from the piano and grinned at them. "You're a great critic, Huneker, but you've never heard anything like that before. Only Vladimir de Pachmann can play like that." With an ominous chuckle, he walked over to their table. . . . "How did you like that, Huneker?" Huneker stayed put but there was a quaver in his voice when he replied. "I never like any composition played backwards. Especially Chopin." The pianist clapped. "You're a bright man, Huneker, but you're still a skunk! For someone who can't even play the piano himself, you're a dirty, critical, son-of-a-bitching skunk!"

. . . "You smell like a toilet, Huneker." Huneker rose to his feet. Suddenly, de Pachmann bent down, grabbed a tankard and, in a flash, hurled the golden liquid into the critic's face. De Pachmann lunged at Huneker, but before he could land a blow he found himself pinioned between two large waiters. Mr. Fleischmann, with his severe, patriarchal beard, approached. "Apologize to Mr. Huneker, Maestro, or I'll have to ask you to leave the establishment." The virtuoso muttered: "Very well, I apologize. Let me go! I apologize!" Mr. Fleischmann nodded his head, the waiters loosened their grip, the little man straightened his tie with dignity and in a tone of profound disgust said: "Skunk, I apologize to you." And he wheeled about triumphantly. The door slammed. (319–22)

Like most stories concerning Pachmann, this one was told many times, with variants. Yet what is more striking than the differences between the versions is their common portrayal of Pachmann as a man inclined to the most theatrical rages. These, like his concerts, were performances, which may be why Huneker, along with Philip Hale in Boston and Olin Downes in New York, remained among his most faithful advocates, notwithstanding the occasional set-to. Nor was Pachmann himself in any way offended by Huneker's description of him as "Chopinzee." (This term has since been used to describe the pianist so often that it would be impossible to begin to cite even a fraction of its appearances in the Pachmann literature.) "Monkeys are your real *Incroyables* [Parisian dandies of the Directoire period]," Luciane declares in Goethe's *Elective Affinities,* "and I cannot understand why people want to keep them out of the best society" (179). It was likely this idea of the monkey of which Huneker was thinking when he called Pachmann Chopinzee.

Later in the year, Chickering published a testimonial to its pianos from Pachmann. "After a few months' [summer] sojourn in the Catskills and at Saratoga," the advertisement began, "during which M. de Pachmann acquired a closer acquaintance with the Chickering Piano, the eminent virtuoso sent to the manufacturer the following":

"The Willoughby," Saratoga, August 25, 1890

The Chickering Piano rightfully stands alone, for on this earth it is not only unsurpassed but unequalled. I can give logical and esthetic proofs of my assertion. When one asks: why do these unique manufacturers attain perfection? the answer is: because they have endeavored to secure (as no others have done) and have succeeded in securing the nearest possible approach to the tone of nature, to what is known as the human voice: the Chickering piano sings like a lovely voice. This is no compliment, but the expression of my innermost conviction, if I may harbor an opinion on this subject.

Yours truly,
Vladimir de Pachmann

In the war of piano manufacturers to gain recognition for their instruments, such testimonials could be immensely valuable—even though a pianist might change his loyalties from one season (or tour) to the next if offered better terms. (In fact, the pianos Pachmann played included models by Baldwin, Bechstein, Blüthner, Bösendorfer, Gaveau, Heintzman, Knabe, New Scale Williams, and Steinway. Some of these he also endorsed.) In his memoirs, Paderewski described an experience in Russia that showed the lengths to which piano manufacturers would go in order to sabotage rival instruments—and the pianists who played them.

As I had been accustomed for several years (when not in America) to play the Érard piano, I asked my good friend Monsieur Blondel to send two Érard concert grands for the Russian tour in 1899. He did so. They were beautiful and I was delighted, but when I came to the concert hall in St. Petersburg, half an hour before the arrival of the orchestra, I found, to my horror, that one of the pedals of the instrument was completely destroyed; and when I tried the piano, I found, between many of the keys, sharp pins standing up. (266)

Piano manufacturers were not the only ones to make Pachmann the front man for a product, an idea, or even a movement. In the *Chicago Inter-Ocean* (28 November 1890), a writer identified only as B. published an essay titled "A Pachmann Fantasy" that reveals the degree to which the pianist was being made an avatar of a movement—aestheticism—from which, at least explicitly, he would remain aloof.[5] As the essay opens, B. is listening to Pachmann play Chopin's *Funeral March,* the notes of which sink "to a half inaudible miserere." Then, at the moment "when the music was faintest in the exquisite melody of sorrow and the audience was intent almost to pain in sympathy," he (or she) hears at his side "a sigh like a stifled sob."

> Turning, I saw in the chair I had thought unoccupied, a slight man of delicate features with a forehead like a saint's, his large, spiritual eyes shadowed by the intensest melancholy, his countenance transparent in the radiance of a singular beauty that seemed wholly apart the physical fineness of the man. The lips were compressed, but the drooping head was eloquent of a sadness that awakened pity and invited commiseration. I leaned toward him and would have put my hand consolingly upon his shoulder, but to my dismay and terror my hand encountered no resistance; what seemed a shadow was as impalpable as air. I felt an indescribable impulse to quit the place, yet there mingled with my fear a sense of assurance and half-yearning compassion—for, notwithstanding I touched nothing, but saw my hand clothed, as it were, with the shadow of mystery, the man and his grief seemed to me as real as life and sorrow. By a great effort of the will I summoned faint voice to whisper:
> "What troubles you, my friend?"
> Without changing his attitude he who sat so dejectedly beside me answered in a strangely musical voice and, as it seemed, in natural full tones, so that I turned to see if others besides myself had heard—
> "He hath my soul. I may not rest. I may not enter into bliss until the time when he shall render it me again."

When the narrator inquires of the figure, "Who hath thy soul?" the figure points "with a feminine finger" toward the pianist, and answers "sadly, but without bitterness": "He who playeth there. He hath stolen from me the blessing of heaven, and estranged me from the realms of joy. I may not enter into peace ere that he give back mine own. See, even now he bends his ear to listen to the murmur of my soul and plays as bidden."

The narrator looks toward the platform, where "the player, scarce touching the keys that nevertheless gave forth tenderest, tearfulest sounds, nodded his head as though approving and obeying some occult minister, listening with greater eagerness and fingering the keys even more lightly till they trembled into sound that was almost silence."

> It was the communion of spirits over the march of the dead, and the player was lost to himself and to the great, still audience that wept, hear-

ing and not hearing. On the instant the music closed, dying into the mere memory of its pitiful sweetness. The player sat as spellbound as the entranced audience, and for the shadow of a moment not a breath too loud disturbed the heaven-born ecstasy of sense. Then he beside me, quickly lifting that shapely head, with sadness gone from the glorious eyes but a world of agony and yearning come into them, cried aloud in voice vibrant with pain, "Voleur! Tu as mon ame!" The player startled from his revery cast a hasty glance toward the audience that now was thundering applause, seemed to gaze at the accusing specter, wiped two glistening tears from his eyes, bowed unsmiling to the audience, and as one with grieving heart quitted the platform.

I turned toward him beside me, angered at first, but at once pitiful as I saw him sink again into the hopelessness of despair; and I said as tears suffused my eyes, "Pray, friend, tell me who you are."

And he answered, vanishing as he answered:

"Alas! I am he who once was Chopin in the world of men, but now with neither men nor angels have abiding place, for that I have no soul."

"Nay, demand your own of him," I said.

"Yea, when that he dieth, not before," came the answer from him I could no longer see. And then, when Pachmann reappeared, he looked toward the empty seat and smiled, and the audience hailed him with bravos.

Admittedly, B.'s rather somber image of Pachmann hardly jibes with the pianist's reputation as a comedian. Yet this very divergence from received portrayals, if inaccurate of Pachmann's onstage character, is revelatory of his playing, the intensity of which torments even the half-alive, half-dead emanation of Chopin himself. A preoccupation with the occult in general—and vampirism in particular—distinguished much fin-de-siè-cle thought and prompted no less august a figure than Walter Pater, in his essay on Leonardo in *The Renaissance,* to write of the Mona Lisa:

> She is older than the rocks among which she sits; like the vampire, she has been dead many times, and learned the secrets of the grave; and has been a diver in deep seas, and keeps their fallen day about her; and trafficked for strange webs with Eastern merchants: and, as Leda, was the mother of Helen of Troy, and, as Saint Anne, the mother of Mary; and all this has been to her but as the sound of lyres and flutes, and lives only in the delicacy with which it has moulded the changing lineaments, and tinged the eyelids and the hands. (125)

For B., Pachmann is the vampire.

In New York, the major musical event of 1891 was the opening of Carnegie Hall. Tchaikovsky, who arrived in the city at the end of April on the *Bretagne,* conducted the inaugural concert on 5 May.[6] He kept a diary during his trip, and wrote several letters to his family from America. Like Pachmann, he found the new world amazing, writing in a letter to his nephew Vladimir Davydov (18–30 April):

> [O]ut of all the arrangements in New York that would most please you, is that every apartment has a toilet room with a lavatory, bath, and wash-basin, and both the bath and the basin have constant hot and cold water. Splashing in my bath in the morning I always think of you. There is elec-tric and gas lighting. Candles are not used at all. If one needs something one does not ask for it in the way one does in Europe—here you ring and say what you want into a tube hanging near the bell. Or if someone downstairs wants to see you, they ring you and tell you through the tube who is there and what they want. This is rather awkward for me as I do not know English. No one, except the staff, uses the stairs. The lift never stops working, running up and down at a terrific speed, taking in and putting out the hotel guests. (*Letters* 489)

On 11 May, traveling by train from New York to Buffalo (he was going to Niagara Falls), Tchaikovsky wrote in his diary:

> I got into the drawing room car. It is like our Pullman car only the easy chairs are placed closer to one another and with backs to the windows, but in such a way that it is possible to turn in all directions. The windows are large and the view on both sides is completely unobstructed. Next to this car was the dining car, while several cars away was the smoking car with a buffet. The connection from car to car is quite easy, much more conve-nient than with us, since the passage-ways are covered. The employees, i.e., the conductors, the waiters in the dining car and in the buffet in the smoking car, are Negroes who are very obliging and polite. (319)

Pachmann, too, was impressed to meet black Americans, and some-times sought out their attentions, as George Copeland recalled in his auto-biography:

> He loved Negroes, and adored being waited on by them especially in din-ing cars when he was on tour. He had all sorts of amusing ideas about food, and he would go into the diner and start dinner at dessert and go backward ending with soup. The entire staff of waiters were aghast not knowing what was going to happen next. And at the end, he was so en-thusiastic about these colored people, that he wanted to kiss each waiter on the cheek before he left the car.[7]

At one concert, in those days of segregation, Pachmann saw a black man standing in the wings; he walked over to him and led him to the center of the stage, telling the audience, "This man I *like*, and for him, and him alone, I will play Chopin's *Étude on the Black Notes.*" At this time, Pachmann would have been unlikely to meet any black Americans who were not in the service professions, especially black classical musicians.

In February 1892, he acquitted himself of three momentous programs at Chickering Hall:

11 (Thursday): Beethoven's "Moonlight" sonata and 32 Variations in C minor, Chopin's nocturnes 9/1 and 3, mazurkas 56/1 and 24/2, waltzes 69/1 and 2, and scherzo opus 54, and Liszt's *Après une lecture de Dante.*

13 (Saturday): Schumann's *Carnaval*, Chopin's *Bolero*, preludes 28/15 and 17, études 25/4 and 10, polonaise 71/2, and rondo opus 16, and Liszt's *St. François de Paule marchant sur les flots*, polonaise no. 1 (*Polonaise mélancolique*), *La leggierezza*, and *Valse-impromptu.*

18 (Thursday): Schumann's *Études symphoniques*, Chopin's ballade opus 23, nocturne 37/2, impromptu opus 36, études 25/3, 10/11, and 25/9, polonaise opus 53, Raff's *Giga con variazioni* (Suite opus 91), Henselt's *Liebeslied* and *Frühlingslied*, and Weber's *Perpetuum mobile.*

His all-Liszt recital at Chickering Hall two months later (21 April 1892) further refuted any impression that he was only a miniaturist. The program consisted of the sonata in B minor, *Harmonies du soir*, *St. François de Paule marchant sur les flots*, polonaise no. 1, *Mazurka brillante*, *La leggierezza*, *Eclogue*, *Cantique d'amour*, and *Tarantella* (*Venezia e Napoli*).

In terms of repertoire, these concerts—together with the 1890 Chopin *cyclus*—were among the most significant that he played in America.

Back in England—she appears to have returned before her husband—Maggie fulfilled a heavy calendar of engagements. At St. James's Hall, she played Beethoven's "Les adieux" sonata, Raff's *Rigaudon*, several works of Chopin (among them two studies from opus 25 and the *Andante spianato* and *Grande Polonaise*), and her *Thème et variations*. Then on 27 June, again at St. James's Hall, she played Chopin's E minor concerto with Cowen. Finally, on 7 July, she gave her last recital of the season. The *Musical Times* (1 August 1891) allowed that while she had greatly benefited by Pachmann's tuition, "she seemed scarcely at her ease" in Beethoven's piano sonata opus 26. It was felt—expectedly—that she was heard to better advantage in Chopin's ballade opus 23 and two studies and in Mendelssohn's *Variations sérieuses*.

Later that year, George Bernard Shaw, with characteristic asperity, reviewed "pianist and pantomimist" Vladimir de Pachmann's performance of Beethoven's third concerto and some Chopin ("including a juvenile *scherzo* which nobody wanted to hear at full length at five o'clock in the afternoon") at a Crystal Palace concert for the *World* (19 October): "De Pachmann is unquestionably a very able pianist, and by no means an insincere one; but now that I have seen, in La Statue du Commandeur, a lady sing a song in dumb show, I want to see a pianoforte concerto played in the same way; and I think there can be no doubt that de Pachmann is the player for that feat." Shaw was becoming the most vocal member of a community of listeners who found Pachmann's onstage mannerisms at best distracting and at worst offensive. Yet the pianist's popularity was showing no sign of eclipse. His audiences either warmed to the intimacy and humor of his behavior or found his playing so ravishing as to obviate every other consideration.

His marriage, on the other hand, was foundering and would soon end. Although their letters have not been found (possibly they were destroyed), other evidence suggests that Pachmann, and not Maggie, was chiefly responsible for its dissolution. It was his habit, in private and in public, to divert his unhappiness over large, and sometimes inchoate, matters into expressions of frustration over small ones. Now a badly cooked egg or a disagreement with his wife over a Henselt étude made him apoplectic. Invariably, once he had calmed down, he would exhort Maggie to forgive him for these paroxysms, explaining, according to their son Lionel, "I can't help it. It's just the way I am." (Here he might have been trying, albeit unconsciously, to intimate his homosexuality, a crucial if unvoiced facet of the way he was.)

The combined pressures of living with an erratic Pachmann, raising children, and sustaining her own career put Maggie under too great a strain for his apologies to count for much. Because she did not want their children to grow up in such an atmosphere of rancour and inconsistency, she asked her husband for a separation. She remained in Paris, while Pachmann went to England, staying with his friends the Defries at their country house and giving the occasional concert. He would not play in London again until 1898.

It is likely that Maggie's affair with Fernand Labori, whom she had already known for several years, began around this time. Labori was in many ways the opposite of Pachmann. Younger than Maggie, he was described by Le Gaulois (6 January 1894) as "tall, blond, of elegant and acute appearance, the expression frank, the voice warm, the movements sober and neat." (A few years later, even the dry legal journal Vie Judiciare would appreciate "his athletic form, the fine head, energetic—that a few grey hairs have begun to soften—the sonorous voice, of a deep sonority, without metallic edges.") During his illustrious career, Labori defended not only Alfred Dreyfus but also Émile Zola, after the publication of "J'accuse" (Zola was accused of libeling the French president and the French army); Henriette Caillaux, who assassinated Gaston Calmette, the editor of Le Figaro, over the publication of the love letters that her husband, France's finance minister, had written to her during the extramarital affair that had preceded their wedding; and Thérèse Humbert ("La Grande Thérèse"), perhaps the most successful con artist of all time, whose downfall exposed unsuspected corruption in the French Left much as the Dreyfus affair exposed it in the Right. Presently Maggie became pregnant by Labori and married him upon finalization of her divorce in 1895. They were to have three daughters—Violette, Denise, and Odette—and a son who died before becoming an adult.

"She divorced me," Pachmann said later, "because I played the étude in double thirds of Chopin better than she." Yet his jocular responses to his divorce never concealed the suffering and remorse it had actually caused him. Years later, in "Looking Back," the pianist Marie Novello recalled meeting Pachmann in London. "I shall never forget the circumstances of that meeting," she wrote, "for the great man greeted me one evening as I was standing outside the artistes' entrance at the Queen's Hall with the strange words: 'Who are you? You look like my wife when I married her.'" Moreover, Pachmann's relationship with Novello reiterated his early tutelage of Maggie:

> I told him that I had just come from Vienna, and he asked me to play to him. That strange meeting was the prelude to a series of memorable Sunday afternoons spent at his house, when he would invariably play a ballade of Chopin. Coming to the big part at the end, he would stop and exclaim: "Now you play this," and he would then get up from the piano and let me take his place.
>
> Sometimes he would play to me for two or three hours at a stretch, and knowing his reluctance to play in private, I was naturally sensible of how greatly I was honoured.

His fondness and respect for Maggie never diminished, nor did the tone of wistfulness that came over him when he spoke of her. Long after they had divorced, he would refer to her as "my wife, Madame Labori."

FIVE

Colleagues

Of all of his contemporaries, the pianist who seemed most the antithesis of Pachmann was Leopold Godowsky, whom the composer and
critic Kaikhosru Shapurji Sorabji would later characterize as "a deeply interesting and significant musician, and a very distinguished mind, for all that a
glowing imagination, poetry, and high fantasy are not his." In Sorabji's view,
Godowsky possessed every quality that Pachmann did not: circumspection,
tact, and reserve. As it happens, though, both men were preoccupied with
attaining an ideal of perfection in their respective spheres, and they shared a
keen sense of humor. Godowsky, in fact, is the author of one of the most famous retorts in all of music history. He was attending the sixteen-year-old
Jascha Heifetz's American debut (Carnegie Hall, 27 October 1917) in the
company of the violinist Mischa Elman, when during the intermission
Elman complained that the hall was too hot. Godowsky replied, "Not for
pianists."[1] Although Pachmann first heard Godowsky play in Chicago in
1893—Godowsky was then head of the piano department at the Chicago
Conservatory—they did not become friends until the turn of the century.

Pachmann was more enthusiastic and voluble about Godowsky's music
than about that of any other composer (always excepting Chopin) and
thought him the greatest master of polyphonic writing after Bach. Godowsky's music was also passionately decadent: Only the author of *The Gardens
of Buitenzorg* could have elaborated Albéniz's already hothouse *Triana*. As
Huneker put it in *Steeplejack,* "Liszt had been [Pachmann's] god, but
Godowsky was become his living deity" (207). When, for its December
1907 issue, *Strand Magazine* asked him to name "The Piece I Most Enjoy
Playing" for a symposium of eminent performers, Pachmann considered
music of Chopin,[2] Weber, and Richard Strauss before giving as his answer
"the arrangements of Godowsky—every one superb, *magnifique, colossal!* I
will not choose any one of them, for I love and admire them all." Later
Pachmann would be passionate about Godowsky's piano sonata in E minor,

regarding it as the most significant piano sonata since Brahms's opus 5 (which he long threatened to play). He predicted, and rightly, that the work would never be a success, however—and for a reason that had nothing to do with its difficulty: "Godowsky dedicated it to his wife," he explained.

Pachmann's advocacy was by no means confined to talk. According to Blickstein, for instance, he attended a recital in London during which Godowsky played his arrangement of the Chopin étude 10/1 for the left hand alone. Many in the audience were affronted by the audacity of the work and ventured to hiss the composer-pianist, at which point Pachmann stood (he was instantly recognized), gave the audience a withering glance, then walked onto the stage and whispered something to Godowsky—who played the étude again. Again in *Steeplejack,* Huneker admitted that Pachmann made Godowsky's music known to him by playing much of it for him in his New York apartment: "[Pachmann] had studied, mastered, and memorised all those transcendental variations on Chopin studies, the most significant variations since the Brahms-Paganini scaling of the heights of Parnassus; and I heard for the first time the paraphrase of Weber's 'Invitation to the Valse,' a much more viable arrangement than Tausig's; also thrice as difficult" (207). In a letter from Berlin (30 September 1900) to Maurice Aronson, Godowsky wrote: "Pachmann is studying hard on my version of 'Invitation to the Dance' and hopes to play it in his second recital. He goes as much, if not more, in extasies [*sic*] over my work, and advertises me wherever he goes. Manager Wolff says that Pachmann is Godowsky-mad!" (Nicholas 46). For his part, Godowsky remembered Pachmann's advocacy by dedicating to him his Chopin study no. 26, after the étude 25/2. Although Pachmann recorded the Chopin-Godowsky étude 10/12 for the left hand, as well as one after 10/5, he never recorded the one dedicated to him.[3] (Nor did he ever play or record either the transcription of the gavotte from Gluck's *Don Juan* or that of a Scarlatti gigue, which Ignaz Friedman dedicated to him.)

Pachmann's theatrical demonstrations at Godowsky's concerts often rivaled those at his own. At one, for instance, he called out from his place in the audience, "'No, no, Leopold, you moost play it like *so*,'" Harold Schonberg writes in *The Great Pianists.* "[Pachmann] played it like so, and then told the audience he wouldn't have given the demonstration for just any old pianist. 'But Godowsky,' he said, 'is *ze zecond* greatest liffing pianist'" (315). *Musical America* (17 March 1917; a report from London):

> When Mr. de Pachmann was not raising his eyes heavenwards in ecstatic admiration of his compatriot's artistry, he was calling his neighbor's attention to some particular finesse of interpretation, or turning to someone behind him to express by eloquent look or gesture his astonishment at

some dazzling feat of virtuosity. The smiles and smirks and nods and muttered ejaculations were, in truth, wonderful to behold. And not less wonderful the contrast he presented to the occupant of the platform, whose attitude at the piano, strangely unlike that of his brother artist, might almost be described as sphinx-like, so rigid are his features and inscrutable his expression.

The good humor with which Godowsky met Pachmann's enthusiasms was sometimes married to embarrassment when Pachmann called attention to Godowsky's presence in the audience of his own concerts. "There's Godowsky," Pachmann would say. "*He* can play the next encore." Or he might cover one of his hands with the other, explaining, "There's Godowsky, I don't want him to see my fingering." (According to Schonberg, Pachmann would do the same when his "alte freund" Rosenthal was in the audience.) Or, wanting to have his friend beside him as he played, he might leave the piano to find Godowsky in the hall, then pull him forcibly onto the stage. (It is said that once Pachmann pulled Godowsky so hard that he tore off his friend's coat. Running back onto the stage with it, he announced, "I couldn't bring Godowsky—but here's his coat!")

Although there have been endless tellings and retellings of the following anecdote, none is so succinct as Gary Graffman's (given in a letter to the author):

> [Pachmann] was about to play some Chopin work at Carnegie Hall, and after placing his hands on the keyboard, he removed them, turned to the audience and said, "But really nobody plays this piece like Godowsky." Turning to the box where Godowsky sat, he beckoned to him, calling, "Godowsky! Godowsky! Come and play this piece for us." According to legend, he wouldn't stop—and the audience joined him—until Godowsky sheepishly got up and came down from his box, went up on stage, and played the piece in question.

There is sometimes a coda to the anecdote in which, Godowsky having played, Pachmann tells the audience, "Godowsky is the greatest pianist of our day; yes, he is even greater than Pachmann. But Pachmann plays more *beautifully.*" And with this statement Godowsky might well have agreed. When he first heard Pachmann, he wrote to an American friend: "[His] playing is like a delicate and exquisitely scented perfume—evaporative, volatile, refined, suggestive, enchanting." He also regarded the fact that Pachmann's playing "defies all laws, all conventions, all analytical dissertations" as a supreme virtue. Thus, for him, was Pachmann's "the most individual form of artistic expression" he had ever encountered.

Although his methods were, to say the least, unorthodox, Pachmann did succeed in bringing Godowsky, who was by nature reticent, into the

popular imagination. To many of his colleagues Godowsky was "the pianist's pianist," but this arcane (and finally pointless) distinction in no way contributed to the successes that made him rich and famous. (Notwithstanding Godowsky's being called "the pianist's pianist," Rachmaninov was generally regarded as a superior artist.) On the contrary, it was Pachmann, with his prescient understanding of the mind of the public, who had brought Godowsky into the limelight—not only by making him part of his comedies but by advocating his music.

Having mentioned him, one might as well consider Pachmann's relationship to Rachmaninov—which has been the subject of no little confusion. The two Russians could not have been more dissimilar in temperament and affect—or effect. Where Pachmann was expansive, playful, and vulnerable, Rachmaninov, as Sorabji wrote in a review of one of his London recitals during the 1920s, remained always "dignified, grave and reserved, never over-stepping the bounds between artist and public, who are quietly and gently but very firmly kept in their place—no orchestra seats, one notices, are ever allowed at a Rachmaninoff recital." Daisy Kennedy (at one time Mrs. Benno Moiseiwitsch) recalls sharing a box at a Pachmann concert in London with conductor and pianist Landon Ronald and Rachmaninov, who had to be seduced into going along.

> So we all went off to the Albert Hall and sat in [Ronald's] rather prominent box. Pachmann came on and did his stuff. He played a couple of pieces, repeated them—talked to the audience . . . and then repeated them again. Pachmann would talk about everything. He talked about his playing, about them (the audience), about himself, about the piano, about the music. . . . Rachmaninov—very tall, very dignified, s-l-o-w-l-y rose from his seat and said, "I cannot stay. He is a Charlatan." Landon and I had to persuade him somewhat vigorously not to leave! We whispered, "You cannot go. The whole audience is looking at you." He had to stay. And I have never seen a more agonised face than Rachmaninov's listening to Pachmann. He just could not take it. We all enjoyed it thoroughly, but were sad to see Rachmaninov so unhappy.

In Kennedy's story, each pianist plays exactly, and only, to type. By contrast, Patrick Piggott, in his book *Rachmaninov,* describes the composer-pianist hearing Pachmann on another occasion—and reacting very differently.

> If Rachmaninov had to play the Prelude [in C-sharp minor] very often himself, he took great pains to avoid hearing it played by anyone else. On one occasion, however, at a recital by Vladimir de Pachmann, a pianist who was as renowned for his unpredictable antics on the platform as for his interpretations of Chopin, Rachmaninov's presence in the audience

was noticed by the celebrated virtuoso, who thereupon raised his hands high in the air and brought them crashing down on the opening notes of the Prelude. Pachmann lingered on the second note (G-sharp) for some time, grinning maliciously at Rachmaninov, who sank his head into his hands in an agony of embarrassment . . . only to raise it again a moment later in delighted amusement as the witty pianist converted the held G-sharp into the first note of Chopin's Fantasie-Impromptu, of which he proceeded to give his usual rippling interpretation. Not all Rachmaninov's colleagues poked fun at the Prelude as subtly as did Pachmann, and its composer was probably more irritated than amused by the letters he received from another colleague, Josef Hofmann, mischievously addressed to "Herr Cis Moll" (Mr. C-sharp minor). (30)

This anecdote is the very apotheosis of the Pachmannesque spirit. It also gives the lie to the dour image of Rachmaninov that Kennedy and others would perpetuate. (Pianist and piano historian Steven Heliotes wrote to the author that Gitta Gradova, a friend of Rachmaninov's, "heard de Pachmann here [Chicago] and said his sound was like chiffon and that it reminded her of Horowitz's pianissimi; quite a compliment coming from her since she was one of Horowitz's closest friends. She once threw Kapell out of her house for comparing himself to VH.")

Finally, Dan Wilson posted a fantastic—but, alas, completely impossible—anecdote about Pachmann and Rachmaninov's music on the Internet:

[O]ne of the stories that had stuck around in the Paris HMV headquarters, and was still active enough in the 1940s for Peter [de Jongh] to have heard it, was that on one occasion Pachmann was in the studio and started warming up with part of the Rachmaninov Second Sonata. The session producer asked Pachmann's keeper whether a full recording of this was possible, as it was not on the repertoire he had been handed. The answer was that Pachmann had to be forcibly prevented from playing it in public, because, while being suspicious of Rachmaninov the pianist as a possible competitor, he admired both the 1913 and 1931 versions of the Sonata so much that he would play them both, interlaced, with additional repeats. This played havoc with any recital timetable as it made the duration of the Sonata unpredictable—anything up to 45 minutes. It also made an issue on 78s impossible.

If the story were true, it would testify to Pachmann's receptiveness to new music even at the end of his life. By 1931, however, he was ill and unable to leave Italy. He could not possibly have played the 1931 version of the sonata in the concert hall, let alone the recording studio, any more than he could have fulfilled his desire to return to America. (His last recordings

were made in 1927.) While it is theoretically possible that Pachmann played the 1913 version of the sonata, it is practically inconceivable: His hands, like Hofmann's, were too small for him to "do" Rachmaninov. Hofmann, to whom the composer had dedicated the work, never played Rachmaninov's third piano concerto—not even on the piano Steinway had made specially for him. According to Gaisberg (*Gramophone,* October 1943), the Baldwin piano that Pachmann played in later years was also a specially made instrument; in "The Grand Old Man of the Piano," Stanley Markham wrote of Pachmann's "beloved piano, with its specially adjusted pedals to suit his short legs," but omitted to name the make of it.

In 1893, Pachmann returned to America.

Of a recital that he gave at Chickering Hall—the first of the tour—the *New York Times* (18 October 1893) pronounced, "If it were possible to take M. Vladimir de Pachmann seriously, he might be pronounced the most accomplished farceur in the world. But it is not possible for any one else to take this pianist seriously, because he takes himself so." The problem, according to the critic, was that while the public understood *Hamlet,* it "does not understand Chopin any more than M. de Pachmann does, and, as we have frequently said, there is no art in which imposition is so easy as in piano playing. . . . If his intellectual equipment were as large as his technical mastery of the keyboard, he would be a great pianist, but it takes brains to make an artist." The critic reserved his sharpest words, however, for Pachmann's performance of Chopin's piano sonata opus 35, which he called, "with the exception of the last movement, simply a piece of grotesquerie."

> He played the forte passages piano, and the piano passages forte, made exaggerated transitions in dynamics and unexpected holds, and otherwise distorted the beautiful work almost as unpleasantly as he distorted his countenance while playing it. He "read" the ballade in a similar manner, and then, seemingly satisfied that he had sufficiently surprised his hearers, played the G minor nocturne very beautifully. His performance of the impromptu was exquisite in color and clearness. It would be a pleasure to give more praise, but, so long as M. de Pachmann persists in treating his art as a mountebank would, he cannot expect much commendation in these columns.

Pachmann obtained a better press (though not without a backhand) from the *New York Times* (1 November) on the occasion of his third recital in the city. He had played the Chopin *Fantasie* "with an intelligence unusual for him and with splendid color, vigor, and variety of touch. It was a notable exhibition of his remarkable technical ability, and aroused the audience to a high pitch of enthusiasm."

"Pianists and Pianism" (*Music,* November 1893) took the form of a dialogue between the writer, Alfred Veit, and "a lady, herself no mean performer." Its subjects were Rubinstein, Bülow, d'Albert, Planté, Josef Wieniawski (brother of violinist and composer Henri), Theodor Ritter, Carl Heyman, and our Pachmann. (Pieces that place Pachmann the musician in the context of his colleagues are significant because they are so uncommon.) Veit's paragraphs on Heyman—a pianist about whom even Hanslick was enthusiastic—are especially valuable because Pachmann was compared to him more than once. "Emanuel Muzio, pupil and friend of Verdi, said to me one day: 'Do not fail to go to Pasdeloup's next concert at the Cirque d'Été. You will hear a new pianist. He hails from Holland and has been compared to Liszt and Rubinstein. His name is Carl Heyman.'"4

> The following Sunday, of course, found me at the Cirque d'Été. After the usual symphony and several orchestral selections, the pianist appeared. The new arrival proved to be of medium height, with uncommonly awkward manners. The way he bowed to the audience was awkward, his walk was ungraceful; in fact, there was nothing about him to predispose one in his favor. But when he began to play Chopin's D-flat nocturne! Has it ever happened to you that you completely forgot your surroundings? It did to me that day. I saw nothing but a graceful swan slowly gliding over a sheet of water, and away off in the distance.—
>
> "The wakeful nightingale in her amorous descant sang."5
>
> Not a hand was raised after the final notes had died away, whether from lack of appreciation on the part of the audience or in expectation of what was coming, I cannot say. The second number on the pianist's programme was Heyman's own "Elves at Play," and rarely has a name been given more aptly to composition or style of playing.

"And have you heard no one to remind you of Carl Heyman?" the lady asks Veit. "Yes," he replies, "in some respects Vladimir de Pachmann does, that prince of 'absolute pianism,' but besides delicacy and poetry Pachmann possesses strength which was not one of Heyman's prominent qualities."6

> Pachmann, to me, taken on the whole, is one of the most satisfactory manipulators of the keyboard. His performances of Raff's "Giga con Variazioni" and Liszt's "Après une lecture de Dante" shall ever remain in my memory as some of the finest specimens of pianism I ever heard. And did his playing of Henselt's "Si oiseau j'étais" not recall the moment when Liszt heard Henselt himself play it, and the author of *Beethoven et Ses Trois Styles* gave utterance to his enthusiasm by the words: "An Aeolian harp concealed beneath wreaths of flowers." It is trying to paint the lily to speak of Pachmann's superiority as a Chopin performer. In the rendition

of Chopin's music his supremacy is undisputed, and for this very reason Pachmann must suffer by that unwritten law which, with the public and certain critics, reads that versatility in art is an impossibility.

By way of developing his argument against this unwritten law, Veit gives examples of it: "Mr. X. plays Chopin admirably—but his interpretation of Beethoven is not to be taken seriously," and "Mr. Y. plays Beethoven admirably—but his Chopin playing reminds one of an elephant trying to dance with a butterfly." "In addition to these felicitous remarks," he continues, "we have the question of nationality"—meaning that (for the anti-versatilists) the musician from the "fatherland" (the German-speaking world) is de facto a great performer of a classical composition. Veit illustrates this point by telling how Sarasate's interpretation of the Beethoven violin concerto was received with only "polite attention."

> Thus Pachmann's beautiful interpretation of the "Moonlight" is greeted with a shrug of the shoulder; an excellent performance of the C minor variations calls forth a knowing wink, and the final opinion in regard to the Beethoven playing of the artist who makes that most uninteresting of Beethoven's sonatas (Op. 54) interesting and palatable is: "Ah! yes. But is his Chopin playing not delightful?"

Finally, Veit commends the acumen and originality Pachmann showed in building his programs, for he was weary of the "same musical menu" served to concertgoers season after season. "I know it is heresy pure and simple to confess it," he wrote, "but I would like to hear Nicodé's exquisite 'Canzonetta,' for a change, in preference to one of those classical *chevaux de bataille* which are trotted out for us every season. Let us take care of the living—the dead take care of themselves!"

> Pachmann's programmes are as varied as they are interesting. Occasionally a bit of Weber, a trifle by Henselt or Raff brighten his programmes, without mentioning his splendid Liszt recitals, which must have been a revelation to the most blasé music lover. Even Pachmann's Chopin programmes contained many novelties. I only need mention that graceful polonaise, in B-flat, Op. 71, which had a fine Mozartian ring about it. The originality of the man is furthermore shown by his challenge of public opinion in playing concertos from notes.

Veit praised Pachmann justly for his programs. He was, for example, attentive to the effect of the sequence of keys and of temperaments of the works he chose. He was not, however, a partisan of the kind of schizophrenic planning later summed up in the phrase "a first half Curzon and a second half Horowitz." For him, the recital proper had to have an internal coherence. He saw the playing of encores as a kind of second recital, one with its own exigencies and etiquette.

In January 1894, the pianist initiated a series of "Pachmann Tuesdays" and "Pachmann Thursdays" at Chickering Hall. The programs for the latter ran as follows—

4 January: Beethoven's "Appassionata" sonata, Schubert's impromptu 142/3, Raff's *La Fileuse,* Chopin's nocturne 9/2, polonaise 40/2, mazurkas 7/1 and 2, études 10/8 and 10, and scherzo opus 20, and Schumann's *Études symphoniques.*

11 January: Weber's piano sonata opus 39, Schumann's *Vogel als Prophet, Jagdlied,* and *Abschied* (from *Waldszenen*), and *Grillen* (from *Fantasiestücke*), Henselt's *Wiegenlied,* Mendelssohn's caprice 16/2 and *Variations sérieuses,* and Chopin's *Fantasie,* études 25/5 and 6, mazurka 33/4, and waltz 34/1.

18 January: Schumann's *Fantasie,* Beethoven's "Moonlight" sonata, Chopin's nocturne 15/1, *Barcarolle,* prelude 28/17 and 12, and waltz 34/3, and Liszt's *Petrarch* sonnet 104, *Harmonies du soir,* ballade no. 2, and *Mazurka brillante.*

On 12 February, Bülow died in Cairo, where he had gone in the hopes of rehabilitating his health. Rubinstein died in November. Their deaths left Pachmann the senior statesman of pianists.

During this second American tour, Pachmann contracted hepatitis under circumstances which have not come to light. Exhausted and depressed, he went to Berlin to consult doctors. He received excellent treatment, and on 9 January 1895 was sufficiently recovered that Hermann and Louise Wolff could present him in a *Chopin-Abend* at the Saal Bechstein (Link-Strasse 42). "Like Paderewski, Vladimir von Pachmann was a Pole [*sic*]," Edith Stargardt-Wolff wrote in her memoirs.

> His playing of Chopin was of the utmost beauty and delicacy. He had the most exquisite touch. There was really no need for him to play to the gallery as he did, with his ridiculous eccentricities. But it seems he couldn't help himself. For instance, after bringing off a difficult passage with bravura, he would kiss his hands or call out, "Bravo, Pachmann!" And conversely, if he was displeased with himself, he would give himself a little rap over the knuckles and say, "Pachmann, you plunker!" Inevitably, it wasn't long before the public was simply waiting for these outbursts and displays, and stopped taking him seriously as a musician.

Stargardt-Wolff goes on to note a "very expensive foible" of Pachmann's that would later receive great attention: his jewel collecting.

He never wore stones in the conventional way, set in a ring or a tie-pin; he preferred to carry them loose in his trouser pockets. He must have spent thousands and thousands on them; once, I remember, he instructed a Parisian dealer to buy a particular pink stone in Warsaw for 28,000 marks. His special obsession was with blue diamonds, and like a modern-day alchemist he spent a fortune trying to turn the fantasy into reality.

Finally, Stargardt-Wolff quotes from a letter to her mother from Marcella Sembrich in which the soprano recalls a concert given with Pachmann in Breslau.

Pachmann was a scream! From the moment he came on, the piano was poorly positioned, the public couldn't see his hands properly. After the first piece, he was indignant that they had failed to "acclaim" him, an artist with a "European reputation." After the next piece, he was peeved that he wasn't called upon for an encore, he always gave encores wherever he played, he had a Chopin étude all ready. Finally, he said, he didn't like to appear with me, he was an artist of the calibre of Sembrich, Patti, Liszt, Rubinstein, or Sarasate, and he should stick to solo billings, not, as he had done here, open for someone else. He couldn't kill off a soprano like me. "I killed off a couple of sopranos recently," he said, "but I couldn't do that to you." And so it went on, all evening. The poor fellow's really not all there. (115–16)

It was at another recital in Berlin that the famous "socks incident" took place, cementing Pachmann's reputation not only as a great Chopin interpreter but as a kind of Till Eulenspiegel of the piano. Olin Downes recorded the incident (*Saturday Evening Post,* 15 March 1930):

It should be explained that the stage at the Berlin Singakademie is reached by a short set of stairs which ascends from the floor to the platform. When de Pachmann ascended these stairs he did so holding before him in a ritualistic manner a pair of socks! So much can be vouched for on the word of eyewitnesses. Then "I made them a speech," said de Pachmann, referring to the audience, "and I told them those socks were sacred to me, because they were a pair that George Sand knitted for Chopin. The next day a critic called upon me. He wished to see those socks, and when I handed them to him he kissed them."

Pachmann wanted to prove what dupes most critics were, and he succeeded. The socks were his own. Twenty years later, while vacationing in Barbizon, in the Haute Savoie, he met the granddaughter of George Sand. She showed him a pair of pants that she claimed had belonged to Chopin, whereupon Pachmann decided to try the socks story on again, as it were.

Once more, he produced a pair of torn socks which he said were Chopin's, and was delighted when the old lady not only believed him but wanted to darn them and send them to Nohant, Sand's home at La Châtre, as authentic *bas de Chopin.*

In time, Chopin's socks were succeeded by Chopin's *paletot.*[7] "The first time we met was at De Pachmann's apartment," Downes wrote. "He played. Before he played he insisted that he must don 'Chopin's *paletot.*'"

> This *paletot,* when he had fetched it, proved to be a frightful old, dirty gray coat, hanging in ribbons from the lower hem, torn in the seams, with some fantastic kind of stuffing—cotton or what?—protruding dirtily from between layers of cloth. Truly a fearsome sight. De Pachmann being small, the fringes of the *paletot* of Chopin dragged along the floor, gathering more dirt as he moved. Add to this the odd little bows and grimaces and smirks, the quick and dexterous movements of his hands and his head, which he would cock on one side like a little bad bird. He played much and well. The manager left to catch a train. Others left. De Pachmann grew confidential:
>
> "This *paletot,* for instance. It may not be Chopin's *paletot.* I don't say positively, you understand. For the public, for the newspapers—yes. Between ourselves, one can't tell. One can't be positive that it's Chopin's *paletot.*"

Harold Bauer, who had long admired Pachmann but never worked up the courage to introduce himself, finally met him in the autumn of 1895 in Berlin. Bauer was practicing in Bechstein's Saloon when two small hands covered his eyes, and a voice asked, "Who is it?" He turned and found himself face to face with Pachmann.

If these were uneventful years—at least publicly—for Pachmann, however (about all we know is that he dined with Busoni and Carreño, in Berlin, in June 1898), they were less so for Maggie. On 4 April 1899, Labori came down with typhoid fever. The illness could not have come at a worse moment, since the couple were in the process of moving from 12, rue de Bourgogne—where they had long had to fend off the "hostile world"—to a small *hôtel particulier* at 41, rue Condorcet. Then in August, Labori, barely recovered, was shot in the back as he was leaving the court in Rennes, where Dreyfus's court-martial was taking place. At first the assassin was thought to have been making an attempt upon the life of Dreyfus, during the prosecution of which he had fired at the wrong man, but an investigation later established that Labori himself was the intended victim. Among the many telegrams he received during his convalescence was one from Marcel Proust (18 August 1899): "Hommage au bon géant invincible à qui cette consécration sanglante manquait seule pour que ce ne fut pas au figuré qu'on parlât pour lui de combat et de victoire, et qui n'a même plus à envier à la gloire militaire le privilège magnifique des soldats: Donner son Sang." ("My respects to the good invincible giant for whom this bloody consecration just missed being metaphorical so that in that case one would not have still been able to speak of his combat and victory. Now he cannot even go on envying the magnificent privilege unique to soldiers destined for military glory: Giving Their Blood.")

SIX

The Demon

Upon his return to America in 1899 for yet another triumphant tour, Pachmann offered a hymn to the Steinway piano—which he would be playing that season—to an interviewer from the *Worcester (Mass.) Spy* (28 September) when asked where and how he had spent his summer. "In the Catskills, at a little place in the backwoods," he answered.

> "Did I play? Not very much; it was too hot. All your America is very hot in summer, I think. But I had a Steinway grand, and how could I help play with such an instrument in the room?" (He paused to run his fingers up and down an imaginary keyboard, his head on one side, his eyes half closed, in ecstatic reminiscence of those summer hours of practice in the backwoods.) "Ah, the Steinway. What a piano! Write this down—it is divine; it is the finest in the world—I could not leave it. I can remember the pianos of 25 years ago; but what a development since. There is nothing so beautiful in touch, so beautiful in tone. Ach! that touch and tone. Mozart and Beethoven, could they hear their compositions performed on a modern piano, would not know them for theirs. The tears would flow from their eyes and run down their cheeks, to hear them."

He inaugurated the musical season of 1899 at New York's Mendelssohn Hall with a recital in October that was attended by Mr. and Mrs. John Jacob Astor, among other ornaments of society. The concert prompted one of the most sensitive and musically detailed reviews ever given to Pachmann (the name of the author of which, regrettably, is unknown). "It was very warm in Mendelssohn Hall last night," the critic wrote, "because of the sultry weather and also by reason of Vladimir De Pachmann—piano virtuoso and Chopin interpreter by the grace of God, as the Germans say—giving his first recital and attracting an audience that packed every foot of room on the floor." Pachmann had changed his program at the eleventh hour, substituting the *Fantasiestücke* 12/3, 4, and 5 and *Vogel als Prophet, Jagdlied,* and

Abschied from the *Waldszenen* for the *Davidsbündlertänze,* a change the critic regretted, since in that day the *Davidsbündlertänze* were "never heard in concert." (Pachmann was to play the *Davidsbündlertänze* in other concerts—at one of which his page turner was Godowsky.) Presently the critic considered Pachmann's performance of Weber's piano sonata opus 39 in such detail that one can really imagine what it sounded like.

The Weber Sonata, Liszt's favorite, has been delivered here in a more sensational, more brilliant manner, but never so beautifully. First, the opening *tempo* was a surprise. It was *allegro moderato,* as marked by the composer, and in the charming fresco decorations, in which peeps forth "Der Freischütz"—but a moment's flashing mask—no effort was made at technical display. Euphony at all hazards was secured, even with a slight loss of the power and pride of Weber's martial spirit. A most sensuous tonal coloring and a flowing *legato,* beyond the dreams of the most avaricious of pianists resulted, and with the Henselt harmonic amplifications—bass figures changed and octaves introduced—the whole composition gained in richness, in massiveness. Very beautiful, indeed, was M. De Pachmann's singing—there is no other word— of the F minor episode. He has gained in power, nervous rather than muscular, and so the working out section was sonorous, if not orchestral.

In the C minor *andante* the soprano voice was *ben tenuto* to a remarkable degree. It is an old-fashioned device to give single tones such prominence, and without pedal help. Here the inner voices were finely differentiated. The octaves in the major section were models of accompaniment figures. There were octaves too in the right hand, in the diminished chord, just before the sixths; this is an innovation. The movement was most romantically read. ["I confide to you the sum of my experiences, my sorrows, my joys," Pachmann said of the andante.] Another surprise was the *menuetto capriccioso,* which was capricious, but not *presto.* The top tones in the Trio were taken languishingly and not at all electrically. But again Weber was faithfully followed and not the dictates of the virtuoso. The Rondo was a true Rondo, purling, exquisite in feeling and *molto grazioso.* Astonishing variety of touch and the right historical feeling characterized the entire performance. The last few bars were lovely, the *morendo* a genuine sigh.

"This artist has, whether by a delicately poised nervous and tactile equipment, or whether because of a sensibility which is extremely rare, a capability of evoking moods the most evanescent, the most nebulously poetic," the critic continued. "There is atmosphere of a curious, morbid, sad-sweet sort in his work that stamps him solitary among his fellow-workers at the keyboard."

Who, for instance, can do such singular things with the "Rondo Capriccioso"? It is not altogether the prim and neatly adjusted Mendelssohn that he gives us in this war-worn epic of the bread-and-butter damsel. Tricksy as Puck, his fingers flashed through the stale bars of the Rondo, letting in a new light, new accents; and when the *coda* was reached the enthusiasm of the audience almost spoiled the well-planned finish. And how he played those simple octaves, the resonance, the *crescendo*—it was astounding! All the more so because it seemed as if this pretty piano piece had become hopelessly stereotyped. The Henseltian *variante* caused the pedagogues present to prick up their ears.

The tiny magician carried himself wonderfully well. Once he made an eloquent apostrophe, a soundless one, to the heavenly powers, signifying his willingness to play all night, to heap up the very cosmos upon the piano, but the heat—then De Pachmann looked triste and dashed off the *coda* of the Rondo, ending all in an E major stillness and topsy-turvying the dynamics of Felix the Refined.

Pachmann brought his program to an end with a Chopin group: impromptu no. 2 ("taken at a grave gait . . . and the last chord—*pianissimo*! This is contrary to Chopin's marking, but it was in the key of the interpretation"); preludes in B minor ("Raindrop"), E-flat, and F major; studies in F minor (played with a "sound, firm, virile touch. The final bars alone took on the air of mystery so native to this study"), F major, and the famous one in double thirds ("at last poetic and not a mere digital *tour de force*").

A flashing of spokes of light and the whistling of the wind—and De Pachmann had begun the B minor mazurka [33/4]. This was given as Zelenski[1] would have it—the program gay, jocular, with an epigrammatic ending. According to Ujjewski it may mean the drowning of the love-lorn maiden and the sounding of funereal bells, a veritable ballade of Poland. Not so De Pachmann. He gave it with dancing fingers, a marvelous *rubato,* and with alternations of tenderness and piquant banterings. The Valse was the old A-flat Valse [34/1]. It was literally waltzed and the Scherzo [C-sharp minor] sounded sardonic and despairing after its ballroom measures. There were some wonderful things compassed in this Scherzo. The figuration of the *chorale* was like an exhalation. And then, in honor of the day, for it was the fiftieth anniversary of the death of the great Pole, the Funeral March was played with all the pathos imaginable and the large audience went home subdued, but vowing that such musicmaking is heard not too often in the land of piano recitals. De Pachmann is now the poet of the piano.

The critics for the *New York Times,* on the other hand, were frequently critical of Pachmann's playing, even if they grudgingly recognized its distinctiveness. "Pachmann's readings are eccentric and sometimes offensive," one wrote (18 October 1899), "but their technical language revels in Swin-burnian tone-tints, and the bewitched ear lulls the brain to forgetfulness." Four days later (22 October), W. J. Henderson, addressing "the curious compound of sensibility and conceit known to the musical world as Pach-mann," observed that his Chopin playing was "not always quite moral," adding that "if Tolstoi had ever heard Pachmann play the nocturnes of the Pole, he would never have written the 'Kreutzer Sonata.'" Six months after that, apparently feeling that Pachmann had gotten off on the morals charge, Henderson effectively tried to erase the pianist from his own performances: "Pachmann's success with the music of Chopin is only another case of good music performing itself." For Henderson, any argument that stopped peo-ple from going to hear Pachmann was worth making.

For audiences as well as critics, Pachmann's playing was becoming in-creasingly representative of its historical moment; one that was defined, in part, by fin-de-siècle literature and the Secessionist exhibition in Vienna in 1897. Some approved, and some did not. In earlier years, reviews (particu-larly negative ones) of his concerts had not troubled to connect them to cultural currents. Now, on the contrary, his playing was being portrayed as objectionable for what it was—sensuous and immoral—instead of what it was not—imposing and athletic. To name him an aesthetic confederate of Swinburne, or to declare that he played a Chopin nocturne so erotically that it would displace Beethoven's "Kreutzer" sonata, was to pay Pach-mann's genius an astonishing compliment—even though a compliment was not intended. The composer himself, as Gide's *Notes on Chopin* makes clear, was also being connected to cultural currents; instead of the morbid and sentimental Romantic, he was—at least for Gide—music's Baudelaire. "Chopin's works used to be called 'unhealthy music,'" he wrote. "*Les Fleurs du mal* used to be called 'unhealthy poetry,' and, I rather think, for the same reasons. . . . I find in both the same use of *surprise* and of the extraordinary foreshortenings which achieve it" (27–28).

Pachmann spent the last months of the year touring at a wearying pace. It was at this point that Willa Cather attended one of his recitals in Pitts-burgh and reviewed it ("Two Pianists"—the other was Joseffy—in the *Courier,* 30 December). Her physical description of Pachmann was partic-ularly memorable:

> Although he no longer affects the long black hair and beard which once concealed his countenance and made him look like a Will H. Bradley il-lustration to a Stephen Crane poem, there is no mistaking the Russian pi-anist's vocation. He wears his hair brushed straight back now, very much à la Toby Rex, and his heavy body and broad, powerful shoulders look queer enough on the absurdly short legs which toddle them about. His feet are small and he is very vain of them.

Cather was one of many writers to remark on the oriental aspect of Pachmann's appearance: "In his thin and bearded days he looked like a wizard of the Svengali type, and even now is not unlike the portly, comfortable magicians of the Eastern fairy tales. The magician resemblance keeps occurring to one as he plays."

Pachmann returned to Europe in the first year of a new century that saw the fame of his ex-wife's husband approaching his own. By now, thanks to his defense of Alfred Dreyfus, Labori was an eminence—and not only in his native France. In London, in June 1901, the "Hardwicke Society," whose members were drawn from the capital's four Inns of Court, honored the lawyer at its annual dinner. When Labori was toasted, the audience rose to its feet and sang *For He's a Jolly Good Fellow.* Wrote French Bar president Chenu, "He was acclaimed everywhere, and the British press celebrated him as the equal of a visiting monarch" (Labori, 268). Pachmann's royal patron, Edward VII, even gave Labori a signed photograph of himself and asked for one in return.

The Pachmann trail now grows faint for a time, reemerging in 1902, when an anonymous critic (perhaps Huneker) described the "rare musical treat" of an afternoon visit by Pachmann to his home. "Without any preliminaries," the writer began, he "at once sat down to the piano—something he rarely does outside of his own rooms and the concert hall—and began to play to an audience of three—a friend who happened to be present, Mrs. Abell, and myself."

> I have often heard Pachmann in public, but he is a man of moods, and I never heard him before in such a glorious mood, nor did I ever before realize what he could do in the way of technic. A fit of virtuosity suddenly seized him and for half an hour he revelled in his most dazzling feats of the keyboard. He played scales in thirds first with the right hand from the top to the bottom of the keyboard, then with the left hand from the bottom to the top, in the same rapid tempo in which he played single scales. Then he did the same in sixths and octaves, it seemingly making no difference to him, the double scale all coming out with the same speed and clearness as the single ones. Then he played chromatic scales in thirds, glissando, the same in sixths, and other tricks. He did the incredible in the way of lightning skips, in single notes and chords and other feats of virtuosity until we were completely awed by the skill of the man. Then he began to prelude, to improvise the most wonderful little cadenzas, runs, variations, &c., until it seemed as if the devil himself were let loose. In fact, as Pachmann sat there in the growing darkness, his profile grotesquely outlined against the window, bringing forth those wonderful sounds from the piano, I was forcibly reminded of Tartini's dream of the

devil appearing at night and fiddling for him that wonderful piece, of which, as Tartini said, his "Devil's Trill" Sonata is but a weak echo. Indeed, with such magical tones coming from the piano, and with the weird appearance of Pachmann in the darkness, it required but little imagination to see in his place the devil himself.

Having given great emphasis to the idea of Pachmann as a demon—a common characterization of the virtuoso—the critic retreats from his own metaphor, as if a little alarmed by its implications, concluding that his playing "was both angelic and satanic."

Near the end of the year, Pachmann played a recital in Berlin that included some "movements from two English suites which he had transformed in tempi and style to suit his own ideas of Bach" and which were judged to be "delightful." On the other hand, the last work on the program, Schumann's piano sonata opus 22, was dismissed as "a perfect musical farce." Subsequently, Pachmann "failed to rouse the audience to the applause he expected and thought he deserved. Nothing daunted, he told them so in very plain language, and of course then a storm of handclappings raged through the Philharmonie, and Pachmann, happy, with a smile from ear to ear, sat down again and gave a da capo performance of the [fourth] movement."

On 22 November 1902, Maggie gave birth to her third daughter, Germaine Marguerite Odette, in Paris.[2]

On 10 July 1903, Pachmann gave the first piano recital in the Royal Albert Hall. Around the same time, a writer using the nom de plume Israfel published what he or she called "A Caramel" about Pachmann that followed in the tradition of B.'s "A Pachmann Fantasy." "In these days when every self-respecting pianist has beside him on the platform a fresh glossy extra piano in waiting—as a huntsman has his second horse—the gentle art of Vladimir de Pachmann comes like warmth in May or a rose in December," Israfel began.

> Under his gracious hand the fiery piano curvets and caracoles exquisitely as a circus steed, answering rather to some subtle sympathy than to mere technical skill. But when stiff five-barred octave passages have to be taken, the rattling of hoofs is not inaudible, and one sighs for the Vaquero-like notemanship of a Mark Hambourg, who, without the aid of the blurring pedal, sails right over the most incredible obstacles that the devilish ingenuity of a Liszt could devise.

For Israfel, Pachmann's "rare art has no more to do with vulgar virtuosity than has faint exquisite attar of roses with the sweet red flower on the bush."

Never was there an art more limited or more entrancing! It is earnest as child's play, prismatic and airy as a soap-bubble, poetic as the evening star. It lacks passion no more than lilies of the valley lack colour. It has scarcely a trace of artifice, merely a naive perfection of coquetry as natural as the blush on a roseleaf. If Paderewski is the king, I would venture to call Pachmann the May queen of pianists.

This startling comparison then leads Israfel into a series of Huysmans-like reveries in which Pachmann is further invoked as an avatar of fin-de-siècle decadence.

His Spring magic is not of Europe at all, the North has no part in him, nor the mystic East, nor the hurrying West: he is of the heady entrancing South. To me his music suggests all the frail starry flowers with symbolic names—tuberoses, oleanders, champak blossoms, and the warm indolent night airs that are faint with heavy perfumes. At heart, he is doubtless an Algerine.

At this point a distinct tone of homoeroticism enters the text, which goes further than B.'s by implying an erotic dimension to Pachmann's relationship with "that fairy prince of composers, Chopin."

George Sand herself was not more amorous of Frederic than is this musical magician, this magical musician. Yet he evokes the spirit of Chopin rather than Chopin's self, sharpening delicately the finer features of that fine soul—reducing the whole man to a ray of moonlight and a breath of honeyed orange blossom. Suggestion is his most potent spell: he is a master of dim suggestion of an intolerable richness—the buried gold burns through the covering earth! He hints the subtler half of what Wagner declares; the April ecstasies of "The Valkyrie" and the wild hues of the Venusberg are held by him in most ethereal pianistic solution. By ecstatic whispers he sets the mind rioting among unheard songs. This musical Keats finds in Chopin a Belle Dame Sans Mercy, a ravishing tormentor, a perilous perfect medium for self-expression. . . . He pictures a dream within a dream; a Southern night wild with the soft-sung ecstasies of bullfrogs and the intoxicating odour of jasmine flowers; a pink sumptuous ice such as only Budapest can freeze; the lovely ruined Ptolemaic temples on the drowned island of Philæ far up the Nile; and Her, who

> left his straight neck bent,
> And round his heart one strangling golden hair.[3]

Like Grieg, Pachmann makes you think of your first love, never of your last. His audience is, therefore, composed almost exclusively of minor poets, since only a few of those rare souls ever attain to the inverted passion expressed by Disillusion.

His is a fairy horse, shod, like Caligula's, with gold. We forgive the rat-
tling hoofs.

Israfel's description of Pachmann's audience as consisting of "rare souls"
attaining to "inverted passion," as much as his characterization of the pianist as a "May Queen," amounts to an oblique announcement of Pachmann's homosexuality—if one that only those "minor poets" who admire
him will grasp. It is as if Israfel—clearly himself (or herself) a wearer of the
green carnation—wants to claim Pachmann for the Decadent movement
much as Henderson did, writing in the *New York Times*. Nor was Israfel the
only observer to have recognized that Pachmann was not "straight." According to Steven Heliotes, pianist Rudolph Ganz—in language less poetic
and certainly less tolerant than Israfel's—told a student that Pachmann was
"as filthy a homosexual as ever lived."

The association between the Decadent style and homosexuality reached
its apogee in the case of Oscar Wilde, who, like Pachmann, married and fa-
thered two sons. (There is no reference to Pachmann in the Wilde literature, so it is unlikely that Wilde heard him, let alone met him.) Wilde was
often put forward as the author of *Teleny*, an underground pornographic
novel published in 1893 by Leonard Smithers, of whom Wilde wrote: "He
loves first editions, especially of women: little girls are his passion. He is the
most learned erotomaniac in Europe" (Sweet 193). *Teleny* tells the story of
a love affair between two men, one of whom is a young Hungarian virtuoso
pianist. The prospectus issued to publicize the novel emphasized the connection by referring to "an article in a largely-circulated London daily
paper, which demonstrated the subtle influence of music and the musician
in connection with perverted sexuality."

Not for nothing had *musical* become an accepted euphemism for *homosexual* in the Anglo-Saxon world at the turn of the century—an association that Israfel reversed, as it were, in his effort to claim Pachmann for the
Uranian tribe.

For his first two tours of America, in 1890–92 and 1893–94, Pachmann had played a Chickering piano. For the 1899–1900 season he played
a Steinway. (Steinway and Blüthner were to remain his preferred instruments.) It was his friendship with Arnold Somlyo, an impresario, press
agent, representative, and one-time manager of the Baldwin Piano Company, and huckster—as well as the prospect of a fourth tour of North
America—that led him to switch his allegiances yet again. This was a daring
move, considering that at that time the Baldwin piano was hardly known.
(Baldwin was also to underwrite, among others, Arrau, Bartók, Gieseking,
and Iturbi.) "The firm that persisted the longest and succeeded the best in
the ascent from mediocrity to distinction," Loesser writes, "was the Baldwin

Piano Co. of Cincinnati. Founded during the days of the Civil War, its products made little stir until 1900, when it received an outstanding award at the Paris exposition. Presently that clownish eccentric and delightful Chopin player Vladimir de Pachmann . . . found that he could project his delicate effects satisfactorily on a Baldwin piano" (*Men, Women, and Pianos,* 574).

For his debut with the Chicago Symphony Orchestra on 10 March 1905, Pachmann played the Chopin F minor concerto. The city's several papers voiced divergent opinions of his success. While all took note of Pachmann's idiosyncratic deportment (one, however, observed that the pianist was "tameness itself in comparison with previous occasions"), as well as of the fact that he played from the score, they disagreed about the extent to which these constituted a distraction. If there was a final word, it was that notwithstanding the distractions, the pianist succeeded in casting a spell over his audience, his performance being "the interpretation of generations past" and "free from morbidness and if not virile, at least far from weakness or effeminacy." At the end, encores were demanded and given: Chopin's D-flat nocturne, étude 10/5, and "Minute" waltz.

On 2 May 1905, there was a big do at the Metropolitan Opera House in New York, a "Musical and Dramatic Performance Testimonial to Madame Helena Modjeska."[4] Pachmann represented the Greek Muse of music, Euterpe, in playing half a dozen works by Chopin: nocturne 27/2, impromptu opus 29, polonaise 26/1, and études 25/3 and 4 and 10/5. The other "eminent artists" who participated were the singer David Bispham, the actors Mrs. Patrick Campbell, Louis James, James O'Neill (father of the playwright Eugene O'Neill), Ada Rehan, and Mary Shaw (a noted suffragist), and Madame Modjeska herself, "in two of her greatest characters": Mary Stuart and Lady Macbeth. Luncheon and tea were served during the intermission, and after the program there was a dinner at "the select Café des Beaux-Arts." Had Pachmann known that he had been invited only because Paderewski had been in a train accident, however, it is unlikely that he would have partaken of any of the meals.

Although Arthur Symons, a key figure of the Decadent movement, was principally a poet, a collection of stories, or "imaginary portraits," is also to be found among his works. *Spiritual Adventures* includes "Christian Trevalga," a portrait of a pianist for which, by Symons's own admission, Pachmann was his inspiration. There is, however, more of Symons himself than of Pachmann in the story, which is a study in obsession and eventual separation from the human community in which Trevalga gives himself up to "the passions of abstract sound," hears "a music which was like what Chopin might have written in paradise," and is finally committed to an asylum, where he dies. Pachmann, though an antic, was not insane and certainly not isolated, whereas Symons did enter an asylum in Italy in 1908.

In fact, Pachmann had fascinated Symons for a number of years. In 1901 or 1902, he had written a sonnet, "The Chopin Player," based, he explained in "The Genesis of *Spiritual Adventures*," on an incident Pachmann had once described to him. First, the sonnet:

> The sounds torture me: I see them in my brain;
> They spin a flickering web of living threads,
> Like butterflies upon the garden beds,
> Nets of bright sound. I follow them: in vain.
> I must not brush the least dust from their wings:
> They die of a touch; but I must capture them,
> Or they will turn to a caressing flame,
> And lick my soul up with their flutterings.
>
> The sounds torture me: I count them with my eyes,
> I feel them like a thirst between my lips;
> Is it my body or my soul that cries
> With little coloured mouths of sound, and drips
> In these bright drops that turn to butterflies
> Dying delicately at my finger-tips?

The Pachmann elements in "Christian Trevalga" clearly derive from the sonnet.

> One day, at a concert, while he was playing one of Chopin's studies, something in the curve of the music, which he had always seen as a wavy line, going on indefinitely in space, spreading itself out elastically, but without ever forming a pattern, seemed to become almost externally visible, just above the level of the strings on the open top of the piano. It was like grey smoke, forming and unforming as if it boiled up softly out of the pit where the wires were coiled up. It was so distinct that he shut his eyes for a moment, to see if it would be there when he opened them again. It was still there, getting darker in colour, and more distinct. He looked out of the corner of his eyes, to see if the people sitting near him had noticed anything; but the people sitting near him had their eyes fixed on his fingers, from which he seemed, as usual, to be quite detached; they evidently saw nothing. He smiled to himself, half apologetically; the piece had come to an end, and he was bowing to the applause; he walked boldly off the platform. (104–105)

When the pianist returns to play again, he looks nervously at the top of the piano, but there is "nothing to be seen."

> He sat down, and bent over the keyboard, and his hands began to run to and fro softly. When he looked up he saw what he was playing as clearly as he could have seen the notes if they had been there: but the wavy line was

upright now, and drifted upwards swiftly, vanishing at a certain point; it swayed to and fro like a snake beating time to the music of the snake-charmer; and he looked at it as if it understood him, and nodded his head to it, to show that he understood. By this time it seemed to him quite natural, and he forgot that there had ever been a time when he had not seen the music like that. (105–106)

At the end of the story, Symons gives the contents of the several "loose scraps of paper" whereon Trevalga "had jotted down a few disconnected thoughts about music." The second is the most Pachmannesque:

> When I am playing the piano I am always afraid of hurting a sound. I believe that sounds are living beings, flying about us like motes in the air, and that they suffer if we clutch them roughly. Have you ever tried to catch a butterfly without brushing the dust off its wings? Every time I press a note I feel as if I were doing that, and it is an agony to me. I am certain that I have hurt fewer sounds than any other pianist. (111)

(Trevalga had already rejected the "thunders" of the pianists he heard in London during his student days.)

Symons's fascination with, and admiration for, Pachmann, was immense—he thought him equal to Verlaine and Whistler—and the process by which he moved toward a comprehensive statement about the pianist (and his playing) merits tracing. First he wrote a review of Pachmann's playing at a Saturday Popular Concert at St. James's Hall,[5] as well as an essay on Pachmann that concluded with the poem "The Chopin Player."[6] Both of these, although originally published in 1901 or 1902, were collected in *Plays, Acting, and Music* (1903). In 1905, "Christian Trevalga" was published. "The Chopin Player" appeared once again in 1906, as part of *The Fool of the World*. On 11 July 1908, a piece on Pachmann and Paderewski came out in the *Saturday Review*. In December 1915, he profiled Pachmann for *Vanity Fair*.

Symons's great summing up of Pachmann, a three-part essay titled "Pachmann and the Piano," was published in 1909 in the second edition of *Plays, Acting, and Music*. Here Symons compares Pachmann to Verlaine, Swinburne, Sargent, and Coleridge, and in so doing seems to be claiming him, once again, for the Decadent movement. Moreover, Symons takes a transgressive delight in reporting the "whispered" rumor that Pachmann "has sold his soul to the diabolical instrument" (250), and hints at the pianist's homosexuality not only by invoking Verlaine but by writing, "When he plays it, music speaks no language known to us, has nothing of ourselves to tell us, but is shy, alien, and speaks a language which we do not know" (240)—that is to say, the artist (like the homosexual) must invent, and explain, himself in a language of his own construction. (Were Symons's loves for women not so well known, one could be forgiven for wondering whether Pachmann was his passion.) One of the paradoxes of the fin de siècle, in historical retrospect, is that the homosexual aspect which is today seen as being its *donnée* was not really perceived in the moment of its happening as being central to it—or was, at most, perceived only by subtle and acute readers and observers. In other words, Israfel's Pachmann "Caramel" could be read in its day with a straight face, while Symons in particular was not writing so much to explicate as to evoke. (He was, after all, a poet.)

It is when Symons turns to works he heard Pachmann play that his essay gains in significance. At these moments Pachmann is less a peg upon which to hang the mantle of aestheticism than what he, in fact, was: a musician. For Symons, Bach's *Italian* concerto formed "the greatest thing" he ever heard Pachmann do. This may seem surprising, even perverse, yet more than one critic who heard Pachmann play a prelude and fugue from the *Well-Tempered Clavier* as an encore (a common choice) judged his interpretation to be not simply dignified but authoritative. Aldo Mantia also considered Pachmann's Bach playing to be exceptional—almost a revelation. It was, as he described it, "very correct" playing (much more so than Cortot's, for instance), especially in private, where there was no audience to take into account. Although Pachmann objected to Wanda Landowska's "guitar" (on a purely aesthetic level, the sound of it displeased him), he was not a priori disposed against the piano's predecessors. Indeed, according to Mantia, he adored the sound of the clavichord and preferred it to the *clavecin* for performances of the *Well-Tempered Clavier*. As for Symons, while he asserts that Pachmann cannot interpret every kind of music, along with the evidence of the *Italian* concerto, he gives his experience of having heard Pachmann play, in private, "a show-piece of Liszt, a thunderous thing of immense difficulty, requiring a technique quite different from the technique which alone he cares to reveal to us; he had not played it for twenty years, and he played it with exactly the right crackling splendour that it demanded" ("Pachmann and the Piano," 251).

What is most interesting (and intelligent) in Symons's account is an almost stream-of-consciousness series of reflections on the element of mystery in music. "Music can never wholly be detached from mystery, can never wholly become articulate," he writes, "and it is in our ignorance of its true nature that we would tame it to humanity and teach it to express human emotions, not its own."

> Pachmann gives you pure music, not states of soul or of temperament, not interpretations, but echoes. He gives you the notes in their own atmosphere, where they live for him an individual life, which has nothing to

do with emotions or ideas. Thus he does not need to translate out of two languages: first, from sound to emotion, temperament, what you will; then from that back again to sound. The notes exist; it is enough that they exist. They mean for him just the sound and nothing else. (242)

Symons reprises the theme of "The Chopin Player" and the passage from "Christian Trevalga" quoted earlier:

[Pachmann's] art begins where violence leaves off; that is why he can give you fortissimo without hurting the nerves of a single string; that is why he can play a run as if every note had its meaning. To the others a run is a flourish, a tassel hung on for display, a thing extra; when Pachmann plays a run you realise that it may have its own legitimate sparkle of gay life. With him every note lives, has its own body and its own soul, and that is why it is worth hearing him play even trivial music like Mendelssohn's "Spring Song" or meaningless music like Taubert's Waltz: he creates a beauty out of sound itself and a beauty which is at the root of music. There are moments when a single chord seems to say in itself everything that music has to say. That is the moment in which everything but sound is annihilated, the moment of ecstasy; and it is of such moments that Pachmann is the poet. (244–45)

If Pachmann was an embodiment of the fin de siècle, it was not because he affiliated himself with that movement but because so many aspects of his biography (and his art) correspond to the preoccupations of the writers and artists who did.

Vladimir de Pachmann.
Photograph by Frederick
Kingsbury.

Marguerite de Pachmann.
Photograph by Frederick
Kingsbury.

CHICKERING HALL

FAREWELL APPEARANCE

— OF —

MR. & MRS. DE PACHMANN

CHOPIN

Facsimile of the MSS. of the E minor Prelude, Opus 28, No. 4.

Largo

SATURDAY AFTERNOON, MAY 17, at 3.

General Director of the Pachmann Concerts, - Mr. F. A. SCHWAB

THE CHICKERING PIANO USED EXCLUSIVELY.

Cover of a program for a concert by Pachmann and Maggie on May 17, 1890.

CHICKERING HALL

SEASON 1893-94.

Pachmann Tuesdays

JANUARY 2,

JANUARY 9,

JANUARY 16,

AT THREE O'CLOCK.

Sole Manager of the De Pachmann Concerts, - - - - *Mr. Frederick A. Schwab*

Cover of a program for "Pachmann Tuesdays" in January 1894.

Vladimir de Pachmann. Photograph by Aimé Dupont.

Vladimir de Pachmann. Photograph by Sarony.

Fernand Labori.

Francesco ("Cesco") Pallottelli and Vladimir de Pachmann.

This was taken when I was thinking of my dear friend and wonderful artist Vladimir von Pachmann his admirer Leopold Godowsky London June 5, 01

LEOPOLD GODOWSKY

Leopold Godowsky. After Pachmann's death, this photograph hung in the Paris apartment of his son Lionel. (Courtesy of Allen Evans.)

MORITZ ROSENTHAL

Moritz Rosenthal, a Pachmann "pupil."

Vladimir de Pachmann and Eugene Ysaÿe, chamber music partners
during the Great War. Photograph by Claude Harris. (Print courtesy
of the National Portrait Gallery, London, and Mr. Jake Harris.)

Caricature of Vladimir de
Pachmann.
(Bettman/Corbis.)

Detail of a postcard of the Royal Albert Hall, London, with a
poster announcing a Chopin recital by Vladimir de Pachmann
in the foreground.

Vladimir de Pachmann *loves* the Baldwin piano. Through the medium of Baldwin tone, this most lyric of contemporary pianists discovers complete revealment of his musical dreams. For a generation de Pachmann has played the Baldwin; on the concert stage and in his home. That loveliness and purity of tone which appeals to de Pachmann and to every exacting musician is found in all Baldwins; alike in the Concert Grand, in the smaller Grands, in the Uprights. The history of the Baldwin is the history of an ideal.

"*. . . . It cries when I feel like crying, it sings joyfully when I feel like singing. It responds—like a human being—to every mood. I love the Baldwin Piano.*"

Baldwin

A request by mail to the nearest Baldwin show rooms, as listed below, will bring you complete information regarding models and prices.

THE BALDWIN PIANO COMPANY

Cncinnati   Chicago   New York   Indianapolis   Louisville   St. Louis   Denver   San Francisco   Dallas

An advertisement for Baldwin featuring an endorsement by Vladimir de Pachmann, circa 1925.

An indication of Pachmann's popularity, from *Good Housekeeping* (1925).

Vladimir de Pachmann. Photograph by Victor Georg. His ring is set
with his celebrated red diamond. (New York Public Library.)

Vladimir de Pachmann. He developed the strabismus in his right
eye during his last tour of America, 1923–25. (Bettman/Corbis.)

The Villino Pallottelli (Via Massaua, Rome).

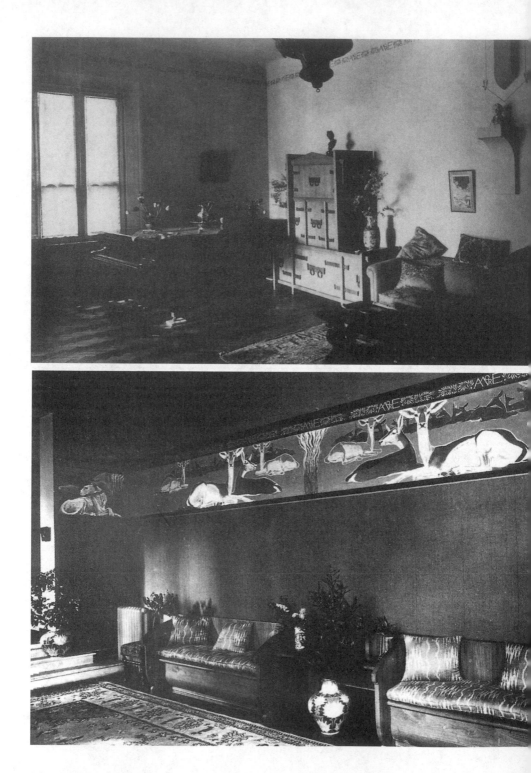

(Above and below) The music room in the Villino Pallottelli, designed by Duilio Cambellotti.

Pachmann and Pallottelli in Rome.

"The Vanishing Years."

Pachmann in a mufti. (Courtesy of Allen Evans.)

SEVEN

"The Face of One's Friend"

Pachmann was looking for a man to act as a secretary and all-around gentleman's gentleman when, in 1905, a mutual friend happened to introduce him to a handsome young Italian named Francesco Pallottelli. He was about twenty-one, and although he had no experience as a secretary—let alone a virtuoso pianist's secretary (his written command of even his mother tongue was imperfect)—he soon found himself on the job.

There is some uncertainty as to where they actually met. Pallottelli himself often claimed that at the time he was working as a waiter, or even as an impresario, in England—as if his established presence in that country might somehow legitimize his relationship with Pachmann or at least lend ballast to his implicit claim that Pachmann's hiring of him had no sexual or emotional underpinning. He led Fred Gaisberg to believe that he had first gone to Pachmann as a pupil. Allan Evans, on the other hand, had it from Aldo Mantia that Pallottelli was a waiter at Ranieri's in Rome when Pachmann met him. Davide Pallottelli, Cesco's nephew, also said that his uncle was a *"poveraccio"* working as a waiter when the pianist befriended him. That Cesco could not keep to one story suggests that the truth lapsed from the standards of *bella figura,* which Italians so highly value.

In any case—and wherever they met—the liaison blossomed into the most sustaining relationship of Pachmann's life. In *The Intersexes: A History of Similisexualism,* Edward Prime-Stevenson, writing under the pseudonym "Xavier Mayne," gives a portrait of the "similisexual" [that is, homosexual] ambience of the era that may help us to understand the (initial) terms of their friendship. "It is to be observed that not all similisexual prostitutes, including thousands of young men who habitually sell their bodies to all passions of the Uranian patron, are homosexual," Prime-Stevenson noted.

> Often they are thoroughly dionistic; dislike and even detest, by natural repugnance, such relations; and have strong preferences for sexual intercourse with women. They violate their natures, turn prostitutes, because too idle to work; frequently to get money to spend on women-harlots.

Many younger or older male-prostitutes have other occupations; earning honestly their real daily bread, they are not homosexual by temperament. By prostituting themselves similisexually—clandestinely they make considerable additions to their modest wages. However repugnant be the embraces and *attouchements* of the Uranians, they accept them complaisantly. (435)

Although any post-Freudian understanding of sexuality is, by necessity, more complex—one might even say more polyphonic—than the early twentieth century's, it is important to remember that Pachmann interpreted his own life according to these older terms.

In the event, Pachmann's relationship with Cesco soon developed into something quite different from the affairs described by Prime-Stevenson—something much closer to a marriage. For one thing, Cesco quickly proved himself to be an unexpectedly capable secretary and not merely what Prime-Stevenson called a "he-heteira." Cesco read music and played the piano himself, although we do not know when he learned to do so. Primarily he concerned himself with the practical aspects of Pachmann's career: dealing with hotels, train tickets, porters, stage managers, and music societies. He was often called upon to mediate between Pachmann and chefs or waiters— a challenging task, since the pianist was becoming increasingly difficult about eating. If something about the preparation or presentation of a dish was not to his liking, Pachmann would return it to the kitchen peremptorily. (Particularly offensive to him were hard meat, cold rolls, and coffee served in a metal pot.) He often expressed a fear of being poisoned (perhaps by one of Paderewski's "Polish patriots") or of "microbes," in anticipation of which the owners of the restaurants he frequented started keeping sets of dishes and silverware aside for his exclusive use. Still, he might insist on washing the components of his place setting himself, with his napkin and a pitcher of drinking water or even wine. Even at Marlborough House, where he played for Queen Alexandra, he washed out his tea cup, much to her amusement. Dmitri Tiomkin, the pianist and film score composer, remembered once seeing the old maestro in a restaurant eating with a straw.[1]

One of the few people who recognized the poignancy of Pachmann's fears was the wife of the concert manager Georges Kugel, who had sat next to the pianist at a dinner in his honor. As Joseph Rezits wrote in a letter to the author, she later told him: "[Pachmann] was the most polite man I have ever encountered. He was always served first (as the guest of honor), but each time a dish was placed before him, he insisted that I eat it first. This procedure seemed a bit unusual, but I followed his wishes. When I related this incident to another musician, he said that 'de Pachmann was always afraid of being poisoned. He would never eat something (at a public gathering) without someone else tasting it first!'"

On other occasions, Cesco was pressed into service as a page turner. He would then find himself onstage with Pachmann, the recipient of the running commentary that the pianist usually directed at the audience. "Isn't that passage beautiful?" Pachmann might say, or "Listen to this phrase." As the concert progressed, he would become more confiding, even—from the perspective of the astute audience member—confessional: "I am sorry I kept you awake complaining last night," Pachmann told Cesco during one concert. At one stopover, the pianist was awakened very late at night by what he thought was the sound of mice scratching. Afraid to strike a match to light his lamp, much less summon Cesco in the adjoining room, Pachmann remained upright in his bed until morning, when Cesco came to wake him up. He developed a high fever, and the concert had to be cancelled. A few days later, Pachmann decided to tell his audience about the incident, explaining that because Cesco had failed to block up the chimney, "mice came down in the night." This was another example of Pachmann's tendency to "go public" with the quotidian details of their life together, as he had done with Maggie.

One curious result of Pachmann's new connection with Cesco was that it aggravated a tendency toward hypochondria in the pianist that would only worsen as he grew older. This was ironic because, in spite of his fear of "microbes," Pachmann was blessed with remarkably good health. Nonetheless, he was forever taking his pulse or complaining, "I've got a pain" or "It's my heart—it's dropped." He was especially preoccupied with the state of his liver, which he pronounced "leevair." (He sometimes admitted that he feigned ill health so that people would pity him. Reassuring Pachmann that he was indeed all right soon became one of Cesco's most exasperating assignments.)

Whatever he may have done behind the scenes, Cesco had scant influence over Pachmann's concert deportment. When the American composer Charles Tomlinson Griffes heard the pianist in Berlin in early 1906, he observed in a letter that Pachmann "talked first of all to the piano awhile and made all sorts of motions to the effect that the stool didn't suit him. Then he got up and went off, and some men came on and pretended to do something to the stool, and he finally began." Although he felt that Pachmann "played some things absolutely perfectly, according to my taste," Griffes disapproved of his behavior, which he characterized as "too disgusting and inartistic for anything. But the audience is still more disgusting. They behave themselves as if in a circus, and the more ridiculous de Pachmann is, the more they like it" (80).

In 1906, Prime-Stevenson arranged for "Xavier Mayne's" *Imre: A Memorandum* to be privately printed in Naples, where the typesetters could not read the text. As in *Teleny,* the eponymous hero is a pianist, yet this book goes much further than *Teleny* in connecting music to homosexuality. At one point, its narrator, having first vehemently expressed his revulsion at "those types of man-loving-men who, by thousands, live incapable of any noble ideals or lives" (116), musicians among them, nonetheless admits that music formed "the very tissue of intimacy, of [his] life" (144) with Imre's predecessor. Music, for Prime-Stevenson, "is the most neurotic, the most 'essential,' the most subtly nerve-disturbing of arts. Music, as a mystery in aesthetics, unites logically with uranianism as a deep problem in psychology. Precisely what music 'says,' when we think it 'says' something, and has such or such a 'message' to us, we really do not in the least know" (395).

> It can be theorized further, that music has an articulate significance, seemingly dangerous. Is it not possibly a language, the broken diction of intenser existences, of which we catch troubled accents?—a speech which if—or *because?*—misunderstood cannot be for the good of mankind? Is the eternally music-loving, music-making, intersexual Uranian verily a sort of creature from another sphere?—still in touch with it?—an "Overman," an "Over-Soul"?—one ever sharply sensitive to the language of his early Somewhere Else, and alert to the chief medium for its communications, however little he or we may *understand* it? (396)

Now the cat was out of the bag: That is to say, for the first time, the mere fact that a man played the piano could "implicate."

Although by no means only decadent artists were interested in jewels, the fascination that fin-de-siècle writers such as Huysmans expressed for them placed Pachmann's own passion squarely in an aesthetic tradition. The poet was bound to respond not only to the colors of jewels but to their mythologies: The name of the garnet derives from the Latin word for pomegranate (whose seeds it resembles), while peridot, "the evening emerald," was once mined at night; the Hindus believed moonstones to be bits of moonbeams; ancients saw diamonds as splinters of lightning; the amethyst was named for the maiden that Diana turned into quartz to save her from Dionysus, whose tears stained her purple; Cleopatra ground pearls into her wine.

In *The Picture of Dorian Gray,* Wilde's eponymous antihero comes to understand that "the senses, no less than the soul, have their spiritual mysteries to reveal." (He already studies perfumes, music, embroideries, tapestries, and textiles as well.)

> On one occasion he took up the study of jewels, and appeared at a costume ball as Anne de Joyeuse, Admiral of France, in a dress covered with five hundred and sixty pearls. This taste enthralled him for years, and, indeed, may be said never to have left him. He would often spend a whole day settling and resettling in their cases the various stones that he had col-

lected, such as the olive-green chrysoberyl that turns red by lamplight, the cymophane with its wire-like line of silver, the pistachio-coloured peridot, rose-pink and wine-yellow topazes, carbuncles of fiery scarlet with tremulous four-rayed stars, flame-red cinnamon-stones, orange and violet spinels, and amethysts with their alternate layers of ruby and sapphire. He loved the red gold of the sunstone, and the moonstone's pearly whiteness, and the broken rainbow of the milky opal. He procured from Asterdam three emeralds of extraordinary size and richness of colour, and had a turquoise *de la vieille roche* that was the envy of all the connoisseurs. (107)

Wilde's decadence came from France and owed in no small part to Huysmans's novel *Against the Grain,* the protagonist of which, Des Esseintes, purchases a tortoise and places it on an Oriental carpet, intending for the sombre tone of its carapace to heighten the carpet's brilliance. In the event, however, the contrast is too extreme, and Des Esseintes resolves to dim the carpet by having the tortoise's carapace gilded. He is, at first, enchanted with this effect. "But he soon came to the conclusion that this gigantic jewel was only half finished, that it would not be really complete and perfect till it was incrusted with precious stones" (40).

> He selected from a collection of Japanese curios a design representing a great bunch of flowers springing from a thin stalk, took it to a jeweller's, sketched out a border to enclose this bouquet in an oval frame, and informed the dumb-founded lapidary that every leaf and every petal of the flowers was to be executed in precious stones and mounted in the actual scales of the turtle. (40–41)

Des Esseintes rejects diamonds, emeralds, rubies, topazes, amethysts, and sapphires as "too civilized, too familiar" (41), choosing instead "a series of stones, some real, some artificial, the combination of which should produce a harmony, at once fascinating and disconcerting" (41): for the leaves of the bouquet, chrysoberyls, peridots and olives, "springing from twigs of almandine and ouvarovite"; for blossoms distant from the stalk, European turquoises, "only a fossil ivory impregnated with coppery infiltrations and whose sea-green blue is heavy, opaque, sulphurous, as if jaundiced with bile" (42); for blossoms in the middle of the bouquet, Ceylon cat's-eyes, cymophanes and sapphirines; and for the edges of the carapace, the hyacinth of Compostella, aquamarine, balass and Sudermania rubies.

In his introduction to the English translation of Huysmans's novel, Havelock Ellis quotes Gauthier's claim that the "style of decadence" is

> nothing else but art arrived at that point of extreme maturity yielded by the slanting suns of aged civilizations: an ingenious complicated style, full of shades and of research, constantly pushing back the boundaries of

speech, borrowing from all the technical vocabularies, taking colour from all palettes and notes from all keyboards, struggling to render what is most inexpressible in thought, what is vague and most elusive in the outlines of form, listening to translate the subtle confidences of neurosis, the dying confessions of passion grown depraved, and the strange hallucinations of the obsession which is turning to madness. The style of decadence is the ultimate utterance of the Word, summoned to final expression and driven to its last hiding-place. Unlike the classic style it admits shadow. (xv–xvi)

This might well be a description of Pachmann's own aesthetic. An article about the pianist's jewel collection in *Musical America* echoed—whether consciously or unconsciously—the catalogs compiled by Wilde and Huysmans:

> Vladimir de Pachmann, the famous pianist, has just added to his collection of precious stones, which is one of the finest in the world, a sapphire-blue diamond, for which he paid a London firm $23,000. It is said to be of a deeper blue than the Hope diamond and to retain its color even under artificial light.
>
> De Pachmann's collection of gems includes diamonds of white from the Transvaal, unique specimens in yellow, brown, green, and deep red tints from Borneo, Brazil, and Australia; carmine-colored rubies, some with blue and violet tints, from Ceylon and Siam; sapphires from Kashmir and Burma, and sea green emeralds from Siberia, Egypt, and South America. In his collection are specimens of every known variety of these four kinds of gems, and his fame as a connoisseur of precious stones rivals his fame as an interpreter of Chopin.

"My love for gems is ideal, abstract," Pachmann himself explained. "I have named most of them. My most flawless diamond has been christened Bach. A wonderful dusky emerald I own is called Brahms. My best opal, the most poetical of all stones, bears the title Chopin. A brilliant ruby, full of scintillating colors, I have dubbed Liszt. Richard Strauss? I have no stone worthy to bear that name." When he had more jewels than the number of composers he admired, Pachmann (according to Mantia) began to name them for compositions: One was a polonaise, another a mazurka, a third a nocturne.

Yet this was not the only way in which jewels provided him with a way into music. He told a reporter from the *Indianapolis News:* "You know that is why other pianists cannot play with Pachmann's colors—they do not know the great science and art of mineralogy. I absorb the colors and the sparkling of my gems and then I reproduce these nuances and tints in my music. That is my secret." Here the pianist almost paraphrases Pater, who wrote in the famously dangerous conclusion to *The Renaissance:*

To burn always with this hard, gemlike flame, to maintain this ecstasy, is success in life. In a sense it might even be said that our failure is to form habits: for, after all, habit is relative to a stereotyped world, and meantime it is only the roughness of the eye that makes any two persons, things, situations, seem alike. While all melts under our feet, we may well grasp at any exquisite passion, or any contribution to knowledge that seems by a lifted horizon to set the spirit free for a moment, or any stirring of the senses, strange dyes, strange colours, and curious odours, or works of the artist's hands, or the face of one's friend. (236–37)

"Look," Pachmann once directed an audience at Carnegie Hall, "look at the ruby I just bought. See how it glitters. See how it reflects the light with its tints." He then put it into his pocket and went to the piano. "Now listen to the way I play this Chopin waltz—and you'll forget all about the ruby."

On another occasion, noticing an American reporter's emerald ring, he exclaimed, "Quelle couleur!" then drew it off her finger and slid it as far as he could onto his own. "You come to my concert tonight," he prompted, returning her ring with a flourish, "and I will play for you alone . . . a living sparkle, a little fountain of green flames, the very color of your emerald stone."

In 1907, Pachmann made his first recordings (for the Gramophone and Typewriter Company, London). He was, in fact, the earliest-born pianist to use recording as an important adjunct to a concert career. His recordings transmit the tone, the nuances, and the license that critics talked about. But they also show—and this point is undersold—that he had a magnificent technique. (Chopin's étude 10/3 is a good example.)

That same year, Pachmann and Cesco crossed from Liverpool to New York on the *Caronia* for the pianist's latest American tour. Although the tour proper was not to begin until October, he had decided to come over early in order to rest as well as to play a dedicatory recital for the Building of Arts in Bar Harbor, Maine, on 3 August. In anticipation of their arrival, Lionel Powell, Pachmann's English agent, had written a letter of introduction for Cesco and sent it to the Baldwin Piano Company, to be forwarded to its various agents across America. "By separate mail we are sending you a photo of Mr. de Pachmann which you may use for advertising purposes," Powell explained. "The young man seated with Mr. de Pachmann is Mr. Pallottelli, who will accompany him to America. Mr. Pallottelli has already acted as his secretary during the last winter season in England and has proved himself to be a most trustworthy young gentleman in whom Mr. de Pachmann and we place the fullest confidence." The purpose of this letter seems to have been to assure puritanical America that Pachmann was bringing the young Italian with him for entirely professional reasons. (A journal-

ist who interviewed the pianist shortly after his arrival in America described
Cesco as "a strange dark young man with a face of singular refined inno-
cence, and hair not very long but of wonderful fineness.")

They spent the summer, which was exceptionally hot, at a Catskills resort called The Sussex. Then they began touring. Perhaps because Cesco
was with him, Pachmann was in high spirits. With reporters he was particularly voluble—and impolitic:

> And other artists? What do they matter to me or I to them? Each of us
> who feels it is his mission to play the piano in public does it in the manner
> peculiar to himself, and the difference of interpretation constitutes what
> music critics call "individuality." It is an influence which regulates the en-
> tire life of its possessor. For instance, I know one famous pianist who
> prefers dabbling in chemistry to giving public recitals and does so only
> when he needs money. Another has a penchant for athletics and is prouder
> of his biceps than the way he plays Beethoven. A third is addicted to the
> "flowing bowl" and that probably accounts for his "liquid tone" which I
> read about. Vegetarians, anti-vivisectionists, Fabians and some who have
> hallucinations that they are composers—all are among my fellow artists of
> the keys.

His pace, on this tour, was brisk. In October, he played recitals in Indianapolis, Cleveland, and Buffalo, at a black church in an unnamed midwestern city, in St. Paul, and, again, in Indianapolis. The *Musical Courier*
(30 October 1907) quoted from the reviews of the Indianapolis concert by
that city's two leading papers. While the *Indianapolis Star* was complete in
its appreciation, it was for the critic of the *Indianapolis News,* who knew his
Baconian philosophy, to offer one of the most exalted paeans to his playing
that Pachmann would ever receive:

> As he played last evening, entrancing his hearers with lovely tone passages
> that slipped along as strands of silk over velvet, singing melody as a
> stringed instrument or an ideal voice, coloring harmonies as with the
> brush of the miniature painter, he was impressive of the ineffable mysti-
> cism of natural phenomena. There can be no flamboyance or pretension
> about this art. There is nothing here to "criticise," but there is only a great
> deal to be thankful for. Nature has provided here an escape from dullness
> and pain; or, perhaps, a revelation of their significance and beauty.

On Sunday, 3 November, Pachmann was at Chicago's Orchestral Hall,
where his performance was presented by F. Wight Neumann.[2] "The most
sensational scene ever enacted in a Chicago concert hall took place in Orchestra Hall yesterday afternoon," the *Chicago Examiner* (4 November) re-

ported, "when Vladimir de Pachmann, the Russian pianist, drove an audience of women into hysteria."

> Many shed tears. Cries and calls filled the air. Some women were on the point of fainting, and the management was forced to turn out the lights and lock the piano in order to drive the frantic women from the hall.
> The frenzy displayed surpassed anything seen in the Paderewski concerts ten years ago, when the "Magnetic Pole" drove throngs of women almost mad.

The article goes on to describe how after Pachmann finished playing (he gave eight encores), the women in the audience "struggled to get near the platform. Hats were displaced and veils torn. Parasols were broken in the struggle."

Pachmann's playing, it seemed, allowed for expressions of sensuality that were socially acceptable even in a restrictive age. A "love of the beautiful" successfully masked a fascination with the morbid and erotic sounds he produced, particularly when he was playing Chopin, and particularly Chopin's *Berceuse*. This was one of the works that best allowed him to demonstrate the *pianissimi*, a *quasi niente* ("almost nothing") to which Olin Downes, who had heard him play it a number of times, paid homage—*pianissimi* being the pianist's *forte*—in 1908 (*Musical America*, 28 March). "It was a marvel of an achievement in miniature, of rhythm and haunting beauty. A piano that was first piano, then pianissimo, then doubly pianissimo, and so on into infinite gradations, until it seemed as if a piano struck by mortal fingers could not be the origin of such tones." Such exquisite playing (his "Pachmannissimo") stretched his audience's nerves to the breaking point and provoked Maenad-like responses—especially among the women. One morning, a uniformed footman even left a small package at Pachmann's hotel with a note attached that read:

> Dear Mr. De Pachmann:—
> I had the pleasure of being at your concert last evening and derived great enjoyment from your beautiful music and your manner of playing it—too much enjoyment by far, I fear, as the accompanying enclosure will testify. I wore the gloves last evening, and feel sure that every woman present went home in the same state. However, I feel that my sacrifice was but a very small one, in the cause of true art. Ruefully, and yet gratefully, yours,
>
> AN ADMIRER

Pachmann then drew forth a pair of gloves split to shreds.

As a sex symbol, Pachmann presents a great contrast to another pianist who was also as famous for his female "groupies" as for his onstage eccentricities: Liberace. It would be obvious to compare the two pianists—both men owned striking jewels and displayed them from the platform—yet the differences between them are more revealing than the similarities. Liberace's attraction to his fans had everything to do with his "persona," whereas Pachmann ultimately seduced with his playing. Also, in contrast to the response of Pachmann's female fans, which was erotically charged, Liberace's appeal was sentimental and, to a regrettable degree, indiscriminately cruel. Liberace was the woman who none of the women in his audience could ever hope to be—rich, draped in furs, adored. He was for them a wish fulfillment.

Yet Pachmann—like Liberace—was not always kind to all of the old dears who came to hear him. The reason was simple and straightforward: Ugliness appalled him. George Copeland wrote in his autobiography of a Pachmann recital in Boston that did not go well for one of a pair of well-known "spinsters" who constituted a faithful part of his audience in that city:

> They were very sentimental ladies, and at the end of some Chopin he was playing, during the great applause, one of the ladies leaned over and handed him a rose. They were both exceedingly plain, and he looked at the woman and then he looked at the rose, and then he looked at her again, and then he put the rose in one place, and picked it up and put it down in another, and then he picked it up and with the rose in his hand he turned and looked at the woman, who was really frightfully ugly. Then he turned and faced the audience, and made the most horrible face, and threw the rose on the floor and stamped on it—and went on with his program.

The violinist Erica Morini, in an interview with Evans, remembered a performance of Beethoven's "Spring" sonata that she gave with Ignaz Friedman in London (ca. 1928). A supper was given in the musicians' honor by Lady Quarrie, whom Pachmann had recently humiliated. Having noticed her in the front row at one of his concerts, Pachmann had told Cesco that he would not perform unless she was removed form his sight. "Pallottelli hurriedly rushed to inform Lady Quarrie that the artist had a 'phobia' for the red color of her dress," Evans writes, "and would not be able to concentrate on his performance." He then invited her to sit with him in his box. "Moments later, a relieved Pachmann emerged and silenced the applause: 'Did you see that lady sitting there?' pointing to a now-empty seat. 'Thank God she is gone. I could not play with her there. She was the ugliest woman I ever saw. Uglier than a monkey!'"

The identity of the woman and the color of her garment changed with each telling of the story. Mantia, for example, heard that the woman, a relative of the queen of England, wore a green dress. "No one is possible so ugly," Pachmann is to have said to Cesco. "Horrible! Horrible! It is impossible to play." Once she had been removed to Cesco's box, Pachmann told the audience, "I am seventy-five and I never saw so ugly a person. She was better than a gorilla."

In conclusion, let the following Chopin anecdote (set down by Margaret Chanler in *Memory Makes Music*) be recorded: "We are told that [Chopin] withered and broke down at a concert because of a lady sitting in the first row with a terrible green bird in her bonnet. He could or would not play unless she moved away" (46).

On 14 November 1907, an interview with Pachmann was published in the *Boston Journal* that revealed him in his most trouble-making vein.

> Brockton, November 13.—As an au revoir Vladimir de Pachmann, the celebrated Russian pianist, who gave a recital at the City Theater last night and departed today, delivered himself of a caustic bit of comment on the lethargy and lack of soulfulness of American audiences and declared that he should never, never again favor the folks on this side of the big briny puddle with any more concerts.
>
> "They are too cool, these American people," said the distinguished visitor, shivering and wrapping himself all the tighter in his long coat. "Appreciation? They have none. Rapture? The word is not in their vocabulary. I shall never play in America again. I am going back to Europe as soon as I can get there. When can I get a boat? America does not appeal to me in any way, shape, or manner. It is too bizarre, too indifferent, too cheap."
>
> There was nothing cheap about the tickets of admission to de Pachmann's concert last night. Nevertheless, he found a full house awaiting him when he appeared on the stage, gave the piano stool a few artistic whirls, plumped himself down, and set the ivories galloping. Everybody was liking it first rate when, along toward the end of his third number, the pianist suddenly stopped, whirled about, and made a gesture of mingled despair and disgust.
>
> The piano was lop-sided, he said. The tone came out crooked. No more harmonies till the instrument was put on the level. There was a great scurry by the ushers for programs, newspapers, bonbon wrappers—anything—and a motley bundle was rammed under one of the legs of the piano. A critical squint or two satisfied the artist and he then proceeded with the recital.
>
> That de Pachmann is a man of eccentricities is known to some of the waiters at the Commercial Club, Brockton's best eating place, but at that they were visibly surprised this morning when, after seating himself at the table, he immediately ordered a pan of water "on the boil." They got it for him and waited to see him drain it, but instead de Pachmann thrust into

it in turn his knife, fork, spoon, plate, butter holder, and napkin. After thus sterilizing them he ate something. He also drank some coffee, but not in a cup. It had to be turned out into a pot. They do it that way in Russia, he said, and he wished to feel as much at home as he possibly could.

Musical America (27 January 1908) published a report from Montréal on "he who more than any one else knows how to get an audience into a happy mood." "It is a very unusual thing to experience at the same time both a sense of admiration for an artist and a restrained desire to laugh at his antics," the critic wrote. "And to add to the odd situation, a tortoise-shell cat clambered onto the platform while de Pachmann played one of his numerous encores after the concert and insisted on showing her appreciation by rubbing against the musician's legs through a waltz movement." (At another concert in Canada—in Calgary—a *black* cat jumped onto the piano while Pachmann was playing. The pianist, amused rather than upset—he was superstitious—or annoyed, announced that he would play an encore "for his friend on the piano": the so-called "Cat's Fugue" of Scarlatti.)

In the middle of January, Pachmann fell ill and remained so for more than four weeks—a period during which he nonetheless continued to play, despite the remonstrances of his physician. In a rare moment, he also sang. The occasion was a Sunday evening reception given by the "Yankee Diva" Lillian Nordica at Sherry's in New York, and his partner was the French baritone Victor Maurel. "We have always known that Mr. de Pachmann had a delightful singing tone in his playing," *Musical America* reported, "but we never heard before that he sang. Possibly the enthusiasm he displayed on Sunday afternoon, when he attended Mme. Carreño's concert at Carnegie Hall, so overcame him that when he was with his good friend, Mme. Nordica, later in the evening, he burst, like a lark in the Spring, into song."

In 1909, the centenary of Chopin's birth, Pachmann returned to England. During the crossing, he turned the ship upside down when he reported that the pouch containing his collection of jewels had been stolen. The captain requisitioned all the cabins and searched the ship; the crew as well as the staff came under a cloud of suspicion that did not lift until three days later, when Pachmann, laughing, confessed that the jewels had been in his pocket the whole time. He thought this was a great joke.

In England, he made another tour of the provinces. A concert in the Queen's Rooms in Glasgow was memorable because he played encores after each piece listed on the program. The evening was brought to a close only because the janitor had put out the lights. (In January 1937, Hofmann, in Chicago, played eighteen encores. A recital by Evgeny Kissin in Bologna, in 1994, came to an end after thirteen encores only because the fire department insisted the theater be cleared.)

Like Chopin, Pachmann suffered acutely from the cold and damp weather in Britain. Longing for sun, for warmth, and for rest, he and Cesco decided to spend the winter in Rome. There he socialized with a number of musicians, among them Giovanni Sgambati and the baritone Mattia Battistini, with whom he and Cesco dined at the Caffé Greco on Via Condotti—a watering hole popular with artists, writers, and musicians since the days when Goethe had lived in Rome. (Among its more unexpected customers was Buffalo Bill.) Pachmann also dined frequently at Ranieri's, the *punto d'incontro* of the Russian colony, where he met Tchaikovsky's brother Modest—and where, very possibly, he had met Cesco. (If so, one wonders how Cesco felt about returning to a scene from his old life.) Yet Pachmann showed little or no interest in the city's archaeological or artistic patrimony, and when Cesco took him to St. Peter's, he only glanced at the façade, then asked the taxi to deliver him to the market at Campo dei Fiori—where he could shop for jewels.

On 6 May 1910, Edward VII, long a friend to Pachmann, died after a series of heart attacks, at the age of sixty-eight. Pachmann was in Paris, where he and Cesco had, or would soon take, an apartment on rue Juliette Lamber, in the seventeenth arrondissement. When he returned to London to give his last recital of the season, he was asked to play Chopin's *Funeral March* in the king's memory. At first he refused, saying that under the circumstances performing it would cause him too much pain. Yet once the lights were dimmed, he put his grief aside and played the *Funeral March* after all.

EIGHT

The Black Hand

On 9 April 1911, the Saturday preceding Palm Sunday, Pachmann presented a mostly Liszt recital in London's Queen's Hall in honor of the centenary of the composer's birth. "A holiday spirit prevailed and certainly the pianist gave a very enjoyable entertainment," a report from London (*Musical Courier,* dateline 19 April) noted.

> Indeed, when presented with a wreath he anticipated the arrival of Pavlova by doing some graceful steps on the platform, holding the wreath over his head. I need hardly mention the enthusiasm of the intensely musical audience when Mr. de Pachmann displayed this side of his genius. The pianist's playing was as flexible and interesting as ever and his remarks were more so.

Presently, he was off to America, with Cesco, once again.

Pachmann once quipped that Adelina Patti made so many farewell tours because on them she "fared so well." He might have been speaking of his own "farewell tours" of America, of which the 1911–12 tour was the latest. Still, this one got off to a rough start. The crossing on the *Mauretania* (which would soon hold all Atlantic speed records) made him seasick, and the special piano stool he had brought with him was seized by customs officials—who declared it to be an "article of trade" and assessed a duty of $2.25—when he disembarked. (Pachmann traveled with his own stool because "one of the most irritating things in the world is a piano stool that is not quite firm.") Upon the appearance of reporters, he declared that he would not be interviewed: "Reporters I hate; critics I hate; New York I hate."

The next day, in his suite at the Prince George Hotel, he was still tired and still in a bad mood. Nonetheless, he gave one of the most fascinating and extended interviews of his life to H. F. Peyser (*Musical America,* 8 July):

> What fatigue, what weariness am I forced to undergo! I am so nervous, exhausted; I am not myself. What an ocean trip—rough weather, heavy seas,

seasickness which kept me in my cabin several days (this particularly painful recollection caused Mr. de Pachmann instinctively to cover his mouth with his right hand). Ah, me! even now do I feel the motion of the boat. The floor rocks under me! And what do I find when I reach this detestable city? Noise, noise, nothing but noise. I cannot sleep, I cannot rest. They are building a house opposite my room and the machines are always going—always, always! That house is full of machines, thousands of machines! They pound and pound and hammer. It overcomes my nerves, it drives away my sleep. My head is like the head of an idiot. I went to bed last night at one. Alas! no quiet, no rest; everywhere noise. I began to fall asleep this morning at six. Then immediately they made the hammering machines begin to work. I am in despair.

When Peyser asked Pachmann if it was true that he had had a bad time at the pier upon arrival, the pianist continued:

Ah! Grand Dieu! Do not let us speak of it. It was awful! To charge duty for a piano stool! How mean! How little! To me, to an artist, to a genius! And those reporters who insisted on talking to me and who annoyed me, though they saw how nervous I was. It was shocking, shameful, scandalous. I hate those men. I hate critics. Mon Dieu! how few critics there are who amount to anything! Critics are a *canaille,* a set of villainous rascals. I can think of only a few whom I esteem. The best one in the world is Dr. [Philip] Hale, of Boston. He is sympathetic, he understands, he adores me. But for the rest—what do I care? *Que m'importent-ils?* I never read what they write. What harm can they do to my genius, my grand genius? What care I so long as my mere name suffices to attract the people, two, three, four thousand of them at a time? The people admire, adore me. To them I am a god. Kings, queens, and high nobility have kissed my hands. What, then, have I to fear from critics? They are all the same, all over the world.

"At this psychological moment," Peyser writes, "the fatal steam-riveter across the street began its deadly work"—whereupon Pachmann began to dilate upon the city in which he found himself.

Oh, how I loathe New York! New York is not America. It is the place where all the humbugs come together. It is the place where foreigners of all nations mingle. The New Yorkers are not Americans. The real Americans are the Yankees from New England. Ah! How different they are and how I love them, one and all! But New York—bah! I should be out of it already if I had a good house in the country.

Turning the interview to more agreeable matters, Peyser asked Pachmann if he preferred American or European audiences. "I am especially fond of English audiences," Pachmann said.

American ones are perhaps more receptive and warmer in feeling. English audiences are often cold, but they are never cold when I play. Mon Dieu, how they love and adore me! You should see and hear them. When I come on the stage it sometimes takes four or five minutes before I can begin my playing, and when I am finished they shout and scream—yes, they scream *comme des brebis* (like female sheep). England is going to be a great country musically. It has been developing wonderfully in late years. When I play in America I always enjoy best playing in Boston [his favorite city in the New World] and in Chicago, though I am also very happy in Los Angeles.

He was again put into an ill humor, however, when the transom above the door gave way just as he was about to be photographed by Peyser's colleague. "There you are," Pachmann said wrathfully.

That is the way they do things in America. I always wonder why Americans are so proud of themselves, why they think everything they do is so perfect. It isn't perfect. The food in American hotels is miserable. American trains are dreadful to travel in—I get as sick in them as on the steamer. And then Americans have the habit of excusing themselves by saying that their country is still too young to do any better. But the land itself is, in truth, not young at all. It must be at least 200,000 years old—no, I guess it is even older than that.

Sunday, 15 October 1911, he gave a recital in Chicago's Studebaker Theater. Karleton Hackett (*Chicago Evening Post,* 16 October) began his review by noting that Pachmann came out on the stage a quarter of an hour late, "which was remarkably prompt for him." Hackett then informed his readers that the pianist now wore his hair à la Liszt and surmised that perhaps this was in honor of the Liszt centenary.

What though he lets his fancy roam free through the music, taking what liberties he chooses with time, rhythm, accent and the notes themselves, still everything that he does is interesting, seems to spring in a way from the music itself, somehow to be in the spirit of Chopin. Another [pianist] will change things, and it comes to us with a shock which we resent, but not so De Pachmann. What he does is pianistically conceived, with the fantasie that never transgresses Chopin's mode of speech, no orchestralization of the instrument, no intellectual recasting of Chopin's thought into something totally foreign to its nature.

Edward C. Moore (*Chicago Daily Journal,* 16 October) began his review of this concert by calling the pianist "a pudgy goblin with a talent for pantomime and a genius for playing the music of Chopin." Whereas Arthur Symons thought Pachmann's playing essentially inhuman, Moore took it to be "more intimate, more human, more alive than that of any other pianist. At least this is the case when he plays Chopin. He comes nearer than any other pianist to creating the illusion that his piano is not a highly organized collection of levers and hammers and wires and sounding board, but something more, on the order of the violin, something to be cuddled and coaxed and made to sing." By way of conclusion, Moore admitted, "It would be of but little avail to endeavor to give a critical estimate of his playing. He is a law unto himself in his interpretations, as in everything else. His idea of conventions is that they are excellent things—for other pianists to follow. . . . He is a creator of beauty—but let no one else try to create it in his way, for failure will be the result. It is a unique secret, and de Pachmann holds the key."

Felix Borowski (*Chicago Record Herald,* 16 October) was astonished as much by Pachmann's "old-time delicacy and charm" as by the fact that Chopin's music "should still move him to so much outward demonstration of rapturous delight." Charles E. Nixon, the critic for the *Chicago Daily News* (16 October), did not fail to understand that for Pachmann, music was more than "mere marks of notation and the metronome."

Dissents were few. Glenn Dillard Gunn, writing in the *Chicago Daily Tribune* (16 October), put forward the playing of Miss Mae Doelling as being of a "better kind." In the *Chicago Inter-Ocean,* Adolphe Brune asserted that "there is no sense in glossing over [Pachmann's] faults"—and he didn't.

Pachmann returned to Chicago for a second recital on 29 October 1911. Hackett and Borowski—also the critic for the *Chicago Daily News*— were just as admiring of his playing as they had been earlier in the month. As for Gunn, whereas previously he had stated his case against Pachmann directly, this time he was cryptic, observing: "A fragment of [Pachmann's] final number, Liszt's 'Tarantella,' showed him in that mood and manner peculiarly his own. This mood and manner are valuable artistic assets, for they comprehend the amateur's ideals of piano playing." Moore wrote only a paragraph about the pianist's second recital, but the last sentence of it is loaded: "De Pachmann gives a very perfect example of what, according to fiction and poetry, a woman's playing at its best ought to be, but what in real life it never is."

Listening to Pachmann sometimes proved too much of a thrill for his American audiences, just as the effort of providing them with a thrill sometimes proved too much for the pianist. His memory began to fail him during his concerts, since, as he explained, "when I get on the platform things make me nervous. The lights especially make me nervous."[1] For the rest of the tour, the lights had to be lowered when he played. "Then what was played was heard with a sixth sense, a keenly emotional, not to say spiritual sense," a Boston critic noted in 1911:

> The unspeakably rich gentleness of the legato section of the E minor study or of the largo of the B minor sonata, had a supernatural directness of appeal that was not to be accounted for merely by reference to a human piano or highly trained finger muscles.[2] It was not until the audience left the hall and got into conversation with itself that it realized how incomplete is the attention ever given to a mere conversation, or any of the doings of daily life, and how complete had been the focusing of attention under the spell of the pianist on the stage.

Pachmann's recital of 21 October 1911 at Jordan Hall (the concert auditorium of the New England Conservatory) prompted the critic Arthur Wilson to write a lengthy essay on the pianist, which appeared in the *Musician* (January 1912). The essay begins by noting that as a result of his brother Simon's death, "It is said that Mr. de Pachmann has fallen heir to a handsome fortune." (Simon's wife and only son had predeceased him. According to Pallottelli, Pachmann made a gift of Simon's library, at least, to the university in St. Petersburg.) Wilson then offers a spirited defense of Pachmann—"the last prophet of a school of pianism that, at his death, will face extinction," whose delicacy of tone provided a welcome contrast to the thunderers.

> It might be a debatable question how great a service to art was the perfection of the modern single piece steel frame of the piano with a resistance power of from 24,000 to 40,000 pounds. In the days of the clavichord it was necessary to play with finesse to play well. Now there are other ways to impress a hearer. Thunders in the bass with the aid of a sustaining pedal are inscrutable to many and profoundly imposing, a heritage not to be charged to Liszt solely, for there are yet those who can testify to his adroitness upon occasion to sculpturesque music of quaint and delicate design, but rather to the various brood who delight their souls in the expansive and ear-filling reverberations of the modern grand.
>
> The pleasure, then, and the benediction to senses to find that Mr. de Pachmann had returned, the magician as of old, creating a haunting spell of elusive beauty by the magic of his touch.

Once again, Pachmann's new fondness for playing in the dark is invoked to suggest the deeply romantic nature of his performances.

> The pianist had the lights turned off above him, and as the cloudy autumn afternoon waned, the outline of the form at the piano—the locks now hanging to the shoulders Lisztian fashion—sank deeper into the twi-

light. It is not a question whether it was or was not an ingeniously devised stage setting. It was a sympathetic frame to the eye for the sensitiveness of spirit of the Chopin that sounded through it to the ear.

The language of this description calls up the séance. With his "intimate" audience gathered round him in a half circle, Pachmann the medium brings Chopin back through his "haunting spell" and "sensitiveness of spirit." Wilson continues:

> In playing such as this the mind of the hearer is not conscious of the *amount* of physical tone. This tone is not a *quantity* to be measured by the marks *p* and *f*, but an *essence*, whose gradations are in intensity rather than volume. Tones which might be measured as the softest are the most elusive, evanescent, the most exquisite in their palpable unreality. Their sheen is seen as from afar, and should one go to take them, it would be with the fear that they would vanish. Tone which is more powerful seems more intimate, enveloping, stimulating, as though fine particles of it pervaded and filled all space, and if all of them were poured in upon the ear, their contact would be an exhilaration to nerves rather than a painful assault upon them.

Pachmann the mystic, then, manages to achieve the almost supernatural feat of penetrating the very nerves of his listeners: He is not only a medium but a hypnotist. "How does De Pachmann avoid the warring vibrations perpetrated upon a defenceless public by the acrobats?" Wilson asks.

> These gentlemen will say that Mr. de Pachmann does not and cannot play *ff*. The metronome can measure the rate of speed at which a man can play, but there is no device sold at music stores to register the amount of noise which he makes. Dynamic graduation of tone is wholly relative, as is all appreciation for nuance in art, as for contrast in life. A few pennies are riches to the child. A tone of only moderate loudness, if properly produced, may be ample to crown a climax with power and distinction, if the scale of values, of which it is a part, has *held it in reserve* until now, and made the mind more alert and the hearing more keen by a discreet husbandry of tone.
>
> But who shall analyze De Pachmann's tone, and say with what degree of stroke, or of pressure touch, or by what combination of both he produces it? The making of individual tones upon the piano does not offer a wide latitude of possible variations in quality. "Color" is to be found more particularly in the treatment of a succession of tones, in the profile of the figure or phrase, where the pianist is then able to inflect, and to impart characterizing, dramatizing values which have their interpretative and emotional import.

By way of conclusion, Wilson shifts his metaphors and aligns Pachmann with nature, yet never quite abandons the conceit that the pianist has a supernatural capacity to become the composer he plays.

> It is in this moulding of the contour of a melodic line that much of the ineffable charm of De Pachmann's playing resides. His rubato is the free, spontaneous, myriad-versioned rhythm of nature, as the waving of a field of grain in the breeze, the swaying tree tops at the approaching storm. It may be thus to-day, and of a different cast tomorrow, yet however it is, it seems the complete and inevitable expression of the thought, as though the hearer should say: "This must have been in the composer's mind. This is the one way it should go."
>
> Is it not this improvisional, this rhapsodic quality which constitutes and illumines the remarkable playing of this man that gives to it the supreme attribute of poetry? It is as though he wove the filaments of each piece anew, a spontaneous creation of that moment, as though yet another time the piano had confided to him its secrets, and he had published them in tone, not as a brazen herald from the housetops, but as a lover would breathe the confessions of his mistress.

In the end, Wilson, having carried Pachmann through a wealth of identities—medium, hypnotist, even Orpheus conducting the orchestra of nature—settles on the metaphor of the lover. Pachmann is Romeo whispering the secrets of Juliet and driving the women in the audience to split their metaphorical gloves.

On 13 February 1912, Harry Truman wrote to Bess Wallace from Grandview, Missouri: "I shall call you up Friday as soon as I can get to a phone and you can decide if I shall come for you or not. It seems as if I should since I shall desert before Mr. DePachmann gets done throwing fits. He is going to play Mendelssohn's 'Spinning Song' and Chopin's great A-flat waltz" (Ferrell 73).

Also in Missouri, Pachmann was engaged to play Chopin's E minor concerto with the St. Louis Symphony Orchestra on 23 (at 4:00 P.M.) and 24 (at 8:15 P.M.) February. "All went well for a while," Paul Martin reported for the *Indianapolis Star*, "until the audience, completely charmed by De Pachmann, forgot the orchestra of which St. Louis people are usually so proud."

> As the program proceeded the enthusiasm of the auditors mounted higher and higher. De Pachmann was at his best musically, and as is his custom, was also indulging in those gymnastics which are almost as entertaining as his music, and in which he delights when he is in particularly good humor. He flirted with his audience. He made funny faces. He

played the solemn chords of the Chopin "Nun's Prayer" with his left hand, waving his right hand in the air, as if to say, "See what I can do with one hand."

At one thrilling moment . . . he bounced up and down in his seat and at the conclusion of a waltz he danced from the stage. These gymnastics, coupled with his superb art, excited his auditors almost to frenzy. When he had played the whirring melodies of Mendelssohn's "Spinning Wheel" the applause compelled him to return to the stage time after time to bow his thanks. Still the audience insisted, and after the seventh bow the lid of the piano was closed to signify that he would not play an encore. The applause was redoubled. Men stamped their feet and shouted. Women waved programs in the air and clapped their hands until they split their gloves [yet again]. Seats were banged up and down, but De Pachmann did not appear.

While all this was going on, the conductor of the orchestra, Max Zach, was becoming increasingly frustrated. At his desk, he waited for the applause to die down, then, when it only grew louder, signaled for the orchestra to begin playing. "As the first sounds of the orchestra were heard above the din people leaped to their feet and the applause for De Pachmann became a crescendo," Martin noted. "The enthusiasm of some excited a counter-demonstration, and those who wanted to hear the orchestra hissed those who wanted more of the pianist." Finally Zach, having "heard the hisses, and apparently believing that they were meant for the orchestra, threw down his baton and signaled his men from the stage." A silence fell upon the audience, the members of which waited for nearly an hour, although neither Pachmann nor Zach reappeared.

St. Louis reporters later interviewed both Pachmann and Zach. "De Pachmann was in a state of extreme temperamental rage over the curtailing of his program," Martin wrote. "As he talked he flourished his hands and tossed the gray mane of his hair." His response was to blame Zach. "Jealousy!" he dissembled. "That's all the trouble. The people loved my playing. From the gallery to the pit they were all in ecstasy. Sacre bleu! What does Zach think? The people can hear him any day. Me—they can hear me once in a lifetime!"

To the same reporters Zach explained, "To maintain the dignity of the orchestra, the only thing to do was to stop there and then."

On 10 March 1912, Pachmann gave a recital in Chicago's Studebaker Theater that provoked a magnificent review by Borowski in the next day's *Record-Herald.*

It is, to be sure, the delightful uncertainty of this performer's actions which make his recitals so fascinating to the crowd. The spectacle of Mr.

de Pachmann crawling from underneath the piano, or, between pieces, explaining some subtle point of art, or gazing with a rapt and passionate expression at some woefully embarrassed person sitting in his immediate neighborhood in the audience is not without a peculiar diversion of its own.[3]

In any event, Pachmann did not disappoint those who "looked for fun as well as music," for when he arrived on the stage he "proceeded to observe the piano stool as if it was an oil painting." Of Pachmann's interpretation of Mozart's A major sonata, which began the concert, Borowski wrote:

Mr. de Pachmann exaggerated much of the gentle sentiment of the piece. It is absurd to put into the reading of a simple variation upon an ingenuous tune the rapturous passion that might fittingly be expended upon "Tristan and Isolde." The performer was, however, much pleased. "Schoen gespielt!" he remarked after the second variation, and toward heaven he cast an ecstatic glance that might have been drawn from a gourmand who had just partaken of a savory dish.

Later in the concert, when Pachmann turned to the music of Chopin, an element of pathos was admitted: " [H]aving forgotten the E major scherzo, [he] advanced to the front of the stage and, holding out his arms deprecatingly, confided to the audience that when one arrives at the age of sixty-four it becomes easy to forget. He attempted another scherzo [the third], but forgot that too, and finally contented himself with the playing of an étude."

A strange, and unfortunately unelaborated, account of this same concert appeared in the *Chicago Daily Tribune* (11 March): "It was the usual De Pachmann performance, save that its grotesqueries were accentuated by the psychic influence of the player on the overflow on the stage. Members of this portion of the audience seemed impelled to emulate the eccentricities of Mr. de Pachmann." (What could this mean?)

Thence to Cleveland, where on 13 March Pachmann gave a recital that Archie Bell, in the next day's *Leader,* judged to have marked an epoch in the city's musical life. A day or two later, Bell had the opportunity to spend an afternoon with the pianist at his hotel and to interview him. "But I found not the eccentric Chopinzee, which concert goers admire so much," Bell began. "I found nothing of the bizarre and almost superman of which the papers have told during twenty-five years."

I met him by appointment, and as he was ushered into the room, there came up to me a jolly, smiling and courtly little old man, bowing in European style until his long gray locks fell over his forehead and eyes. He held out his hand and shook mine afterward in genuine Yankee fashion. Perhaps the etiquette of the thing was to have met de Pachmann as one meets a bishop. Afterward in our conversation he said to me: "Emperors, kings, queens and princesses have kissed those hands when they were outstretched to them." Perhaps they were not to be rudely shaken with the genuine "glad to meet you." For this man de Pachmann is an egotist. That is, he knows and believes that he is great, and although he begs the pardon of the one with whom he is talking for the personal reference, he does not hesitate to say, "I know that I alone in all the world play that perfectly." (quoted in Adella Prentiss Hughes, 149)

Presently, and for one of the few times in his life, the pianist spoke openly of his limitations and his way of effacing them in public.

"Pachmann is his best and most severe critic," said the pianist. "Remember I am sixty-three years of age. I have always been playing and hearing others play. I know myself better than any other can know me. I know that there are certain limitations, size of hands, physique, and other things; there are things that I cannot play. There are certain compositions of composers whom I play regularly, that I would not attempt in public. You never hear me play those things. That's how I do my tricks—I only do what I can do perfectly. I know that the world never had a pianist who could do certain things that I do, as well as I can do them, and I do some of these things in public. How do I know this? The critics did not tell me. The critics have told me nothing, but the great giants of the musical and art world have told me. They know better than the critics. People would not crowd to see me if I could not please them. There's the answer. I am no fly-by-night pianist, but I have been playing every year for forty—yes, for many years, and people know exactly what they want to hear." (149–50)

Pachmann now returned to New York, where on 13 April he played a recital that elicited some charming reviews. The *Musical Courier* ("Variations") reminded its readers, "Not for [Pachmann] are ranting, melodramatics, and orchestral sonorities on the piano. He lets others claw the keys; he caresses them. He does not try to be the Atlas of the piano, but rather the Ariel. He works not in atmosphere of fire, like Pyracmon, but in Dorian mood of 'flute and soft recorders.'"

Noting that this was supposed to be the pianist's last American tour, the same publication summed up:

All of us will miss Vladimir de Pachmann, dispenser of delicate musical emotions and disciple of an art that is none the less beautiful for representing the characteristic tonal expression of a generation that knew not the vigorous anvil blows of our twentieth-century Young Siegfrieds of the piano, and did not imperiously require the virtuosos of that instrument to be giants in intellect and prodigies of passion. Much gentler and infinitely more gracious will be the memories left vibrating in the American musical mind by rare Vladimir de Pachmann. Peace and primroses attend his further wanderings and his continued profitable application of the luminous scale and the fluttering pianissimo!

Musical America (27 April) took the occasion of Pachmann's farewell recital in New York to distinguish his unique order of piano playing—which the *New York Times* had described as concerned "with grace, fleetness, elegance, exquisitely perfect mechanism" from the "school of to-day" (the orchestral style of piano playing). The writer, acknowledging that neither order was complete, called for a marriage of the two: Piano playing "can progress to a stage where dynamics are kept within the bounds of beauty, where much of grace, elegance and singing tone are retained, and, at the same time, where there will remain a grasp and power quite sufficient to reveal the deepest in music."

On the personal front, a rift appeared to be opening between Pachmann and Cesco, who had learned much under the pianist's tutelage and was now far more sophisticated than the young waiter Pachmann had spontaneously taken into his employ. Although the details are sparse, what is clear is that more and more Cesco, now in his mid-twenties, was going his own way while he was with the pianist. Not only was he investing in questionable business ventures. He had also taken to playing jazz piano and "lo ragtimes," which drove Pachmann crazy. (Perhaps he played jazz and "lo ragtimes" *in order* to drive Pachmann crazy.) Then, when Pachmann made public, in New York, the fact that he had received a "Black Hand" letter threatening him with death if he returned to Chicago for a concert on 28 April, Cesco's reaction was curiously muted.

The "Black Hand" (*Mano Nero*), Jay Robert Nash writes in *Bloodletters and Badmen,* was "an extortion racket practiced by Sicilian and Italian gangsters (many of whom were members of the evil brotherhoods) for approximately thirty years—1890 to 1920—against the unschooled, superstitious immigrants of the 'Little Italy' settlements sequestered in major Eastern, Southern, and Midwestern cities" (57).[4] A note would be sent to a prominent and wealthy person demanding money and threatening to kill the victim (or the victim's family) if it was not forthcoming. The Black Hand was so called because "in most cases, the outline of a hand dipped in heavy black ink was impressed at the bottom of the note" (57). Nash continues: "The violence displayed by Chicago Blackhanders against their victims was devastating; it consisted mostly of bombings that destroyed whole buildings and several families in each attack. Little Italy—the area contained within Oak and Taylor Streets and Grand and Wentworth Avenues—was a Black Hand playground, more appropriately a slaughterhouse" (59). Black Hand killings peaked in 1910–11, when thirty-eight people were shot to death at the corner of Oak and Milton Streets alone.

Pachmann's manager, F. Wight Neumann, made the threat public in an interview with a reporter from the *Chicago Examiner.*

> De Pachmann, like most geniuses, is eccentric, emotional, impulsive and inclined to be arbitrary, if not autocratic. He has been terrified by a black hand or anarchist letter, sent to him from some one in Chicago when he was in this city last month. The letter threatened him with death, and, though in all probability it would not be followed by any attempt upon his life, he cannot be persuaded that he would be entirely safe if he came to Chicago.

According to an article in the *Record Herald* (8 April 1912), this letter informed Pachmann that he would be "blown up." On the same date, the *Chicago Tribune* quoted Cesco's summary of the situation:

> [The letter] was full of obscenity. It worried De Pachmann, *although there was no reason why he should have been frightened* [italics mine]. It was signed with the initials "D. C. M." When he got back to New York after his trip through the southwest he decided on the Chicago cancellation because he was worn out by the strain of the trip, because of disgust over receipt of the letter, and because of the lurking fear that anyone who was crank enough to send such a letter might possibly turn to dangerous ways.

Although the Chicago police offered to provide the pianist with bodyguards or an escort of detectives in plainclothes, Pachmann refused to return to the city. He had good reason: He was far from being the only celebrity to have received a Black Hand letter. Actress Laurette Taylor had gotten one during the spring of 1912 and promptly gone into hiding.[5] Paderewski had received one in 1913 and suffered a breakdown as a result.[5] Incredibly, however, upon learning of Pachmann's decision, Neumann told a journalist for the *Chicago Inter-Ocean* (8 April), "The old man is a coward! I don't know whether the Black Hand letter is a joke intended to scare him or not, but he is just the sort to get all kinds of fright at the receipt of such a letter." This cruel and inelegant dismissal of the validity of Pachmann's fear—to which many deaths bore awful witness—speaks strongly for Neumann's lack of regard for the pianist's life; clearly, Neumann was more concerned about the box office receipts he stood to lose than about Pachmann himself. (Cesco's own attempts to play down the situation suggest motives that are not much better.)

The Black Hand letter, together with the news that he was to inherit a share (approximately $300,000) of his brother's estate, prompted Pachmann to abort his tour and to return to Europe, with every intention of retiring. Although he had made a lot of money over the course of his career, he had spent much of it on jewels (and Cesco) and could not have afforded to retire without the serendipity of the inheritance. (In fact, just a short time before, Arnold Somlyo had persuaded him to invest in a film company that turned out to be a swindle—resulting in the pianist losing a considerable share of his fortune. Whether Somlyo was the swindler or was swindled himself is unclear.)

Cesco did not go with him. He had either quit Pachmann's employ or been released from his duties.

Before departing, Pachmann spoke of Europe to some reporters: "It is far over the ocean, and even though I feel a young man, my years are many. Matthew Arnold said, was it not, that the melancholy part of old age is that as our bodies grow old, our hearts grow young.[6] So it is with me." Then he embarked, alone. He told no one where he was going.

It would be several months before Cesco started looking for him.

NINE

"The Sky Is Changed!"

Pachmann went on to Abbazia (now called Opatija), an Adriatic resort
two hours from Trieste in what is now Croatia. (Much more recently,
the pianist Ivo Pogorelich settled there.) The town's history began with the
founding of a Benedictine monastery in the twelfth century, to which the
church of St. Jacob was added in the fifteenth century. In 1844, a merchant
from nearby Rijeka named Iginio Scarpa came and built a villa (Villa Angiolina) and gardens there. (One of the plants he brought to Abbazia was the
Japanese camellia, now the town's official symbol.) This was the beginning
of Abbazia's touristic history, for in addition to its superb geographical position, it offered a salubrious climate. Indeed, it was sometimes called "the
Austrian Nice." In 1884 the first hotel in town—the Quarnero (now the
Kvarner)—opened its doors; the Kronprinzessen Stephanie (now the Imperial) opened the following year. Presently Abbazia became a watering hole
for royalty and the official sanatorium of the Austro-Hungarian monarchy.
Emperor Franz Joseph and Empress Elisabeth[1] sojourned there, as did King
Carol I and Queen Elizabeth of Rumania, Kaiser Wilhelm II, King Oskar
II and Queen Sofia of Sweden, and the princes Philip, August, and Leopold
of Sachen-Coburg—as well as writers Anton Chekhov and James Joyce
(who taught English at the Berlitz School in nearby Pula), violinist Jan
Kubelik, dancer Isadora Duncan, Hungarian operetta composers Franz
Lehár and Imre Kálmán, and Gustav Mahler.[2] Here Pachmann, always a
friend to the titled and the famous, lived comfortably, playing the piano
only rarely. He often went to the cinema (the first one in Abbazia had
opened about 1910), but not to the theater, since he could not stand the
usually inferior playing of the musicians in the orchestra pit.

In late March of that year (1913), *Yato*, Marguerite Fernand Labori's
"lyric drama" in two acts after a poem by Henri Cain and Louis Payen, was
given its premiere at the Opéra de Monte Carlo. (It would have its first performance in Paris at the Gaieté Lyrique the following April.)[3] Unfortu-

nately, we do not know if Pachmann attended or what he thought of it if he did. Then in September, accompanied by their four young children and a governess, Maggie and Labori sailed to Montréal, where he had been invited to attend the annual congress of the American Bar Association. Labori's fame had continued to grow in the years since the Dreyfus affair, and after touring the country, the family returned to Montréal, where he was award-ed a degree *honoris causa* by McGill University. Thence to Boston, where he had surgery for appendicitis and received flowers from President William Howard Taft each day during the five weeks of his recuperation. Upon re-covering, he gave a lecture at Harvard University. They sailed from New York to Europe on the *Lusitania,* on which they were given the royal suite.

As for Cesco, during the first months of Pachmann's "retirement" he al-lied himself with a number of dubious projects in New York, none of which panned out. There is some suggestion that he had found a new bene-factor, who he hoped might do more for him than Pachmann had. But this seems not to have panned out either, and Cesco—without immediate pros-pects—turned his thoughts, once again, to Pachmann.

It was at this point that he began working behind the scenes with Li-onel Powell to arrange a tour for the almost septuagenarian pianist—even though the almost septuagenarian pianist had not been asked if he wanted to tour. What Cesco and Powell were banking on was the hope that Pach-mann would be missing the limelight so much that he would readily agree to their plan as soon as it was presented to him. And they were right: Pach-mann, whom Cesco found in Abbazia, proved to be as keen to return to concertizing as his handlers had hoped, even though he now had no practi-cal need to do so.

A vintage example of Cesco's pay-as-you-go attitude toward human relationships was the affair he now began conducting with the daughter of the owner of Pachmann's hotel in Abbazia, behind the pianist's back. This was not the first affair that Cesco had had with a woman (in this regard he perfectly illustrated Prime-Stevenson's paradigm of the "he-hetaira"), yet the fact that it came immediately in the wake of his reunion with Pach-mann made it seem particularly callous. Now, having dispatched Pach-mann to London and installed him there, Cesco returned to Abbazia. When the affair did not work out, he went back to London—and to Pach-mann—whereupon the spurned and perspicacious mistress sent a telegram to Cesco blaming Pachmann for "interfering" and threatening to come to London in order to kill the pianist.

A quarter of a century earlier (*Star,* 7 March 1890), Shaw had written of Pachmann's memory lapses: He "passes off mishaps of this sort so effec-tively that he has been suspected by evil-minded persons of bringing them about on purpose." Although the memory lapses that had haunted Pachmann during his 1911–12 season in America persisted during the 1913 tour, he lost none of his humor in handling them. Most pianists, when they suffer a memory lapse, simply pause to collect their thoughts, then begin again; in rare cases, they may leave the stage to consult, or even to return with, the music. (There are also numerous examples of pianists attempting to find their way by more novel means.) Rosina Lhévinne recalled Pachmann dealing with the same problem in a manner anything but banal:

> In the middle of a Sonata he completely forgot where he was in the music. Without any hesitation, instead of going behind the stage, he went forward and up the aisle. He walked like a lunatic, staring straight ahead he slowly went to the very back of the hall. There he jumped on a chair, reached up and stopped a clock and said in a loud voice that the ticking of the clock had disturbed him. Then he returned to the piano and resumed playing. (Mitchell 145)

Similarly, on those infrequent occasions when his technique let him down, he took refuge in a wonderful bit of cleverness. Victor Seroff wrote in "A Memory of de Pachmann" (*Bravo,* January-February 1962) that "if he had to play a rather difficult passage, he would stop before attacking it and say to the audience: 'I know you all think it is very difficult. Not at all. It is all your imagination. You should practice it a long time very slowly. Like this.' And he would play it very slowly, which was very simple indeed. Then, without ever playing the passage at proper tempo, he would finish the piece."

In October of that year, in the *Musician,* G. Mark Wilson offered a refreshingly literal description of Pachmann's hands. In all the previous ink devoted to Pachmann, his hands had been described metaphorically. Wilson, by contrast, described what they looked like. "Compared with other famous pianists," Wilson began, "[Pachmann's] hands are the smallest of any playing at the present time."

> They are rather odd in shape, the body of the hand being long and narrow, while the fingers are short and thick. He asserts that pianists with short fingers have greater command over the volume of tone, style of touch, rapid execution, etc., on account of the decreased though steadier leverage which of necessity they must adopt. Evidence of great muscular development is at once apparent in the hands. This is particularly noticeable when viewed from the side. The wrists are large and powerful, but like the fingers are as flexible as finely tempered springs.

Wilson's article is especially valuable because those plaster casts of Pachmann's hands known to have been made (they were photographed and the photographs of them published) have been either lost or destroyed.

In all the years that he visited London, if he did not rent a house or a flat, Pachmann stayed at the Hotel Ronveau at 2–3 Golden Square (near Piccadilly Circus, at the south end of Carnaby Street); his wedding reception had been held there, and he had become close to the French wife of the hotel's proprietor, Peter Leon. By 1914, however, the Ronveau had lost its lease and been pulled down, and "Madame Peter" was living again in France. At the end of the season, Pachmann hired a touring car that sped along at the then extraordinary speed of forty miles per hour and visited her in the great cathedral town of Troyes, whence he and Cesco continued on to the Haute Savoie to spend the summer in a house they had rented on Lake d'Annecy. Powell visited, as did Pachmann's sons Lionel and Adrian (the more athletic of the two), with whom Pachmann was photographed. It is an odd picture, full of unease: Pachmann is seated, with his sons standing behind him. All three are dressed in casual suits and wear hats that obscure their expressions. Neither son rests a hand on his father's shoulder, which would have been not only a comfortable but a conventional pose.

When Lionel and Adrian were boys, Lionel later recalled, and their father would visit them in Paris, he would often treat them to dinner at a deluxe restaurant such as Henry on the rue St. Augustin (just off the Avenue de l'Opéra); if the dinner was especially good, Pachmann would show his appreciation by playing a piece for the chef and his staff on the restaurant's piano.

Curiously enough, however, Lionel claimed to have heard his father play in concert only three times. The first occasion, which he described to several interviewers, was in 1909 at Bechstein Hall in London. At this point, Lionel was at the beginning of his own career as a musician. Having first summoned him to the stage, Pachmann introduced the embarrassed young man to the audience with a monologue along the lines of the following: "Ladies and gentleman, this is my son. As you see, he is taller than me. He, too, is a musician. As a pianist . . . (Pachmann made a face). As a composer . . . perhaps. But as a theoretician (Pachmann kissed his fingers), a most learned man! A professor *en attendant* at the [Paris] conservatoire." Pachmann then bade Lionel to sit beside him while he played the first piece on his program, all the while making remarks and giving him instructions. When the piece ended, he sent his son back to his seat with the admonishment to remember all that his father had told him.

The second time Lionel heard his father was a year or two later. Pachmann had agreed to share the stage at the Royal Albert Hall with Jan Kubelik, who owned the Villa Rosalia in Abbazia. Pachmann was to open the concert with a Chopin group, after which Kubelik would play some solos; then, together, they would play Beethoven's "Kreutzer" sonata.

That afternoon Lionel, as he told it, rode with his father in a taxi from the Hotel Ronveau to the Albert Hall. Already Pachmann was in an ill humor, thanks to an encounter in the hotel lobby with an old man who had announced his pleasure at the prospect of hearing him "accompany" Kubelik; this sort of thing never went down well with him. When they arrived at the hall, a constable approached the taxi and demanded that the driver, who was looking for the artists' entrance, move on. When he hesitated, the constable asked whether his passengers already had tickets to the concert, which was sold out. The pianist was uncomprehending. "But he is Pachmann," Lionel explained to the constable, who immediately showed them to the artists' entrance. By this point the combination of the old stranger's effrontery at the hotel and the constable's failure to recognize him had pushed Pachmann over the edge. "I, a ticket?" he kept sputtering to his son, who did his unsuccessful best to console him.

In the event, Pachmann's mood improved once he was in front of his "friends" in the audience, whom he proceeded to gift with so many encores that Kubelik, waiting in the wings, became almost as irritable as the pianist had been half an hour before. Sharing the stage with Pachmann was never easy.

On Lake d'Annecy, he and Cesco gave frequent garden parties as well as evening parties. During one of these a storm arose so suddenly and with such violence that the electricity had to be turned off. Candles were lit, but soon the drafts inside the house extinguished them; the thunder grew louder, and all conversation ceased.

> The sky is changed!—and such a change! Oh night,
> And storm, and darkness, ye are wondrous strong.[4]

When the storm had passed, and the electricity was turned on again, Cesco went to look for Pachmann, who had disappeared. Presently he was found hiding under a table, invoking the name of the Virgin over and over again.

Mostly, however, the weather was glorious. On a particularly magnificent evening, Lionel recalled, his father threw open the French doors so that moonlight would flood over the piano; he then played the "Moonlight" sonata. In *The Great War and Modern Memory*, Paul Fussell writes, "Although some memories of the benign last summer before the war can be discounted as standard romantic retrospection turned even rosier by egregious contrast with what followed, all agree that the prewar summer was the most idyllic for many years" (23).

> It was warm and sunny, eminently pastoral. One lolled outside on a folding canvas chaise, or swam, or walked in the countryside. One read outdoors,

went on picnics, had tea served from a white wicker table under the trees. You could leave your books on the table all night without fear of rain. . . .

For the modern imagination that last summer has assumed the status of a permanent symbol for anything innocently but irrecoverably lost. Transferred meanings of "our summer of 1914" retain the irony of the original, for the change from felicity to despair, pastoral to anti-pastoral, is melodramatically unexpected. (23–24)

This idyll came to an abrupt end with the assassination of Franz Ferdinand and his morganatic wife, Sophie, duchess of Hohenberg, in Sarajevo on 28 June, their wedding anniversary. (It was also St. Vitus Day, the Serbian national holiday.) Austria declared war on Serbia—by cable—on 28 July. Germany, Austria's ally, declared war on Russia on 1 August and on France on 3 August—the date Britain declared war on Germany. On 6 August Austria declared war on Russia. On 12 August Britain and France went to war with Austria.

Pachmann's response to news of war was decisive and pragmatic, indicating that he suspected the conflict would not, as others said, be over by Christmas. First, believing that French currency would soon be rendered valueless, he changed all of his paper money into silver. Then, as a precaution against food shortages, he bought rabbits. The mere prospect of hunger terrified him. "There are two things for me in the world," he once said: music and gastronomy. "On my deathbed it is my fervent wish that I may have the strength to eat a good, hearty last meal!" (Pachmann would have agreed with Alice B. Toklas that cooking could produce "something that approaches an aesthetic emotion.") On Lake d'Annecy, his posture seems to have been one of retreat, but when the summer ended, he was ready to play in public again. He believed that it was the artist's sacred duty to communicate with and to console his public, particularly in a time of confusion and horror.

With this goal in mind, he and Cesco set off for England, where Pachmann was billed as "The World Famous Russian Pianist, who has two sons fighting at the front." (Adrian received the Croix de Guerre and three citations for conspicuous bravery at Verdun and other fields of battle.) This calculation seems to have exempted him from the hostility to which a number of foreign-born musicians were subjected in Britain during the war—a hostility that Robin Legge had attempted to diffuse in the *Musical Courier* (18 November 1915), writing: "The war will benefit us here if it will keep away all the second rate foreign musicians. But we are not going to advance very far if we are to insist on living, like a camel, on our own hump!"

Additionally, and no less calculatedly, Pachmann was to participate in many benefit concerts for the English Red Cross. "Although sixty cents was the lowest priced seat obtainable for a concert for this fund," W. J. Bowden wrote in the *Musical Courier* (16 December 1915), "an audience of considerable dimensions occupied the Philharmonic Hall [in Liverpool] when de Pachmann again appeared, together with the brothers Eugene and Theodore Ysaÿe, and Mme. [Elsa] Stralia, a coloratura soprano, hailing from the Antipodes." In fact, Pachmann and Eugene Ysaÿe, both of whom were managed by Lionel Powell, often shared the stage on behalf of the Red Cross. At these concerts Pachmann played last because, as the *Musical Courier* again reported (6 January 1916), "it would be impossible for Ysaÿe, the serious, to follow Pachmann, the comic (albeit a fine artist)."

Adrian de Pachmann was now a lieutenant in the French army stationed at the front. On 7 January 1916 his mother wrote to tell him that Labori's health was deteriorating. In this letter, which she later included in *Labori, ses notes manuscrites, sa vie,* she refers to her husband as "Père," indicating that at least one of Pachmann's sons had elected to ally himself more closely with his stepfather than with his father—or that Maggie wanted him to do so. Both Adrian and Lionel also chose to become French citizens. Pachmann, by contrast, was becoming more and more a darling of the Anglo-Saxon world, and on 31 January 1916, the Royal Philharmonic Society presented him with its gold medal in recognition of his contribution to British musical life. At the gala concert at the Queen's Hall, he played Chopin's E minor concerto with the orchestra under Thomas Beecham. Beecham claimed that later, in the green room, Pachmann bit the medal to make sure that it was really gold. (Although Paderewski is listed among the recipients of the medal, he is believed to have declined it, since his name would appear only on its edge.)

In May, *Musical America* reported (inaccurately) that the "so-happily-dubbed Great Chopinzee of the pianoforte does not trouble himself very much to learn things that have not been in his musical system for many long years, but he had one novelty on this London program. It was a Berceuse by Walter Imboden, to which the subtitle 'Bruges' is appended by way of localizing its significance." This subtitle was by then ironic, since for Pachmann's audience Belgium meant not a romantic medieval past but Ypres and Flanders Fields. Although no musical response to this Berceuse seems to exist, the very title would have called up the glorious model of Chopin for Pachmann's listeners, quite independent of how much, or how little, the work could be characterized as "Chopinesque." On the other hand, Imboden's *Valsettes,* dedicated to Pachmann, were once characterized as "Schumannesque." Imboden's name recurs in the Pachmann literature, though no musical source except Refardt's 1929 *Historisches-biographisches Musikerlexikon der Schweiz* lists it. Terence Pepper of the National Portrait Gallery, however, writes that a Walter Imboden of Kensington "registered on 7th October 1909 at what is now the Public Record Office at Kew (and was then Chancery Lane) a photograph he had taken of Pachmann in London,

3/4 face." This Walter Imboden is also listed in the National Phone Directory for at least two issues in 1909, at which time he lived in one of five flats at No. 1, Horton Street, Kensington.

It was on this tour of England that Pachmann suffered a change more disruptive to his life even than the war itself: Cesco married.

While arranging concerts for the benefit of the Red Cross during the Great War, he had met a young Italian woman named Alice (or Alicia) de Fonseca. Born on 6 October 1892, Alice was the daughter of Edoardo de Fonseca, a proto-Fascist and editor of the Italian magazines *Novissima* and *La Casa;* as a young woman, she looked rather like the actress Celia Johnson in the film *Brief Encounter.* Alice had been sent to school in England in the hope that she might marry an English gentleman; instead, she did what her Florentine family least wanted her to do: she fell in love with a short Italian from the Marche. Earlier, Cesco had assured Pachmann that he and his new wife would look after him once they were married, adding, "If you feel lonely, you can live near us." Pachmann corrected him: "I will live *with* you." Presently, of course, Cesco and Alice understood that *they* would be living with *him.*

Although the trio sought to promote an air of amicability, this domestic arrangement set the stage for a battle of wills between Alice and Pachmann (and to a lesser degree, between each of them and Cesco) that would last until Pachmann's death. Cesco got everything: the chance to begin a new relationship without having to sacrifice an old one. Indeed, their shared resentment at the casual recklessness with which he had created the ménage provided Alice and Pachmann with a rare point of common cause. Yet despite the unhappiness and anger that Alice legitimately felt at having to keep house with her husband's homosexual benefactor, she was no shrinking violet. When she caught her eight-year-old son Duilio smoking, her grandson Sergio recalled, she hit him on the face with a bread board, breaking his nose.

After his marriage, Cesco wrote a small booklet about Pachmann. (Published for sale at Red Cross benefit concerts,[5] the English translation is pointedly dedicated "To My Wife"; the Italian edition bears no dedication.) In June 2000 I bought a copy of this booklet that indicates the degree to which its owner treasured Pachmann; indeed, this copy is almost a reliquary. It has been bound in leather and the cover gilt stamped:

V. de P.
1917.

In the lower left hand corner are the initials "H. H. H." (for Herbert Hugh Harvey), while on the inside of the flyleaf are pasted two clippings from the

Daily Telegraph (the obituary of Pachmann and an article about the leather bag from which the pianist had been inseparable for half a century). In the book proper are additional pastings: an advertisement for Pachmann's Columbia recordings, the *Evening Standard* review of his Queen's Hall recital on St. Patrick's Day 1917, and an appreciation of him by Landon Ronald from the *News Chronicle*. The photograph of Pachmann and Pallottelli on page 13 has been signed by both men and dated 21 May 1917; on the same page, a card reading "With compliments F Pallottelli Going to H[?]" has been tipped in.

The booklet includes an amusing account of Pachmann's daily life at home. Here we learn that he liked to play hide and seek before lunch; that at lunch and dinner his conversation turned on the quality of the food; that he preferred to play the piano at night (a preference he suppressed after Cesco and Alice had children); and that he hardly ever went to bed before 3 or 4 A.M. On tour, he never missed a train, and only once, according to Cesco, did he miss a concert—following the night that the mouse kept him awake. Nor did he understand, according to Cesco, how money deposited in a bank could earn interest. In short, Cesco portrayed Pachmann as a child—and if Pachmann was a child, then Cesco was his guardian. His presence in the pianist's life was now not only necessary but commendable. Yet Pachmann had lived quite successfully for fifty-seven years before Cesco came on the scene.

Pachmann's relationship with Cesco and Alice in some ways resembled E. M. Forster's with Bob and May Buckingham. In his youth, Bob, a policeman, was Forster's lover, and when he first announced his intention to marry May, Forster was hostile not only to the idea but to the girl herself. Later, however, he grew to love May deeply, becoming as dependent on her as he was on Bob. For his part, Pachmann began to believe, in time, that Alice might be a friend to him and, albeit guardedly, brought her into his confidence. He never entirely trusted her, however—and with good reason. Alice made no secret of her annoyance at his practicing, and sometimes expressly forbade him from doing so. Nor was she reluctant to embarrass him in front of his colleagues. (When Harold Bauer came to dinner, she asked him if he needed to study as long as Pachmann did to learn a certain work.) In a very real sense, the member of the Pallottelli family who most appreciated Pachmann was the cocker spaniel Cio-Cio-San—named for the heroine of Puccini's *Madama Butterfly*—who would often sit on a chair and listen while he practiced.

On 14 March 1917, Labori died. A business card inscribed to Pachmann's pupil Allan Bier and dated June 1917 by Pallottelli tells us that at this point Pallottelli was established (professionally if not residentially) in

Paris, at 51 Avenue de Villiers, 17ieme. The printed portion of the card reads "François Pallottelli / V. de Pachmann's / Touring Manager / Partner of / R. H. Schneider Co. / 84 rue St. Lazare / Paris." (The "Partner of" portion, however, has been crossed out and the address on Avenue de Villiers written beside it.) Whether Pachmann was also in Paris, and communicated with Maggie at the time of her husband's death, we do not know.

Alice and Cesco's first son, Virgilio, was born on 11 August 1917.

By 1918, the year he turned seventy, Pachmann felt that he had come to a crisis in his musical life: When his muscles were tired and stiff, he could not produce the tone that had made him a legend. This deterioration of his mechanical gift, in turn, interfered with his ability to communicate with an audience that he so prized in himself.

Though a large part of his admiring public was willing to overlook his decline, he was too serious an artist to be satisfied giving less than his best. He therefore decided that he would restudy, rephrase, and refinger (playing passages written for one hand with both hands, for instance) his entire repertoire according to a new principle which would lessen the stress on his muscles. This "new method," as he called it, became an obsession for him.

The function of all reputable methods is, finally, a modest one: to allow the pianist to do the most playing with the least and most relaxed movement. Yet Pachmann, with an admixture of panache and bombast, trumpeted his new method as nothing less than "a revelation" that "came from heaven." Indeed, in an interview included in her book *Modern Masters of the Keyboard,* he told Harriette Brower:

> The first benefit of my Méthode to the player is that he can produce a *natural tone,* made without effort. I can play hours and hours without fatigue. I could play the whole twenty-four if I didn't have to eat a little and sleep some. . . . Ah, the poor piano! But *my* piano will yield lovely tones because I treat it in the right way. Why not caress it like this? Listen to these little upward passages; how delicate and shadowy! How ethereal they can be made if the heart speaks through them by means of the fingers! And the fingers, doing their part through right adjustment and correct choice, glide up and down the keyboard with little or no effort or exertion. (35–36)

Pachmann felt that if he had a reputation as the founder of a new method, his playing would be heard differently. Whether the new method was unique or bluff, his promotion of it as of use to all pianists, instead of as merely providing a new lease on life for his own playing, would lend weight to his performances. "Yes, I intend to write out my Méthode," he said near the end of the interview; "it shall be set down in an orderly manner, for the benefit of those who come after me. But not yet—I have no time; I must go on tour. After all that is over—then—perhaps—" (39).

He never did write it down, although he spoke of it for the rest of his life, explaining in a 1925 article on how he kept young published in *The Music Lover's Portfolio:* "My new method brings health to the body, abolishes fatigue, makes for straight wrists, adds to the beauty of the hands, and induces tranquillity. Five valuable advantages." Indeed, the linchpin of the method was a straight wrist position. "It does not consist of high, stiff wrists," he told Brower; "that would be very bad—abominable! You see I move my wrists up and down freely when I play. But my hand and arm I hold quite level, with the outside of the hand on a line with the arm, not turned in or out at the wrist" (34). There was, however, some confusion as to whether "straight wrist" meant "stiff wrist." Pachmann spent a lot of time correcting the error in interviews he gave, and on 20 September 1923, Cesco wrote a letter to the editor of the *New York Times* setting the record straight once and for all:

> The letter of Hugo Goerlitz brings up the point of the "stiff wrist." This statement was a misquotation of Mr. de Pachmann which has already been corrected in several papers. What Mr. de Pachmann said was "a straight wrist." In an interview with John Alan Haughton of *Musical America,* issue of Sept. 8, 1923, Mr. de Pachmann said regarding the "stiff wrist": "Could anything be more absurd? Can you imagine playing the piano or doing anything else with stiffened muscles? They simply misunderstood me, those reporters, or they don't know a lot about the piano. Now what I did say was this: 'I now play without any lateral motion of the wrists, and the line from the angle of the second joint of the hand to the elbow is the diameter of a circle.' In other words, such lateral movement as is required has the elbow as the center of a circle and not the wrist joint." The above statement is a correct report of the maestro's view.

The origin of the new method was Clementi, who was, according to Pachmann, "against the use of the thumb on a black key. I wondered why, and thought it over until I discovered that Clementi's reason was that there was an undue strain on the wrist, with consequent fatigue." Even Virgilio Pallottelli was brought into the act, photographed in 1923, at the age of six, being taught Pachmann's "straight-wrist" technique for an article in the *Literary Digest* (3 November).

Only some of the works in Pachmann's repertoire lent themselves to his new method. Indeed, he remarked philosophically, "You can't play everything"—an admission that, together with the fact that he never wrote the method down, does much to diminish his claims for it.

The only known extant footage of Pachmann, made about 1928 and lasting less than a minute, shows him recording a piano roll. Here—in the flesh, so to speak—it is possible to see both his application of the method and the personal charm that audiences found so endearing in him. Upon being presented with the finished roll for his signature, Pachmann lifts his arms in wonderment and smiles with the surprised delight of one receiving an unexpected gift. He then signs it "V. de Pachmann"—the final "n" flowing into an aristocratic paraph.

On 11 November 1918, the Armistice putting an end to the Great War was signed in the Hall of Mirrors at Versailles. (Paderewski was the signatory for Poland.) That same year, the Spanish influenza pandemic broke out, killing more than twenty million people before the end of 1919. For a man terrified of "microbes," as Pachmann was, the pandemic was a nightmare. Even at home, after all, he would wash his plates and silverware in a bowl filled with water or wine, unless he happened to be animatedly telling a story and therefore forgot. This precaution appears to have paid off, since he emerged from the pandemic unaffected. So did his sons. On 14 April 1919 the *New York Times* reported the marriage of Adrian, who had come to the United States with the French High Commission, and Edith Sproul, the elder daughter of Mr. and Mrs. George D. Sproul (a publisher and dealer in rare books) of 222 Riverside Drive. The wedding had taken place the preceding Saturday afternoon at the bride's home, the Rev. Charles G. Sewall officiating. It was further reported that in September the couple would be moving to Paris, where Adrian was connected to the law firm formerly headed by his stepfather. There he would act as correspondent for prominent New York law firms, among them Evarts, Choate, Curtin & Leon and White & Case.

Pachmann did not attend. He was in Rome that season, playing, on occasion, under the auspices of the Accademia di Santa Cecilia. In his *Ricordi del Presidente,* the president of the Accademia, Conte Enrico di San Martino Valperga, recounts a story about the pianist, whom he professed to admire as much for his character as for "his marvelous mechanism, the perfection of his touch, the *genialità* [in Italian, both genius and geniality] of his interpretations" (139). Here the count wrote that once "at the home of his friend Pallottelli," the violinist Mischa Elman was being accompanied in the "Kreutzer" sonata by a pianist who also proved to be a "wonderful artist" (140). Pachmann, as was his wont on these occasions, made life miserable for his colleague of the keyboard. When the unnamed pianist played—in Pachmann's view—badly, Pachmann would turn to the guests and grimace, perhaps even give him the thumbs down. If, however, the pianist played well, Pachmann would pat him on the back and say something like, "Not bad, good, very good, I like this." The count could not decide whether he admired more the pianist ("probably of German origin") or the patience with which he forebore Pachmann's phrase-by-phrase scrutiny of his playing with Christian resignation—"I say Christian but probably I should have said Jewish" (140).

Presently, the count goes on, Pachmann acceded to the audience's supplications that he himself play, and after explaining that his new method was unique in all the world, he launched into a Mendelssohn scherzo. In the middle he stopped, turned, and confided to his listeners that only one other pianist could have performed the work as well as he did: Liszt—on the condition that he had practiced nothing else for three months.

The count concludes by mentioning that for many years Pachmann had been staying at the "casa Pallottelli," where he received "a loving hospitality and where all the peculiarities of the maestro, whose great goodheartedness and sincere affection were held in esteem, were accepted with patience and grace" (142). This was the typical Italian perspective on Pachmann's relationship with Cesco, reversing its terms so that Pachmann became the dependent and the secretary the benefactor. Such an account provided a balm to Cesco's ego by glorifying his role in the pianist's life.

On 6 January and 23 February 1920, Pachmann gave additional recitals in Rome. His piano, on the latter occasion, was one from Turin's Fabbrica Italiana Pianoforti, since Cesco was interested in promoting instruments from the company and had arranged to have one sent to the *filarmonica*. When Pachmann arrived at the auditorium, Cesco lied to him, telling him that Steinway had been unable to deliver the piano he had requested and that he would have to play this new one instead. Pachmann was upset and performed for less than an hour. Then at the end, before he went out to play his *bis,* Cesco asked him if he would tell the public that it was a "very good piano." As Mantia recalled in a 1980 interview with Allan Evans, Pachmann dutifully returned to the stage, saying, "They said me to tell you this is a good piano."

Cesco's determination to use Pachmann to promote an Italian make of piano prefigured his imminent involvement with the Fascist movement, for which he was being groomed by Alice and his father-in-law. (In the caption to a photograph of Pachmann and the Pallottellis published in the *New York Evening Post* on 3 May 1924, Alice is described as "a friend of Mussolini.") Fired by his new nationalistic tendencies, Cesco decided to reestablish himself in Italy, and in 1920, along with his family, he returned *in patria.* Pachmann went with them. Now, from late June until September or October, the pianist stayed in Fabriano, a medieval town in the Marche, near the Umbrian border, that was famous for its paper works. (The art of watermarking originated there.) Not coincidentally, Campodonico, the village in which Cesco had been born and had grown up poor, was a *frazione* of Fabriano, located about fifteen kilometers to the west. Pachmann spent the late autumn and winter in London, where Powell would secure an apartment for him and the Pallottellis in Great Portland Street. In the early spring he returned to Rome for a few weeks. Then it was back to England for the spring season and Fabriano by the end of June.

Today Fabriano is neat and affluent, with a Bang & Olufsen shop across from the Palazzo del Podestà (built in 1255) and the Sturinalto fountain (built in 1285). The streets are cobblestoned, and there is a large shady park. Poplars abound, blanketing some of the streets in spring with a fine white down, almost like snow. In addition to its paper works, Fabriano has a number of beautiful churches and civic buildings, and claims as a son the painter Gentile da Fabriano (1370?–1427), whose *Adoration of the Magi* hangs in the Uffizi. The town's theater is named for the painter.

Campodonico, by contrast, has the harsh, unyielding look of many Umbrian villages. Most of the old stone houses are boarded up now, casualties of the earthquakes that rumbled through this part of Italy in 1997. Five years afterwards, most of the villagers were still living in temporary wooden houses, oblong and narrow, a cross between log cabins and mobile homes, while they waited for their own houses to be rebuilt. There was even a temporary post office. Otherwise, Campodonico has changed much less over the last seventy years than Fabriano. It has the feel of an outpost, and one can understand how a boy like Cesco, growing up there, might have longed for that larger town which was to him "the city."

Certainly his return to Fabriano, with Pachmann in tow, had something of a "local boy made good" quality about it. Or at least this was the impression that Cesco sought to create, given that the money really belonged to the old pianist on whom he wanted people to believe that he was bestowing his kindness. The Villa Gioia—an emblem of success in the small world of Fabriano (one writer likened it to a castle of "once-upon-a time")—would have been beyond his means otherwise. Located at the top of the Via Martiri di Kindu, it had sublime views both of Fabriano itself and of the gray mountains beyond it; indeed, the villa's very position suggests domination. The house is large, with many windows, and its plaster façade is decorated with antique majolica plates and tiles. Today it is owned by one of the foremost commercial families of Fabriano.

The fact that Pachmann did not like Fabriano at first—he thought the people provincial and tiresome, found the town dusty and dirty, and suffered from the mosquitoes—cements the impression that his purchase of the Villa Gioia was made at Cesco's behest. Before long, though, he grew fonder of the place. Pachmann often opened the windows before he played, and it was said that the farmers working the fields outside would sometimes stop to listen, even in the rain, while a Chopin nocturne floated over the hillside. In prosaic fact, the hillside beneath the villa is too steep to be farmed.

Clarence Lucas (*Musical Courier,* 28 October 1920):

> London, October 5, 1920.—Could any other pianist than De Pachmann draw an audience large enough to fill Albert Hall? I do not know the players who draw best in the other great cities of the world, but I have had the best kind of evidence that De Pachmann is the favored pianist to the London public. Yesterday afternoon the huge hall was filled to hear him. His audience would have crowded all the other concert halls of London put together. He was greeted with the warmest enthusiasm and he was evidently in the best of moods. Having bowed slowly and profoundly to the four points of the compass, he strode to the center of the stage and began a series of pantomimic gestures which would have done credit to the Russian ballet. He rubbed his hands and smiled, showing that he was in good humor. Then he patted the muscles of his arms and felt of his wrists to show that he was fit for the task ahead of him. Then he raised both hands very high, assumed a tragic expression, and pounded away at the air like Macbeth clutching at the imaginary dagger. He shook his head violently that the audience might know that he despised piano pounding. In fact the mere suggestion of banging the keyboard upset him completely and he covered his ears with his hands and shuddered. Recovering himself, he smiled significantly at his spectators, put his hands outstretched in front of him as if playing on an imaginary keyboard, moved his fingers up and down and indicated by his eyes and elbow gestures that he would play in a gentle and undemonstrative manner the compositions set down on the program. These visible and intelligible gestures were accompanied with an inaudible stream of Pachmann polyglot on which a few fragments of English, French, and German syllables were detected floating. Having finally inspected his Steinway and satisfied himself that all the strings and keys were in place, he cast aside, metaphorically, the comic mask of Thalia and took on alternately the masks of Terpsichore, the dancer, and Erato, the muse of amatory poetry. But why say more about the playing of an artist who was famous before most of the readers of the *Musical Courier* were born!

In a letter to Florence Barger (10 November 1920), E. M. Forster described attending Pachmann's 3 November concert with his mother. "We sat close under Pachmann's nose," he wrote, "and he seemed delighted to see us, nodding and making remarks in a variety of languages. His madness is not offensive—rather a dear old happy man I thought and his playing quite exquisite, the only defect being a lack of force which doubtless proceeds from age. I should hear him again if I got the chance" (318).

During the few weeks that he spent in Rome each year, Pachmann received many visitors, one of the most celebrated of whom was Moriz Rosenthal. When Pachmann asked him to play, Rosenthal commenced a Chopin mazurka. Pachmann was delighted, for he had not considered that "the Napoleon of the Pianoforte" (as James Gibbons Huneker called him) might have an intimate and poetical side. (Several years earlier, however, Arthur Johnstone had described beautifully this aspect of Rosenthal's playing, commending a performance of the Chopin *Berceuse* that brought out "all the delicate moonshine filigree of the right-hand with infinite subtlety.") Pachmann was genuinely fond of Rosenthal's playing of the mazurkas, and later—rewriting history a bit—took to referring to him as "my pupil."

Arnold Somlyo, one of the marginal figures who made extra cash off Pachmann's reputation (and confidences), "transcribed" many stories about his client and then supplied them to the press—one of them, titled "What De Pachmann Taught Rosenthal," being about a piano lesson the older pianist gave to the younger one many years before. According to Somlyo, "It so happened that both pianists were in Vienna at the same time" (other sources locate the story in Berlin or Rome) when Rosenthal resolved to learn from Pachmann the "secret" of playing Chopin's mazurkas. When he called upon him and solicited a demonstration, Pachmann said, "I will play the F major mazurka [68/3] for you."

De Pachmann puttered about among the book-cases and shelves and hunted for fully five minutes before he finally brought forth a worn and battered old volume labelled: "Mazurkas, by Chopin." Another prolonged search resulted in De Pachmann's finding a huge pair of horn spectacles, which he adjusted carefully on his nose before he placed the Chopin book on the piano rack and turned painstakingly to the F major mazurka. Rosenthal was mystified. De Pachmann, the pianist of the limitless repertory and the amazing memory, to play a two page piece from the notes, and that piece the F major mazurka, familiar to all amateurs!

Very carefully, De Pachmann began to play, reading note for note from the page and glancing carefully at his fingers to see that he put them on the right keys. Laboriously he plodded through the mazurka, in the stiff, angular style of a schoolboy, with not a vestige of that grace, daintiness, and poetry so characteristic of Pachmann's real performances. When he struck the last note in the composition, he closed the book, took off his spectacles, sighed, and turning to Rosenthal, said sadly: "A very difficult work, my dear friend, yes, a very difficult work." For a moment or two, Rosenthal, who had been listening in utmost amazement, was nonplused, then he recognized that De Pachmann was a diplomat of the old school. Reaching for his hat, Rosenthal murmured his thanks, and was bowed out with Chesterfieldian grace by his imperturbable host.

On another occasion Rosenthal managed to turn the tables on his colleague. Charles Rosen (from a letter to the author): "I do not know much about Vladimir de Pachmann, except the story of my teacher, Rosenthal, who once heard him play the Etude in thirds but not at his best in a salon, patted him on the back and said, 'Now you have the tempo, you can put in the thirds.' Of course I know de Pachmann invented the standard fingering for this piece."

Pachmann adored Rome, the atmosphere of which—its brightly colored houses, its sultry weather—reminded him of Odessa, and at Cesco's urging, in 1921 or 1922 he bought a villa and garden at the corner of Via Nomentana and Via Massaua. Today, on Via Massaua, modern apartment blocks alternate with elaborate villas in the style that the Italians call "Liberty" (Art Nouveau). The traffic noises are inescapable, and the urban sprawl is depressing. In the 1920s, however, Via Massaua was almost in the Roman *campagna*. The houses—then fashionable and new—served as the trophies of the class that would evolve into the Fascist bourgeoisie. (The aristocracy, by contrast, lived in palaces in and around the old city center.) Many of the street names memorialized Italy's failed efforts to colonize Africa: In addition to Via Massaua (named for an Eritrean port that was occupied by Italy in 1885), there were Via Asmara, Via Assab, Via Mogadiscio, Via Ogaden, and Via Tripoli. Pachmann's neighbors later included Mussolini himself, whose Villa Torlonia was only a short way down the Nomentana from number 377.

Cesco had commissioned Duilio Cambellotti—who had designed fourteen stained-glass windows for the Casina delle Civette at Villa Torlonia—to restructure the "Villa Virgilio," as well as to design and build a new portico, vestibule, and music room composed of a small stage for Pachmann's piano and an arrangement of cushioned benches (also designed by Cambellotti, who was something of an Italian Charles Rennie Mackintosh or Frank Lloyd Wright) for his listeners to sit on. There was a monumental fireplace in Carrara marble inset with majolica cymas (now missing). The walls were decorated with a frieze consisting of an anagram of the word *amore* and olive leaves, as well as an enormous fresco (130cm×345cm) depicting lions and lionesses, dogs, lynxes, and gazelles—as if the animals were waiting for an Orpheus to come and tame them. As it happened, Cambellotti already had a connection to the Pallottelli family, having designed the cover for *La Casa*, one of the magazines published by Alice's father. (The magazine was dedicated to "the aesthetics, décor, and care of the modern home.")

There is no getting away from the fact that Cesco had excellent taste. The decoration of the villa, if rather severe, put it at the cutting edge of Italian design at that time. By hiring Cambellotti, and then giving him free rein to oversee every aspect of the villa's transformation, Cesco was in effect providing the designer with the opportunity to create a showplace—one that would bring prestige and attention to them both and that could be featured in *La Casa*. And yet it is hard to imagine that Pachmann—who paid for it all—found it a comforting place to live. (Notably, in photographs of the music room, not a single object connected to Pachmann or suggesting his specific presence is visible: not the Etruscan vase given to him by the czarina; no pictures of Maggie or his sons; not even any of his music.)

Tellingly, the Villa Virgilio is known today as Villino Pallottelli; it still stands, although its street address is now 3 Via Massaua, the entrance on Via Nomentana having been closed off when a five-story police *caserma* was built over the garden. Although the address of the *caserma* is 1 Via Massaua, 377 Via Nomentana is still viable: It belongs to the Fina gas station—of the European sort that is no deeper than a sidewalk—tucked between the *caserma* and the old Roman road to Nomentum.

As for the villa itself, it is now occupied by the Suore di Ns. Signora Ausiliatrice. Its walls are painted a clear pale yellow and inset with twenty majolica plates painted with animals and twenty square majolica tiles figured with children's faces like those at the Villa Gioia in Fabriano (for which Cambellotti was also responsible). The frescoes were painted over during the 1970s, however, and the stage of the music room and the lower part for listeners were split into two rooms.

Among the visitors to Via Massaua in those years were the violinist Mario Corti, Ignaz Friedman, Leonid Kreutzer (a pupil of Essipov), Luisa Tetrazzini,[6] and Aldo Mantia, who studied Pachmann himself as much as his way of playing. Mantia learned at once that Pachmann was an extremely generous man—one might even say generous to a fault—with the result that Cesco had to keep him under surveillance, in case he should try to give away something irrecoverable. To Mantia himself, Pachmann gave cuff links that he said had belonged to Chopin ("You must always wear them when you play," Pachmann said), a snuff box, a library of books about Chopin, and a glass (paste) sapphire.

His eccentric behavior was by now becoming endemic to his personality, something he engaged in offstage as well as on—and sometimes at the same time. Nor was he always Forster's "dear old happy man." Gaisberg writes (*Gramophone,* October 1943) that at a concert in Bradford, "an altercation in the wings of the stage became audiable [*sic*]."

> A peevish, irritated voice with a foreign accent was heard and a little dumpy man backed out into the open, still haranguing an unseen somebody. . . . He stumbled and caught himself in the rough boards of the platform. "Yes, now I remember this rotten floor [from] last year. I told you to have it repaired—have it repaired for me the great de Pachmann. You did not do it. I am the great de Pachmann, why do you treat the great de Pachmann in this way." All this while still addressing the unseen and with his back to the audience.

In 1921, he performed throughout Italy, where critics compared his performances to the commedia dell'arte, calling him the "Pulcinella [Little Flea] of the Piano." He also played in England; by Cesco's reckoning, he appeared in more than one hundred concerts.

TEN

Talking to the Moon

During the summer of 1922, Pachmann signed on for a two-year tour of North America under the auspices of the Baldwin Piano Company, to begin in October 1923. He then departed for performances in England, taking Alice—and, of course, Cesco—with him. He instructed her to find for him the elusive red diamond he had long coveted for his collection. (If she and Cesco were using him and his money in order to live grandly in Fabriano, it appears that he was perfectly willing to make his own demands of the couple, who had taken to calling him "Papy.") When Alice actually did find the stone—a testament to her acumen—Pachmann feigned to be cross, telling her that had she not done so, he would not have had to spend so much money. In any event he had the diamond set into a ring. In the photograph by Victor Georg accompanying an article on the pianist in *Good Housekeeping* (February 1925), it is possible to see the ring on his left hand.[1] This is the only one of his jewels he ever wore. (Although the red diamond was the jewel Pachmann chased after the longest, it was not the one for which he traveled the farthest. On more than one occasion he spoke of a "wild adventure" in Borneo, where he might well have stopped on his way to Australia. No evidence, however, has come to light to prove that he actually concertized in the Antipodes.)

Pachmann often visited the old English music halls, which presented a greater range of entertainment than is usually thought to be the case today. Prima ballerina Anna Pavlova might share the bill with, say, a mesmerist. One of his favorite music-hall performers was the "Laughing Scotsman," Harry Lauder, several of whose records, according to Cesco, the pianist owned. He also enjoyed the clown Barclay Gammon, famous for his undisguised imitation of Pachmann himself. (Pachmann's only objection to Gammon's performance was that Gammon made him smile too much; sometimes, he reminded Gammon, he was "triste.")

On 5 November 1922, he gave a Chopin recital at Royal Albert Hall. An anonymous concertgoer who annotated his program from this recital recalled that when, at one point, Pachmann's memory failed him, the pianist "kept on playing Chopinesquely and turned his head to us while still playing 'Ca c'est pas du Chopin'; but he soon found his way back to Chopin." Pachmann also made a tour of the provinces on which he was accompanied by Harold Holt, an employee of Pachmann's manager, Lionel Powell. Holt's favorite story about the pianist became almost as famous as the "socks" incident in Berlin.

One Sunday morning, in Dundee, Pachmann announced his wish to have a bath. Cesco dutifully filled the tub for the pianist, whereupon Pachmann declared that he would not bathe until a clean sheet was first placed in it to protect him from the microbes of other bathers. The tub was emptied, the sheet laid, the tub refilled. Pachmann then demanded to know the exact temperature of the water. Cesco told him that it was "just right," but the pianist found this answer unsatisfactory. Holt went out to find an open chemist's shop, where he could buy a bath thermometer. By the time he returned with this article, the bathwater had cooled, so once again the tub had to be emptied and filled.

Then there was the matter of soap. Cesco offered Pachmann a piece he had only used once, but this would not suit him. Again Holt went to the chemist's. Being wise to Pachmann, he bought several pieces of soap, each a different color. (Pachmann then decided that only green soap would do.) Again the tub was emptied and filled. All seemed to be set for Pachmann's bath, except that the bath towel had not been put on the radiator to be warmed. *Now,* an hour after preparations for the bath had begun, everything was in order—but Pachmann decided he did not want to take a bath after all.

By this point, Pachmann was obviously a little mad—and his madness showed up during concerts to a degree that it had not before. Indeed, even those who in the past had been indulgent of him found cause to complain. He kept his audiences waiting for half an hour ("In Russia my concerts always begin half an hour late," he explained—although he had not played in Russia for many long years). He refused to play certain encores and demanded the removal of unattractive persons from the audience on threat of canceling the performance. In other words, he gave abundantly of all that was most intolerable in him and sparingly of that which seduced and charmed.

What was the origin of this "madness"? No doubt, at least in part, it owed to the strain in Pachmann's character that was at once obsessive, paranoid, and self-dramatizing. And yet one must not discount the legitimate causes that lay behind his ill humor and occasional bad behavior. After all, by 1922 he was seventy-four years old and playing a heavy schedule; this was necessary if he was to earn the money that Cesco required to maintain his grand Italian lifestyle.[2] If he was resentful—and the story of the bath suggests the resentful acting up of a child—he had good reason to be. What was unfortunate was that his audiences had to bear the brunt of an anger that should have been directed at the Pallottellis.

In early 1923, Pachmann was in Berlin, where he gave "interpretative lessons" to the Polish stepmother of Yve Menzies. "What I have to say about Vladimir de Pachmann . . . is all rather negative," Menzies wrote in a letter to the author (8 April 2000). "As a result of what she called her previous rigorous German musical training, . . . [my stepmother] realised that there was no point in her continuing interpretation lessons from de Pachmann unless she wished to follow in his footsteps." Twenty years later, the stepmother studied in London with Solomon, who apparently "very nearly refused to give her lessons purely on the grounds that she had been a pupil of de Pachmann!"

Dolly Pattison, the Rome correspondent of the *Musical Courier,* spent a summer afternoon with Pachmann in Fabriano and found him in fine form. "Not alone is he proud of the agility of his fingers, which is prodigious," she wrote in a profile of the pianist published 13 September 1923, "but also that of his feet and limbs; while conversing on the subject, up he springs like a youth, saying: 'Look now,' and runs around the terrace of the garden, up the stairs of the veranda and down again, without losing breath or seeming tired. 'You see, I can run as though I were eighteen.'" Having shared with Pattison his sympathetic remembrances of America—he execrated only the American custom of drinking ice water, which horrified him (most Europeans still feel the same way about it)—he confided to her that he had two treasures. The first was his new method, which he demonstrated by playing a work of Liszt's "with remarkable brilliancy," Brahms's waltzes, Godowsky's *Karneval,* and a Chopin nocturne "hardly known." (To think there was ever a time when any Chopin nocturne was hardly known!) In response to hearing the waltzes, Pattison exulted: "It was wonderful—it was extraordinary—it was everything! Brahms, under his fingers, did not seem the heavy footed mastodon almost all pianists present. Here was brilliancy, lightness. Birds, butterflies flew across the keyboard; then again, according to the coloring of the tempi, sturdy solemn oaks bent their branches. It was a dream." The second of his treasures was "'one of the rarest exemplaires of the red diamond,'" the like of which only czars had once possessed. "But the poor Czar," Pachmann sighed, "who knows where the Bolsheviki have sold his?"

In August 1923, Pachmann sailed to America on the White Line's ship *Majestic* from Cherbourg, accompanied by Cesco, Alice, Virgilio, and Eva, their cook. If he let so many years pass between his visits to America, it was perhaps because his anxiety about sailing—acute under the best of circumstances—had been heightened by the sinking of the *Titanic* in 1912 and the torpedoing of the *Sussex* in 1916. (Enrique Granados died in the later accident.) In *My Many Years,* the second volume of his autobiography, Arthur Rubinstein writes that when he sailed to America on the *Majestic* in January 1923, he met Pachmann and visited him daily during the crossing:

> At my next visit to the old pianist, I told him, "There is a lady, one of your great admirers, who is terribly anxious to be introduced to you." He made a disgusted face.
>
> "A lady? I'm an old man, I'm in bed, what can I do with a lady?"
>
> "She is the Marchioness of Cholmondely. Her husband is a Chamberlain of the King." His face became more sour.
>
> "What do they want of me, Chamberlain, lady, March . . ." I felt I had to give him more details. "She is the granddaughter of the great banker Baron Gustave de Rothschild." My gambit produced an expression of admiring wonder.
>
> "Rothschild?" He rubbed his thumb and forefinger together. "Very rich!" he said. I nodded.
>
> "All right," he said. "Bring her tomorrow at noon. I will get out of my bed."
>
> Sybil [the marchioness] thanked me effusively. At noon next day, I knocked on Pachmann's door. It was opened by his secretary. "Please take a seat, the Maestro will be right with you." We waited a good quarter of an hour. The door opened and Vladimir de Pachmann entered in a black frock coat with silk lapels, stiff white collar, and a tie, in black shoes, and with diamond rings all over his fingers (he was a famous collector of diamonds of different colors). He shook my hand and then, pointing at Lady Cholmondely, he asked a little too loudly, "Rothschild?" Sybil blushed. She did not know that this name had done wonders with the Maestro. He walked up to her, made a short bow, and looked disapprovingly at an emerald brooch that she wore. "Bad stone, your emerald," he said, "but look at my beautiful diamonds!" and spread out his ten fingers, which were covered with them. Sybil was so scared to death by this whole show that she was unable to utter a word. She stood up, whispered a few polite, inaudible words, and left the cabin, followed by me.
>
> At lunch she tried to tell the whole story to [her husband] but laughed so much he couldn't understand a word of it. For years it was enough to pronounce Pachmann's name for her to burst into uproarious laughter. (277)

Rubinstein's rubbishy anecdote is easily dismantled. First, Pachmann did not sail on the *Majestic* in January 1923. More to the point, the pianist, who had counted more than one royal among his familiars (even friends), would hardly have been impressed by a garden-variety marchioness, no matter how rich her antecedents. He himself was—or had been—anything but poor. Once, in fact, he had even scored off the Grand Duke Constantine: He was walking along the Nevsky Prospect in St. Petersburg when the grand duke, an amateur musician, saluted him with the words "Good Day, colleague"—whereupon Pachmann replied, "Since when have I been a grand duke?"[3] It is true that had the marchioness's emerald indeed been inferior, Pachmann would not have hesitated to tell her so. At the same time, we know that only one of his diamonds (the red one) was set; all his other stones were loose. Thus, had he been inclined to make a show of what he owned (and this he never did; instead, his jewels were the stepping stones, one might say, that permitted him to metaphorize his playing), he could not possibly have done so in the way described.

What is most confusing about the story, however, is the celerity with which Sybil goes from being "scared to death" of Pachmann to being amused by him. (A small point of illogic: If "she was unable to utter a word," how could she whisper "a few polite, inaudible words"? Moreover, if the words were "inaudible," how did Rubinstein know they were "polite"?)

If I have given more space to Rubinstein's account than it deserves, it is because it seems a particularly harmful one. In truth, he fobbed his own preoccupations off on Pachmann. It was Rubinstein who cultivated the titled and the rich. Indeed, if every reference to the aristocratic and the famous, not to mention every passage of a self-congratulatory nature, were to be excised from it, his autobiography would be a thin performance indeed. Rubinstein's smugness ill conceals the anxiety he habitually showed in the presence of greater pianists. (One of his techniques for diminishing his colleagues was to identify them as homosexual—Horowitz most famously. He uses the same tactic, more obliquely, when he has Pachmann ask, "I'm in bed, what can I do with a lady?")

As for Pachmann, though he said many extraordinary things, he never spoke ill of the dead. The worst he did was to hold that Liszt once told him that he played a certain Chopin work as well as the composer himself; he said this some years after Liszt had died and was unable either to corroborate or to deny the story. In any case, Pachmann never compromised Liszt's reputation. Rubinstein, by contrast, was malicious with forethought.[4]

The pianist had prepared two core programs and a nosegay of encores for his North American tour (including Mexico). The first program included Bach's *Italian* concerto, Beethoven's *Pathétique,* Mozart's *Fantasie* in C minor, and smaller pieces by Schumann, Mendelssohn, Liszt, and Brahms;

the second was all-Chopin. Interestingly enough, Dr. C. Ward Crampton, "the noted authority on superior physical condition and longevity," examined Pachmann before the tour and pronounced him "in fine physical condition, fit to concertize for ten years more" (*Chicago Journal of Commerce,* 6 October 1923). Presently the *Musical Courier*—always a friend to Pachmann—published two photos of the pianist under the title "Vladimir de Pachmann Then and Now" (1 November). One dated from his second American tour (it had appeared on the cover of the *Musical Courier* for 18 October 1899), while the other—a new portrait by Victor Georg—showed the pianist "seventy-four years young, with (right) F. C. Coppicus, head of the Metropolitan Musical Bureau, his manager, and Signor Pallatelli [*sic*], his secretary and companion for eighteen years." This was one of the few occasions on which Cesco's extraprofessional role in Pachmann's life was acknowledged in print, if only obliquely.

Upon arriving in New York, Pachmann gave an interview to the *New York Times* (29 August) that would haunt him for several months. The interview was vintage Pachmann. He began by admitting that he had become intensely Christian, saying the Lord's Prayer twelve times a day. Then he showed the reporter his passport, which had been issued under the rule of the Romanovs and was as thick as a Russian novel. Finally, when asked to name the greatest player in the world, he answered, "I am the great player the grandest player." It was this last remark which provoked criticism and which proved to be a measure of the extent to which times had changed: Skins were getting thinner. Pachmann's calculatedly unstudied opinions of his colleagues published in the *New York Times* on 30 August only antagonized critics (and pianists) further. How, they asked, could Pachmann have the chutzpah to say of Josef Hofmann that he had been going downhill since he was nine years old? (How many of them, though, had heard Hofmann when he was nine years old—as had Pachmann himself?)

Still, Pachmann was a legend to the generation that had come to maturity since he had last visited America; literally so, since this generation had heard of him (and heard his recordings) but had never seen him. It was with Pachmann as it was with Liszt himself, for as Schumann wrote in a review of the older virtuoso's concerts in Dresden and Leipzig (1840), "If Liszt were to play behind the scenes a considerable portion of poetry would be lost."

On this, his final farewell tour of North America, Pachmann decided to be more Pachmann than even he had ever been. And with much of the public, at least, he succeeded extravagantly, as the *Musical Courier* (18 October) testified after the first New York recital of his tour, at Carnegie Hall on 11 October. (The tour proper had begun 1 October, with an all-Chopin recital at Massey Hall in Toronto.)

Never having heard him in former days, this writer cannot judge whether or not the marvelous "straight wrist" method which he discovered for himself five years ago makes him play better than he used to or not (evidently he thinks so, for a good part of his front-row explanations were devoted to it); but if so he must have been a phenomenon, for today his playing in compositions which particularly appeal to him proclaim him as still in the forefront of the greatest contemporary pianists. For a man of his age, it is simply remarkable.

After remarking on the works on the program, the writer concludes:

> The huge audience [Godowsky, Levitzki, and Lhévinne were in it] was evidently greatly delighted with the playing of the veteran, for applause was plentiful and hearty; and it was equally pleased with his sallies and pantomiming, which often earned a hearty laugh even in the midst of his playing, something that is more or less disturbing to those who take music too seriously. De Pachmann, however, is to be regarded not solely as a pianist but also as a musical institution. One of his pranks was to play, as an encore, a bit of the so-called Minute Waltz as the little girl beginner would do it and then to give the whole of it as de Pachmann does it, with a feathery lightness that is inimitable. After the final number there was the usual crowding around the stage and further lecturing and playing by the pianist, who appeared much pleased at having an audience so close that he could address it with greater ease than under ordinary circumstances.

For others of this generation, however, Pachmann's performances were at best an impertinence and at worst an irrelevance. For them, the desire of the nineteenth century (the 1890s particularly) to escape into, or through, what Constant Lambert called in *Music Ho!* "a more highly coloured and less moral world" (139), which Pachmann embodied, was not only alien but evil.

Pachmann's physical appearance had often been described as oriental. Now his playing was seen, sometimes pejoratively, to possess the same origin. At that time, "oriental" meant North Africa and the Near and Middle East instead of Asia: Algeria and Syria were the "Orient." Kaikhosru Sorabji (*Chesterian,* December 1919) deplored the approximate, pay-as-you-go use of this word and sought to define it by identifying works of contemporary occidental art that manifested the truly oriental. After praising Aubrey Beardsley's pictures as being as polished and finished as "a marvellous piece of lacquer," Sorabji interrogated music for his examples. Russia, notwithstanding its deeper connection to Asia than to Europe, "does not show anything more profound than quite externally 'orientalistic' influences often and perhaps most frequently of an utterly superficial type." (The same may be said of Puccini's *Madama Butterfly* and *Turandot*.) It was in France that Sorabji found happier examples. Debussy's *Prélude à l'après-midi d'un faune* might, he wrote,

> with much greater point and verisimilitude have been entitled "Après une lecture de Hafiz" or "Omar" (not the Omar of Fitzgerald *bien entendu,* which is as much Omar as the "Variations on a Theme of Handel" [Brahms] are Handel). Debussy's incomparable little masterpiece has so much of that peculiar commingling of languid extasy and passionate voluptuousness, which is so essentially a characteristic of the odes of the "Prince of Persian poets," as John Payne well called him.

The song of the Sirens from the nocturne *Sirènes* was, he continued, no less evocative of nostalgia of the Orient. Ravel, on the other hand, he identified with Japanese works of art:

> There is the same love of working on a small scale, within a restricted area as it were, the same prodigious care and microscopic attention to details whose very existence is not even suspected by others. There is the same avoidance of the grandiose and of the Olympus-storming methods, the same keen alert observant intelligence that one feels so powerfully behind a Japanese ivory carving, and the same malicious ironic wit. . . . There is also the same *appearance* of simplicity and *naiveté* which is the very last refinement and subtlety of an extremely cultured and highly civilised intelligence—a simplicity that is as far in the world as it can be from simplicity.

Still in France, Roussel's *Évocations* "most powerfully evoke the *idea* of India."

Sorabji's consideration is of unique value for the reason that he himself, being of Parsi descent, was an "oriental" and understood what that meant to—and in—Europe. Indeed, he was one of the few men of the day able to distinguish between the illusion of the Orient (Godowsky's *Java* suite, or Rudolph Valentino in *The Sheik,* or even Maggie's opera *Yato*) and its essence (Van Gogh's paintings after Hokusai).

By the twenties, as Pound wrote, the pianola had replaced Sappho's barbitos. According to Constant Lambert:

> Unable to find exoticism in the strange and distant, we force ourselves to dive down into the familiar, and what is conveniently called Low Life provides the exotic motive for the post-war artist. The grubby gamins and snotty little brats that haunt the pages of Gide and Cocteau have taken the place of Pierre Louys's pitiless courtesans; and Swinburne, were he alive to-day, would write about a very different sort of queen. (140)

(What Lambert neglects to describe is the degree to which orientalism remained an aesthetic property, if a devalued one. Thus, Abram Chasins's kitschy *Three Chinese Pieces,* Charlie Chan movies, Suzie Wong.)

Still, the nineteenth century's Orient remained a place of which an older generation could dream, and if Pachmann's devotion to this anachronistic vision (if not to Debussy or Ravel) annoyed the new breed of listeners and critics, it continued to charm his contemporaries. Younger listeners did not pause to consider that it was exactly this vision which had made Pachmann an "authentic" voice of Chopin. Nor did they stop to consider that the man Pachmann was, in effect, from the East—as had the author of "A Pachmann Pastel" in now remote 1891: "[Pachmann] has the subtlety of the East and much of its sensuousness. His play has the lulling quality of an Oriental drug, and this little fellow with his malicious smile and snappy, sarcastic eyes can weave for you a story that is as fascinating as a procession of thin ghosts curling from burning opium."

Thus one of Pachmann's performances of the *Pathétique* sonata was interrupted by "bursts of ironic applause" from an audience. Deems Taylor, writing in the *World,* and Lawrence Gilman, writing in the *Tribune,* leveled at Pachmann the charge that in essence he was an irresponsible steward of music. (Taylor actually walked out on one of his concerts.) By contrast, the New York drama critics, realizing that the best show in town that season was not on Broadway but at Carnegie Hall, rose to Pachmann's defense. The resulting "War of the Critics" was one of the liveliest and most sensational episodes in the city's journalistic history. The Algonquin Round Table's Alexander Woollcott, writing in the *Herald,* refuted Taylor in a response later collected in his book *Enchanted Aisles.*

> De Pachmann seemed to us to be caressing that piano and to be evoking from it a voice of gold, but then, too, there was Chaplin at that piano, there at times was such brilliantly expressive pantomime as that with which Paul Clerget glorified the Ames revival of "L'Enfant Prodigue." There was *Deburau* himself. Nay, there was *Pierrot* grown old and free and given to talking to the moon.
>
> As everyone knows, de Pachmann, with many winks, chuckles, groans, and appeals to heaven, keeps up a continuous, murmurous chatter about the music he is invoking. To himself, to the spirits of the dead, to any within range of his half-whispered monologue, he talks about that music, about how it came to be written, how Liszt played it, how he hopes to play it, how beautiful it is, and so on, and so on. It is chatter which only a few can hear distinctly and of which the eccentricity sets the remoter or more woolly witted auditors into a fit of the giggles. If you are nearer you see how the moods of the melody—fear, hope, anger, love, gayety, despair— write themselves on every aspect of his mobile face, in every line of his re-

sponsive body. If you are nearer still you can hear enough to know he is now exultant in a free and childlike way at his own astonishing dexterity, now mortified at his own shortcomings, now grateful to whatever god brought the wonder of music into an ugly world. (4–5)

"Such communicativeness in the world of affairs or on the concert platform," Woollcott continues, "may be an infirmity, but, after all, it is a part of de Pachmann, and one did not come away from Bernhardt's last 'Camille' denouncing her for being a grandmother with a wooden leg. It is barely possible that de Pachmann could be made by a grim management to keep his behavior orderly, his face straight, his mouth shut. But probably he would burst" (5–6).

> To those sitting further from the stage it may be—nay, it must be—maddening to have the most delicate transitions of the Chopin nocturnes drowned in the empty laughter of giggling neighbors. But it was the whole implication of the more ferocious reviews that these "antics," these "monkeyshines," these "capers" were the tricks and manners of an old showman who was going to attract an audience by fair means or foul. Yet really weren't they rather the candors of an artless and quite simple person who would have behaved in exactly the same manner had the hall been empty and who would have had just as good a time alone with the composers? Many of these "monkeyshines" were prayers, for de Pachmann was not talking to A-2, A-4, A-6, A-8. He was talking to God. (6–7)

In conclusion, Woollcott takes on Taylor himself, observing that the music critic "did not stick it out."

> He went away in distress, "feeling a little ashamed of caring so much about music in a world where so many excellent people didn't mind a bit what happened to it." Well, that makes two of them, for, though Mr. Taylor's implication was rather to the contrary, we have a suspicion that there was another person in Carnegie Hall that night who cared as much about music as ever man cared since the first note sounded across the void. The other man's name was Vladimir de Pachmann. (7)

Woollcott was one of the few writers sensitive enough to recognize in Pachmann's "candors" the natural effusions of "artlessness" rather than a calculated ploy to attract publicity. The music critics were to have the last word, however, for now that their colleagues at the drama desk were reviewing music, they decided to review drama. Taylor, who had a regular column, "Music," that ran Monday through Saturday, and a feature essay, "Words and Music," that ran on Sundays in the *World*, responded on 21 October in a piece titled simply "The De Pachmann Way," in which he demonstrated how *A Doll's House* would sound if Mrs. Fiske were to play Nora in the de Pachmann manner.

NORA—I have waited so patiently for eight years; for goodness knows I knew very well that wonderful things don't happen every day. *That's a tricky speech.* Then this horrible misfortune came upon me; and then I felt quite certain—*I don't know what's come over that electrician; the lights are awful to-night*—that the wonderful thing was going to happen at last. *My throat's bad again. I must remember that aspirin!* When Krogstad's letter was lying out there—*did you notice that the property man forgot it to-night?*— never for a moment did I imagine that you would consent to accept this man's conditions. *Watch my change of voice in this next speech:* I was so absolutely certain that you would say to him: Publish the thing to the whole world. And when that was done—*how's that for technic?*

HELMER—Yes, what then?—when I had exposed my wife to shame and disgrace? *Can't I say anything but the lines, Minnie?*

NORA—*I should say not! Who's the heroine of this play, anyhow?* When that was done, I was so absolutely certain, you would come forward and take everything upon yourself—*awfully good house to-night*—and say: I am the guilty one.

HELMER—Nora!

NORA—It is a thing hundreds of thousands of women have done.

HELMER—Oh, you think and talk like a heedless child! *You jumped a long speech just there.*

NORA—Maybe. *Oh, Lord, so I did!* But you neither think nor talk like the man I could bind myself to. *My throat certainly is sore to-night.* As soon as your fear was over—and it was not fear for what threatened me, but for what might happen to me—*there aren't many women could get over a parenthesis like that*—when the whole thing was past—*I pray Gott I can remember the rest of this darned speech*—as far as you were concerned it was exactly—*Ibsen showed me how this should be played*—as if nothing at all had happened. Exactly as before I was your little skylark, your doll—*Alec Woollcott thinks I'm the best actress in the world; dear man!*—which you would in future treat with doubly gentle care, because it was so brittle and fragile. *Mon Gott, what a beautiful speech!*—Torvald, it was then it dawned upon me that for eight years I had been living—*I saw Janet Achurch play this scene once; Mon Gott, she was terrible!*—here with a strange man, and had borne him three children—*now watch how I take this climax*—Oh, I can't bear to think of it! I could tear myself into little bits. *Ah, bravo, Fiske! Bravo!*

Pachmann's behavior onstage created a vicious circle: The more unsure he was of how his audience was likely to receive him, the more unpredictable he became; the more unpredictable he became, the more he was open to censure. Much of his public conduct had always owed to anxiety:

He felt that if he could pierce the membrane of formality and judgment that separated him from his audience, then he would be playing not for a "public" but for "friends."

In any case he was much more at his ease with audiences outside New York, where the musical press was less likely to attack and, in fact, more likely to understand him. Eugene Stinson (*Chicago Daily Journal*) told his readers that "most assuredly [Pachmann] belongs to the period when carriages struggled over the muddy roads of Europe, and life was a succession of wonders." Also from the Windy City, a correspondent for the *Musical Courier* (25 October) observed: "De Pachmann is a great showman, but he is also a very great pianist. Mannerisms that would not be tolerated in any other pianist are permissible with him and even demanded. . . . [But] These mannerisms would be absolutely intolerable even in De Pachmann if he did not play as he does." The correspondent concluded, "It would be puerile . . . to analyze the innumerable qualities of this virtuoso, but as a final tribute, let it be said that the De Pachmann of today is superior to the De Pachmann of yesterday."

Of a concert at Symphony Hall in Boston, the *Musical Courier* reported (1 November): "Notwithstanding his seventy five years, Mr. de Pachmann soon convinced his tremendous audience that he was in full possession of his celebrated abilities both as pianist and as monologue artist. We do not frown on this pianist for his antics, nor do they interfere particularly with our enjoyment of his playing."

Significantly, Pachmann restrained himself at a subsequent concert in New York in the hopes of obtaining the approbation of the critics who had been hardest on him. To his probable chagrin, the *Musical Courier* (22 November), which had always been sympathetic to him, now complained that he had "double-crossed the large audience that went to Carnegie Hall to hear him on Friday evening, November 16."

> He played an all-Chopin program—but never a word did he utter all the evening, though he fidgeted with the restraint and it seemed from time to time as if those eloquent hands must burst into speech. After his first recital, some of the critics had called upon him to stick to his muttons and omit the running comment, and he did it, determined to show that he could play the piano without delivering a lecture at the same time. Yes, he did it—and with his silence there went, at least for one hearer, half the attractiveness of his performance.

Pachmann's situation was what would later be called a Catch-22. If he acted up onstage, the press objected; if he did not act up onstage, the press objected. To make matters worse, the 1923–24 musical season in America was an embarrassment of pianistic riches, with the result that Pachmann's performances were subjected to even greater scrutiny. Every pianist of stature was touring—among them Cortot, Friedman, Hofmann, Levitzki, Lhévinne, Nyiregyhazi (so popular that Valentino asked him to be a judge in the contest to choose "the most beautiful girl in America" from among the eighty-eight contestants the movie star himself had selected), Paderewski, and Rosenthal. Further excitement was generated by the arrival of Mieczyslaw Münz and the debut of Cherkassy. (Heliotes: "Shura Cherkassy, whom I knew quite well, told me that he met and played for de Pachmann here in Chicago in October 1923. When Shura (then just a child) finished playing, de Pachmann bent down and said, 'Now kiss Papa Pachmann on the head.'") The English pianist Mme. Peppercorn was also touring.

The presence of so many pianists in one country led to inevitable collisions of personality. Pianist Ethel Leginska[5] (née Ethel Liggins) was provoked to write a letter to the *Musical Courier* (25 October 1923) and the *New York Times* (21 October 1923) in response to the interview in which Pachmann had called himself "the great player—the grandest player."

> The interview given to the New York papers recently by Vladimir de Pachmann has come to my notice, and in the name of modern pianism and sincere musicianship I protest indignantly that such things should appear without public resentment from the many splendid musicians in America today. True, they may consider such piffle not worthy of serious consideration, but then again there is a large body of music students in this great country a few of which might be influenced by such stupid statements.
>
> Having waited in vain for some of my colleagues to answer these assertions, I have decided to express my own opinion.
>
> De Pachmann quite modestly calls himself "the greatest pianist in the world" and impudently declares that both Hofmann and Rachmaninoff are "third-rate pianists." That De Pachmann has made a name for himself as an exquisite performer of small pieces cannot be denied, but where is the big sweep, the gigantic power, the colossal brain of a great pianist such as Liszt (with whom he so discreetly (?) compares himself), or a Rubinstein, of olden days—of a Hofmann, a Busoni, or a Rachmaninoff, of today— where the superb musicianship of a Harold Bauer or a Gabrilowitsch? (By the way, the latter can play a mazurka of Chopin with quite as much charm as De Pachmann.)

Leginska goes on to recount "a little experience I had with him some years ago":

> During one of his Queen's Hall concerts in London, I was taken into the artist's room to meet him. Upon being introduced as a coming young pianist, De Pachmann lifted his hand to my mouth in order that I might

have the honor of kissing it. Being not at all inclined to avail myself of the opportunity, I gave him, instead, a good British handshake. With a howl of indignation he went hopping about the room, first on one foot then on the other, exclaiming, "She bruk' my wrist! she bruk' my wrist!" while a circle of doting De Pachmann enthusiasts glared at me for my "gross affront to the master."

Leginska concludes,

De Pachmann, in making the public statement he did, spoke as if America were still as musically ignorant as it was twenty-five years ago. On the contrary, probably now there is no other country in the world better able to decide for itself, having had all that is best in music and the world's greatest artists. Assertions that thus reflect upon the intelligence of the musical public here should not go unchallenged.

Patriotism, as Dr. Johnson famously defined it, is "the last refuge of a scoundrel"—and Leginska's epistle does nothing to contradict that definition. (It is exceedingly odd to find an Englishwoman being jingoistic about America.) First, Pachmann did not belong to the world of modern pianism; for her to condemn him in its name was as ignorant as it was unkind—Pachmann being the child of a century that was not hers, a century in which "life was a succession of wonders." Second, his claim to be the greatest pianist in the world was founded upon his rejection of the orchestral style of piano playing. ("Why torture [the piano] to perform what an orchestra can do much more effectively?" he often asked.) Though the claim might be arrogant, he was the only true "pianist" before the public, ergo "the great player—the grandest player."

Leginska's diminishment of Pachmann for playing small works attests, more than anything, to an anxiety that many women pianists have faced: the belief that to be great, they must play huge works and have a "big sweep," "gigantic power," a "colossal brain." Indeed, it is inconceivable that Leginska, or any major female pianist of her day, for that matter, would have even considered emulating Pachmann's interpretive ethos. (Eighty years later, many women pianists still feel that they have more to prove than men if they are to succeed.) Leginska's praise of Bauer, for one, does not acknowledge that he adored Pachmann, which is to say that she lacked the vision to understand Pachmann as the pianists *she* adored understood him. Yes, in his interview, as well as when Leginska was introduced to him, Pachmann was being grand. But surely he had earned the right to be grand.

The pianist, composer, and socialite Anton Bilotti answered Leginska's letter in the pages of the *Musical Courier* (31 January 1924). "I feel much honored by the fact that DePachmann has shown a friendly interest in me and thinks well of my future," he wrote.

I admire him very much, and it is a rare privilege to know him. He is a wonderful pianist and a wonderful personality. I, for one, regret the recent severe criticisms of this great artist. He does not talk at his recitals just for effect or publicity. It is his natural manner at the piano, and his remarks come spontaneously and from the heart—he does the same when playing alone at home. Naturally he could not play as he does and not know that he is great, but I do not think that he considers himself the only great pianist. He particularly admires Paderewski and Godowsky.

What was omitted from the letters of Leginska and Bilotti was acknowledgment of the alacrity with which Pachmann would condemn his own playing if it was bad. As dearly as he wanted to be admired, he deplored any admiration that he felt he had not earned. In London, after giving a concert with which he was unhappy, he played Beethoven's sonata opus 111 as an encore. In so doing he affirmed his belief in a technical and aesthetic standard that had not been met—either by himself or by his audience. When he was on his form, though, his piano playing was the most perfect to be heard.

Music history records a handful of keyboard "duels": J. S. Bach *v.* Louis Marchand, Domenico Scarlatti *v.* Händel, Mozart *v.* Clementi, Beethoven *v.* Steibelt, and Liszt *v.* Thalberg. The *Chicago Daily News* (22 November 1923) reported:

> A battle, of which the piano keyboard is the field, fought in the presence of a competent jury of other artists, composers and critics, the receipts and side bets (if any) to go to an education fund for a promising young American pianist. That is the challenge flung to-day by Moriz Rosenthal, Polish virtuoso, who arrived in Chicago for his first visit in seventeen years, in the face of Vladimir de Pachmann, another master of the piano, who is—by his own admission—the world's greatest.
>
> "De Pachmann spoke disparagingly of me and other artists in his latest interviews," explained the "little giant of the keyboard." "Well, I will play him. I will play him and I shall not be afraid of the outcome."

The duel was never fought. A few days later (30 November), in fact, the *Chicago Music News* dismissed the gauntlet Rosenthal had thrown down as "clever advertising," and not only for himself: Regardless of his motive, both his and Pachmann's concerts in Chicago that season drew full houses.

An article on Pachmann published in the *Concert Bulletin* ("Official Program of Selby C. Oppenheimer's Attractions") prior to his arrival in San Francisco the following month handled with greater sympathy the things he did onstage besides play the piano. "But aside from his wonderful skill there is also his bubbling, irrepressible personality to be dealt with," the writer proposed. "It is a tribute to the marvelous individuality of the man that they must talk of him. Some praise, some blame, his custom of interpolating short speeches between his selections, and carrying on a continuous monologue while playing. But they all say something. The vivid and sparkling personality of the man forces it from them." (The penultimate sentence of the article recalls Wilde's famous aphorism, "The only thing worse than being talked about is not being talked about.")

Harold Bauer's unpublished memoir "Dinner with Pachmann" (New York, 17 June 1924 or 1925) is an almost stream-of-consciousness narrative in four languages in which Pachmann is the principal speaker. No document better illustrates what Pachmann *sounded* like.

Message from Pachmann through manager: Why don't I go to see him? Excuses—I don't care to go. Second message through secretary: "Mr. Pachmann would like you to call on him." Excuses—I don't think he can remember me, it is so long ago, etc. Meet Pachmann, who says: "Why did you not come to see me?"

I answer laughingly: "I thought you did not like pianists."

The old man pats me on the back: "Oh, you are not a pianist, come and dine with me."

This is irresistible, and I accept. Mr. and Mrs. Pallottelli, beautiful apartment Central Park, house owned by Heifetz. Fearing too much piano-playing, I had bandaged a finger. Hot evening in spite of terrific thunderstorm in the afternoon.

Pachmann comes in, unshaven and dirty, bows to me like a Chinaman for five minutes. "Mr Pauer? no, Bauer Pauer—Ach, it is so long, à Londres, nicht war? O yes!" clasping his hands and looking up. "Sie sind der grosse Pauer Bauer je vous ai entendu that wonderful beautiful piece marvellous, the arrangement in octaves of Weber's *Perpetuum Mobile*. Grossartig! I kiss your hands."

I answer that I regret it was not I. I never played that piece.

"Aber wass! Mais oui, c'était vous, in London that marvellous piece. No? No?? I am very glad because that is a disgusting, disgraceful piece, no artist would play it."

I present my rose. "A single flower for the unique artist."

"For me! Ah, that was well said: the unique artist (confidentially)—it is true, of course. Pallottelli! you hear what Mr. Bauer says: for the unique artist. Did he not say it? Ach, mein lieber Freund, I went to see Wagner, he kiss my hand. Pallottelli, did he not kiss my hand? Nonsense, you were not born. I am an old man but young again since I discover my méthode. Godowsky tell me (you know Godowsky, ach, my Lep! As composer the greatest. Yes, pianist, polyphonic technique and he make me discover my méthode but I play better) Godowsky tell me (did he not tell me, Pallottelli?), 'Vladi, it is sublime, you play like God.' 'Dear Lep,' I answer, 'God did not discover my méthode.' Wait, Mr. Bauer, I shall show you my fingering. Kolossal! You can only say it is perfect. How do you do? I am glad to see you."

We go in to dinner. He hammers on the table with a spoon. "Mr. Bauer, you do not listen when I speak to you. I tell you I played in St Petersburg, Chopin F minor concerto, and Rubinstein would not conduct, disant que je parlais trop au public. O what a Jewish pig. But happily my von Bülow was there. O my Bülow, the great artist (sein Spiel war doch ein bischen trocken) and he conducted while Rubinstein, ah ha! the great Rubinstein, ja! yes, I tell you, he was green, yes, and blue, yes, and yellow, yes, and brown, yes, and black! Yes. Jealousy. Ah Ha!"

"Pappi," says Mrs. Pallottelli, "don't you know those pieces by Godowsky yet? You have played them thousands of times, every day two hours."

"Nonsense, not two hours, one hour. An artist must play every piece [to play it] every day. Mr. Bauer, I ask you, is that too much? One hour with my Godowsky, his polyphonic technique. The lovely waltzes, as great as Beethoven. One hour a day. I am an old man, that is my pleasure in life. Eating is not everything. I cannot love any more. And no teeth." (showing his gums) "O yes, the storm today, I could not shave. I prayed to God. Who knows, it might have been I. Tell me, you are afraid in the storm? You go under the bed, behind the door, and you pray, n'est ce pas? Of course, you are an artist, and one hour a day for yourself (only in the morning when nobody is there) is not too much. You see I am not shaved, but for the public it is different. Il faut, nicht war? I make my chin smooth and white, like—like—like this. But today in a hurry, no soap, no hot water, the storm. I have a Gillette, cold water and so quick, just a little you know on the eyebrows, not stiff and white and old. The appearance, aha! Mr. Bauer, you do not drink. We have plenty of wine, but I must strain it for you. What do you know, some flies perhaps. You will play for me later. What do you say, a sore finger? It does not hurt much."

He goes out with a young man and whispers to him, comes back looking very shy. "Tell Mr. Bauer what I say."

Young man solemnly says, "Mr. de Pachmann thinks you bandaged your finger because you were afraid to play for him."

"So I am," I say, "but if you will play for me I will play with my sore finger." I play Bach Partita.

"Beautiful, sublime, what a touch! Liszt did not have such a touch, nor Tausig nor Thalberg (I never heard him) nor Reisenauer. O how I hate Reisenauer! Dead. Yes. You are a great artist. I kiss your hand. Ach! Adelina Patti when she heard me play, she wipe her eyes. What use to sing wenn man so auf dem Klavier singen kann? Did she not tell me, Pallottelli! O oui. I teach you my fingering and you will be a good pianist. But I whisper to you: trop de [illegible word; Verscheibung?]. It is a disgusting sound.

Since Liszt, no pianist has pleased me like you. Ask Pallottelli if I did not tell him. Ask him." (Pallottelli winks.) "You know, these critics do not understand you. They do not appreciate my genius here. Only two cities in the world—in the world!—where there are good critics. In Rome, great critics. They appreciate my genius. I tell them about you. They know what it means if Pachmann says you play well. Berlin, great critics. They appreciate my genius. Only two cities. O yes, one more—O the lovely beautiful man. Dr. Wolff. Doctor of Music. He is a genius. Only a genius can understand a genius. I used to be modest, but I can say since I discover my méthode I am no longer modest. Dr. Wolff appreciates my genius. I show you his criticism. I only show it to my friends. Where was that place, Pallottelli? Lancaster. Ja. Lancaster. Three cities in the world where there are great critics. Rome, Berlin, Lancaster. All the others are fools and dogs. Jewish swine I call them. No, I cannot play for you. Die Gesellschaft gefällt mir nicht. She [Mrs. Pallottelli] says I play too much. Poor Pachmann! One hour each morning, is that too much? Eating is not everything, and I cannot spoil my hands if the music does not suit my méthode. O my méthode! Nothing is perfect, but my méthode, you can only say, that is perfect. And such time to make my fingerings. And new programmes. Only one piece by Mozart—tum—tum tum tum tum tum tum—you know, C minor *Fantasie*. I play the sonata [A major] last season, nobody can play it like I, but it is a stupid piece. I put it in the fire. But it suits my méthode. Never tired. Other pianists, ugh! pianists! play two hours, three hours, and they fall down sweating. I play twenty-four hours. Never tired. But practice without cuffs, without sleeves. You must watch the straight wrist. Ach, what fingering! And always wash your hands. Everybody has dirty hands, and you would not touch a lady's face with black fingers. Moi qui vous parle, I wash my hands three times since dinner. Aber nein, I can not play to you. It is true that you do not know how I can sing on the piano. Such a pity you cannot hear me play the slow movement of my *Pathétique*. Tum Tum Tum. Paderewski is a good man, a great man. He hates the Jews. I tell him to his face in Chicago—Pallottelli, did I not tell him to his face?—Five pieces you have no equal. Five pieces, ja. You play the *Variations sérieuses* and after the theme I wipe my eyes. Ha Ha! The A-flat polonaise, all the others, stupid, they lie down their heads on the octaves, you stand on them. Aha! That was well said. Schumann *Fantasie*, grossartig. La grandezza. Pallottelli, what was the fourth piece? I do not remember, but I do not like it. And the last Beethoven sonata, Tum, Tum, Tum. Without equal, I tell him to his face. Grand. Noble. Polish. Yes. Paderewski was honored to hear such words from me. He tell me so. And the other pianists in the artist room, they were black and green. Jealousy. I am not jealous. I tell Paderewski to his face. Did I not tell him to his face, Pallottelli? Five pieces. All the rest I play better. Tout à fait entre nous, mon cher ami, I play better than Liszt, better than Rubinstein, better than

Paderewski, but I whisper you, one thing Pachmann has not, yes? La grandeur. The grandness. If I must play for you, I first wash my hands. And I wipe the keys. Pfui! the dirty keys. You have played on my piano— And you must not smoke cigarettes near my piano. The ashes might fall inside and spoil the action. With cigars is different." Goes out and returns with a dirty rag. "I keep this napkin for my piano keys. I wipe them. Excuse me." Goes out again, comes back with long brown ragged coat and stands bowing in the doorway. "Chopin's coat. He wore it. I would not sell it for $100,000. One must have money, n'est ce pas, but I do not like to sell. Mr. Bauer, are you not interested in my méthode? You must sit near me and see my fingerings. The piano is so beautiful. I like Steinway. What is this piano, I always forget. O yes, Baldwin. But the finest piano in the world I find in Canada. What was that piano, Pallottelli? Heintzmann. Yes. Heintzmann is the finest piano in the world. Imagine, it plays itself when you blow on it, what it sounded when I play with my méthode! Now you hear something. Watch my méthode. Tum, Tum, Tum. Ach, the memory! I am old like Beethoven. Time to go. Quelle tragédie quand je ne sérais plus là. [Pachmann said this a quarter of a century earlier, and then not for the first time.] Singen, das kann Niemand mehr. Chopin's coat, old too, perhaps I live so long as that. Old but pratique, comfortable. Tum, Tum, Tum. I cannot remember. Pallottelli, can I remember my *Pathétique?*" He says yes. "Well . . . Tum, Tum, Tum, Tum, Tum, Tum, Tum, you see my thumb? Kolossal, wass? . . . There, you never hear that again like that. I must say: Bravo, Pachmann! I play E major scherzo by Chopin on my programme of course the best scherzo, nobody can play it without my fingering.⁶ I cannot teach my fingering, I will not sell, why should I give away? Brahms, yes, I know Brahms in Vienna. He kiss my hands. Rhapsodie en si mineur I play, they all try to play it, but they do not know till they hear me."

"There are other rhapsodies by Brahms, Mr. de Pachmann, do you play them?"

"*One* other. Tum Tum Tum Tum. Not good."

"Pardon me, Mr. de Pachmann, *two* others."

"*One* other. Tum Tum Tum Tum. Not good."

"I assure you, two others. One in E-flat."

"So? Then not in the same collection. I do not know it. It is not good. You know my B major nocturne? Chopin was with Liszt and frightened when they knock at the door. Brrrrr! Frightened. Liszt said, 'Do not be frightened.' Aha! Nobody knows this story. Dramatic, Ah! I wipe the keys, you wipe your eyes when I play—Ha Ha! Tum Tum Tum Tum. Wonderful, yes? Pallottelli, he says I am unique. O what a great artist you are. But too much soft pedal, a disgusting sound. I never play soft pedal."

"Mr. de Pachmann, I thank you for your charming hospitality, and fear I must now leave you. It is late."

"Never late, but I do not play in the evening. I would not play any more. J'avais fini déja. You are great as composer, and I enjoy your conversation, ein hoch gebildete mann. You are a learned man, a scholar. You understand my genius, like Bach and Beethoven and Chopin. Bach a little old sometimes, like Mozart. Adieu, mon cher maître, you honor me. I come to the door with you. Liszt came to the door with me in Weimar. Good-bye. O the intelligent conversation not like others. Auf Wiedersehen. Good-bye. I have pleasure to show you my méthode. Unique, perfect, wass? Aha! Next time I play you."

Elevator door closes on me.

In an interview quoted in the *Musical Courier* (26 June 1924), Pachmann asked a journalist to say that he had "lived for the last seven years on the Godowsky *Walzermasken*." They had revived his interest "not only in art, but in life":

> "If I had not found them, I am sure I should be nothing but a doddering old man, basking in the sun of our villa outside Rome. These, by the way, are the nine numbers from the *Walzermasken* which I selected and the order in which I play them· Französisch, Wienerisch, Legende, Satire, Karneval, Abendglocken, Eine Saga, Tyll Eulenspiegel, and Humoreske." Bad weather has kept the veteran pianist in New York until the present, but he will soon leave for his summer home in the same little village of up-state New York where he spent a summer thirty-five years ago.

The "little village" was Saratoga. Resting and gathering strength for the coming season, Pachmann would sometimes walk among the cows in his hat and Chopin's *paletot*. These morning strolls to the barnyard produced the cow-milking story immortalized by Schonberg in *The Great Pianists*: "The seventy-six-year-old pianist said it would never do to let his fingers stiffen and claimed that milking cows was better finger exercise than anything devised by the mind of man" (314).

Of his first appearance in New York for the 1924–25 season (Carnegie Hall, 17 October), Olin Downes wrote with his usual understanding, once again proving that of all the New York music critics of the time, he knew Pachmann best (*New York Times,* 18 October).

> It would be possible to exclaim in irritation at the passing eccentricities which have exasperated many a sincere admirer of Mr. de Pachmann's art, and to allow such a reaction, and differences of opinion concerning his wayward and willful interpretation of certain passages, to overshadow what is a more important fact, namely, that when Mr. de Pachmann rises to his full height as a musician and a pianist—and it is not to be forgotten that underneath his fooling and his "causeries" lies a profound knowledge

of his art—he gives performances of a unique poetry and beauty which will die with him, and that often constitutes revelation in a single phrase.

As in Britain in 1922, Pachmann became corrosive under the strain of touring. The slightest provocation, especially from a reporter, was enough to set him off, so much so that Cesco now introduced members of the fourth estate as writers, architects, or even "actors who love music." And as the pianist's weariness increased, his anger verged into hysteria.

In *Speaking of Pianists,* Abram Chasins claims Godowsky invited him to hear Pachmann play in New York in the early 1930s. (Chasins was wrong about the date, of course.) When he expressed reluctance, Godowsky told him, "If he plays for one minute the way he used to, it will be worthwhile being miserable for the rest of it" (148).

"I went," Chasins wrote. "The hopefully awaited minute never arrived. The whole thing remains a nightmare, and I wish that I had never gone, for now the mere mention or sight of Vladimir de Pachmann's name makes my heart sink and flashes before my mind's eye a sickening picture of a senile, tragic old man" (148).

Godowsky also invited Josef Hofmann, but he reportedly refused, explaining that it would be "too painful."

With precious exceptions, few of his listeners at this point seemed to understand that Pachmann's ability to play depended to an enormous degree on the state of his relationship with Cesco. Olin Downes was one of these exceptions. In two accounts, the latter a reminiscence (*New York Times,* 22 January 1933), he wrote of an incident that took place in the spring of 1925. The scene was a dinner party in Springfield, Massachussetts, at which the pianist, who was to play Chopin's F minor concerto the next day, was in a foul humor—worsened by the presence of Downes's companion, a critic who had "forcefully [that is, negatively] chronicled" in the press one of Pachmann's concerts the year before. Upon seeing the pianist, the critic asked whether he remembered "the delightful time we had together last season." Pachmann answered, "'Yes-s-s,' with a hissing intake of the breath, and an icy regard, 'Yes-s-s, I remember.' Presently dinner was served," Downes wrote in the reminiscence—and all of Pachmann's suppressed fury and indignation burst forth.

> Suddenly he whirled about in his chair, glaring malignantly. He thumped the table with his fist and shouted, "As for you, I know you! You are a damned hypocrite. What did you mean by inviting me to your house and then writing what you did about me in the paper? I know every word of it. My secretary's wife translated it for me. I understand you for what you are"—and by this time he was beyond control. Beside himself, in a paroxysm of temper, he was throwing the food, right and left, on to the floor.

The room was in a turmoil. No one could stop him, until, with a violence that matched his master's, "Cieco," the secretary, also present, leaped to his feet, denounced de Pachmann in fantastical French which included the word "cochon," informing him that he was not ever to bring his wife's name into the conversation, and, slamming a door, rushed out of the room.

Downes's earlier version of what happened next is more emotionally revealing:

> This proved salutary. I never saw a face change as de Pachmann's did. He looked and looked, dumbly, helplessly, in utter consternation, at the slammed door, and then, with a mute glance around, an unspoken bid for help and succor, burst into tears. He wept audibly, copiously, miserably. He was a poor old man, alone, without a friend. His very bodyguard, protector, and light of his eyes had rejected him in his need.

Although Cesco was soon induced to forgive Pachmann, it is the swiftness with which the pianist's fury turned into supplication that is most revealing here, particularly given the entire neutrality of his reference to Alice. Betrayal hurt Pachmann more deeply than anything, and at this dinner he believed that he had been betrayed twice: first by the critic, and then by Cesco, who knew what store the pianist set by loyalty. Through the lens of this episode, a "portrait of a marriage" begins to come into view: Cesco, the "light of [Pachmann's] eyes," willing to menace and panic him with the withdrawal of his affection if he did not do as he wanted (and Cesco had invited the offending critic); Pachmann, needful of family and stability, willing to be humiliated in order not to be alone. If Pachmann so valued stability, it was in no small part because Cesco deprived him of it—both by threats of emotional withdrawal and by making him responsible for their income at an age when he could not do so with equanimity.

Incidentally, Pachmann's performance of the F minor concerto the next day (conducted by Moldenhauer) was adjudged by Downes to be superb. "This was the reward of the pilgrimage," he wrote.

> In truth no one did play, or ever will play, the Chopin F minor concerto as de Pachmann played it. It had under his fingers an unearthly beauty, and if it is said that when he sang on the keys the ineffable song of the larghetto angels wept over the golden bar of heaven, it is only a little more than the truth. Indeed, the music had a haunting and seraphic melancholy, a freedom from every thralldom of this world, only to be evoked by the supreme artists and the pure in heart. There sat that little fellow, who had the face of a French abbé and connoisseur of the eighteenth century, and the lineaments of a monkey, mixed up in one, and he knew that beauty, and was at ease and confident in its company, and brought it down to earth for us.

This was the last time Downes heard Pachmann play.

Pachmann's absolutely last American recital was at Carnegie Hall on 13 April 1925. The next day the *New York Morning-Telegraph* described the scene when Pachmann came to the end of his printed program: "The crowd, unwilling to lose sight of the little figure, swooped down to the footlights and would not go. The stage throng was augmented by a rush from the wings and, surrounded by applauding admirers, the maestro played his swan-song to America. It proved to be the 'Gondolieri' of Haenselt." At the end, the pianist "received flowers and salvos with the urbanity of old mummified Seti in the British Museum, whom he resembles in his fleeting periods of facial repose."

> Vale de Pachmann! Nor decade, nor perhaps century will come ere your equal or the personality to match you is heard here!

Of the more than $2 million that Pachmann earned for his 110 concerts on this last tour of a New World that had never seemed newer or more remote from the one into which he had been born, Cesco claimed half for himself, ostensibly to pay for the upkeep of the Villa Gioia and the work on the Villa Virgilio. All Pachmann's own, however, was the piano he had played in Shamokin, Pennsylvania: This instrument had so pleased him that he had acquired it and had it shipped to Italy, and when, three years later, Con R. Graeber—who had presented Pachmann's recital in Shamokin—visited him there, Pachmann took him immediately to the music room to show it to him.

ELEVEN

The Exhaustless Genius

When Pachmann returned to England in 1925, he managed both to offer a season and to record for HMV at Hayes on 26 June. He was back at Hayes on 15 December, when he recorded the waltz 64/1 and gave a prefatory speech: "I will play for you the D-flat major waltz of Chopin—at first I play like is written down—afterwards the slow movement, little slower than usual—and afterwards, I think staccato, à la Paganini—and then again à la Chopin, the [inaudible], and finish the waltz." The disc leaves us with a rare sense of what it was like to attend one of Pachmann's concerts.

He performed in Manchester in November and received a significant review from Samuel Langford in the *Guardian* (reprinted in the *Pianola Journal*). Before writing of the concert that occasioned the review, Langford recalled Pachmann playing in Manchester, in 1885, "Mozart's D Minor Concerto as it has never been played since, with an irresistible animation which seemed to beam not only from the music but from his whole being." Langford recognized that Pachmann "has always been one of the first purists of his instrument, and has been almost first a lover of the pianoforte, and a lover of music afterwards. 'If I played it like the rest I would not play at all,' he said of something on Saturday, and it is in this extreme conscientiousness of the exacting purist that he plays everything."

Langford considered at some length Pachmann's performances of Mozart's *Fantasie* in C minor and Chopin's scherzo in B-flat minor—"As a feat of velocity and polished execution it was astonishing," he wrote of the latter—then turned to Pachmann's seven encores:

> He began his encores with the little D-flat Valse, indulging his favourite ninths in the left hand, which are a fastidious addition of which Chopin himself might have been proud. Then came a little Barcarolle of Henselt, also with charming additions from his own hand, and then the pianoforte was closed. Yet he came back after a while and gave the little-played B major Nocturne [of Chopin]. Then came a dazzling performance of the

"Black Note" study [of Chopin] with the middle section given in a marvellous lyrical manner, and the final octaves taken in contrary motion. It
was this piece also, we think, which he enriched in the harmonies by a su-
perbly sustained ninth—a real stroke of genius. Then he went back to the
favourites of days gone by—the E-flat Rondo of Weber, which he played
with marvellous vigor and velocity. Could any other player in the world
have equalled this feat to-day? Not satisfied with this triumph he went on
to the "Rigoletto" fantasia of Liszt, strewing the notes of the cadenza passages around him with a true Oriental lavishness. One began to forget his
age, for he had worked himself into a sort of youth once more, and his
opulence and rapidity of execution enabled one to sense the true Pachmann, the exhaustless genius of the piano. We had almost forgotten what
we thought was the greatest musical feat of the recital. Few would associate Pachmann with Brahms, yet it was in the composer's rugged "Rhapsody" in B minor that we found him wrestling, and that quite triumphantly, with heroic ideas. He played the purist here, too, and we should
not have guessed, from the satisfying result, that Brahms was, as Liszt said,
the worst of all pianoforte writers.

Queen Alexandra died that autumn, but Pachmann refused to play Chopin's *Funeral March* in her memory at a concert in November at Bourne-
mouth. To the *New York Times* (27 November), he explained that he had
last played the *Funeral March* after the death of the late queen's husband,
Edward VII, on which occasion he had vowed never to play it again.

Once again Pachmann retired from performing—though not from talking. On 24 January 1926, the *New York Times* published a group of short
interviews with personalities of the day—one of them Pachmann—about
how they kept healthy. Here the pianist described his eating habits:

> I take three meals a day. For breakfast, strong coffee and rolls, and two
> brown-shelled, lightly boiled eggs. Rice or spaghetti, some stewed meat—
> cooked according to the custom of the country [Italy]—a white vegetable,
> fresh fruit, and strawberry jam which I love to eat out of the spoon, is a
> delicious lunch for me when it is accompanied by good red wine. I never
> go without my wine. For two years I was in "dry" America, but I always
> had my red wine.
>
> At 4 o'clock I take a cup of tea when I am in England, or a glass of milk
> fresh from the cow—if I happen to be in the country, near a farm.
>
> Then in the evening I am happy to eat, after my soup, two boiled eggs
> again, some more meat tenderly cooked—my teeth are not as good as once
> they were, and I refuse to have new ones put in my mouth—a special
> home-made cake which must only be made by my perfect Italian cook who
> travels with me everywhere, coffee and wine, and perhaps a liquor. Before I
> retire, a little something—a chocolate or a cake or a crust of bread.

I never eat before I am to play, but after a concert I will have a fine supper, with champagne and all the things I like. My favorite vegetable is the giant Californian asparagus, and my favorite fruit a big, juicy watermelon. I am happy to sit alone for an hour with a watermelon. I can eat it all.

Pachmann follows this charming and rather childlike account with his opinion of smoking and exercise:

The doctors will say that the nicotine is bad for you. Well—I still smoke eight cigars every day. The doctors say you must have exercise, walk in the air or play with the ball. Well, I have never taken any exercise in my life unless you count the four hours a day practice at the piano. I have a beautiful little summer house at Fabriano, in Italy, with lovely gardens, but I never walk out in them. All the fresh air I want comes to me through the window.

(That he took no exercise in Italy is not strictly true. He played golf—there is a photograph from this period showing him putting—although he preferred cards: Patience, which Adrian had taught him, and Whist, during one game of which he surprised his fellow players by asking them to show him their hands.)

On 27 March 1926, in order to beguile time, Pachmann played a recital at the Teatro Quirino in Rome to benefit the Corso Estivo di Musica di Villa d'Este. (This time he played a Baldwin, the "Stradivario" of pianos.) According to Cesco, it was the success of this and other small Italian concerts that persuaded Pachmann to return to England to play before a tremendous public—if only for a single season. The profile of the pianist published in the program for the benefit concert of 27 March, however, suggests that it was Cesco himself who urged the English tour on Pachmann, who is quoted as saying that he wants to sing his last song to "this nation of poets"—the Italians. (The Machiavellian Cesco's tirelessness in ingratiating himself to the Fascists may also explain this hymn to the Italian people.)

In any event Cesco won the day, and in 1927 the "man of a thousand farewells" was giving concerts in England at age seventy-nine. That Cesco's pecuniary interests were now prevailing over Pachmann's artistic ones was evident from the venues at which the pianist appeared. "A new departure in supper entertainment was inaugurated at Mayfair Hotel [yesterday], with Vladimir de Pachmann as the attraction in a Chopin recital," the *New York Times* reported (31 October 1927).

The supper and reserved table seats cost thirty shillings, the dining room accommodating five hundred.

Sir Francis Towle, who closed his "Midnight Follies" recently, arranged the concert, which he asserts is the most expensive musical supper concert ever given in Europe. It will continue Sunday evenings indefinitely, and the promoter anticipates full houses, as the law bars Sunday cabarets.

It was on this visit that Pachmann returned to the recording studio—the Small Queen's Hall—for the last time on 3 November 1927. According to Gaisberg, Pachmann was always glad not to go to Hayes, since traveling in a motorcar invariably nauseated him.

This aversion dated from a motor accident he sustained in America a few years ago. One rainy evening, after a recital in Cincinnati, a car was carrying him and his secretary to a supper party to be given in his honor, when it overturned. As the little pianist was extricated from the wreckage more dead than alive, he is said to have remarked pettishly: "Now we shall be late for supper and they will have eaten all the food." (*The Music Goes Round*, 193)

On 9 February 1928, a recital by Lionel de Pachmann at the American Students' Club in Paris (on the Boulevard Montparnasse) was reviewed in the *Musical Courier* under the heading "Pachmann Junior." "In the simple and clear manner of playing Chopin he is plainly the son of his famous father," the critic (C. C.) wrote. "His public appearances are rare, however, as he devotes the better part of his time to composition and teaching." In addition to works by Chopin, Schumann, and himself, Lionel played "a poetic and dreamy composition called Elevation, by his colleague [and his father's friend] Bilotti." In April, Lionel gave a recital of works by Chopin and himself at the American University Club.

In addition to being the centennial of Schubert's death (an anniversary that occasioned notable concerts of the composer's music on both sides of the Atlantic), 1928 also marked Pachmann's eightieth birthday, which he celebrated by making an impressive "Grand Tour" of Europe. This time, the idea for it was his own: He wanted to go out in a burst of glory and not playing in hotel restaurants, singing for other people's suppers. Once again he gave concerts in London—although a May recital at the Royal Albert Hall is sometimes remembered as his farewell to the capital, he also played there in the autumn—as well as in Berlin, Vienna, Paris, and perhaps other capitals besides. Steven Heliotes has suggested that Vladimir Horowitz may have heard Pachmann during this jubilee tour: Pachmann always raised his fingers to show the number of encores that he would play, and Horowitz—alone among all the pianists who have followed Pachmann—did the same.

In March, Pachmann gave two *Klavier-Abend*s in Berlin (Philharmonie): The program of 15 March was a Chopin recital, whereas on 29 March he played works by Weber (D minor piano sonata), Chopin, Mendelssohn, Schumann, Brahms, Tchaikovsky, Godowsky, and others. Hugo Leichtentritt (*Musical Courier*, 12 April) reported that the first concert by "dear, old Pachmann," absent from the city's concert halls for twenty years, "was nothing short of sensational."

> The adjectives "extraordinary" and "original" apply in this case not only to the aged artist, but also to the public, which took an active part in the melodramatic scenes, which he staged with his mixture of speech, mimic action, and piano playing. The audience besieged the platform, eager to see the jovial Pachmann as closely as possible and to catch all his humorous and quaint remarks. When finally the police arrived to restore order in the auditorium, Pachmann eloquently pleaded for his admirers, saying that they were all his friends, even if they had paid for their tickets!
>
> Quite apart from all fun, however, Pachmann must still be rated as a great and unique artist, in spite of his eighty years. His Chopin playing, though lacking in power and passion, still breathes a poetry, an indescribable charm of tenderness, which seems to have almost vanished from the world.

From Vienna, Paul Bechert (*Musical Courier*, 10 May) wrote, "Pachmann was with us, after many years—too late, I fear. The bewildered audience mistook for symptoms of old age what has always been the grand old man's personal note, namely the colloquial character of his recitals. An old lion—but still a lion."

On 1 June, he wrote a letter to Bauer that exemplifies his tongue-in-cheek self-aggrandizement.

> My dear Mr. Bauer-Pauer (Pauer-Bauer?):
>
> This is only to accompany these pictures and send you my best greetings. I regretted not to see you lately, as I admire you as a good pianist, really *good*, indeed, when you play well, it is almost as good as when I play badly and I think how better you could play if you had more opportunity to hear Me and to have My advice once in a while. But, in spite of that, my dear Mr. Bauer-Pauer (Pauer Bauer?) you certainly are a *good* pianist and I wanted to tell you my sincere appreciation. I hope you will have a nice vacation and manage some day to come and study with Me and learn how to play the Piano, as I do.
>
> Yours sincerely,
Vladimir de Pachmann

On Monday, 4 June, he played publicly in Paris for the first time in more than forty years to benefit the Accueil Social Franco-Américain. The city was much changed from the one in which he had first played in 1882:

earlier in the year, Stravinsky had conducted two concerts of his own works at the Salle Pleyel, and Gershwin, visiting the French capital for the European premiere of his *Concerto in F* (Théâtre de l'Opéra, 29 May), was the toast of the town. A few days before the concert, a reporter for the *New York Herald* called at Pachmann's hotel in the rue de la Paix to interview him, but found only Cesco. (It is interesting to note that for the American writer, Cesco remains a "secretary," not the great impresario he was in Italy.)

> "De Pachmann has gone shopping again," the secretary said in obvious distress. "He is an amateur of precious stones, and when he gets started from one little shop to another, there is no telling when he will get back. It's not so bad, his buying jewels, for he loves them and knows what he is getting, but in his enthusiasm, he usually stops some taxi-driver or porter to show his new purchases—diamonds, rubies, or emeralds. De Pachmann trusts everybody—and the strange part of it is he never loses anything. The strangers he encounters are too surprised to act."

Many of Pachmanns's interviews began with a pretense of his being out, with the result that Cesco could then relate a story about him before he made his entrance. It turns out that on this occasion Pachmann had in fact been resting and not shopping at all.

> The weather was so hot he could not sleep, [Pachmann] added, with a glance of rebuke toward the sunlight pouring through the window. Moreover, he had just emerged victoriously from spiritual struggle involving the most vital things in his eventful life and had decided, in the tranquillity of his old age, to face once more the familiar scenes of Paris, which he had avoided forty years because of the sentimental associations involved.

(This is incorrect. Although Pachmann had not played in Paris for forty years, he had, in fact, lived there on and off since his marriage.)

For the concert, a benefit performance under the patronage of Marshal Ferdinand Foch and the American ambassador, the Salle Gaveau was adorned with roses and the audience was formally dressed. The program was printed on fans, the obverse giving a photograph of Pachmann and the reverse the program itself: Chopin, ballade opus 23, études 25/3 and 4, scherzo opus 54, nocturne 27/1, preludes 28/3, 15, and 19, mazurka 24/4, impromptu opus 36, and polonaise 26/1; Mendelssohn's prelude 35/1, Schumann's *Novellette* 21/6, Brahms's rhapsody 79/1, Tchaikovsky's waltz 51/1; and Godowsky's *Tyll Eulenspiegel.* In addition to diplomats and ornaments of French society, the crowd included a large American contingent—and Maggie Labori.

In a long and complex career, Maggie was to be the only woman with whom Pachmann ever formed a long-standing romantic bond. Of all the players in his life, she is also the most difficult to know. Although some writers have sought to represent her as a sort of Alma Mahler—a woman of genius to whom men of genius were drawn, in a long and sometimes precipitous succession—there is really no basis for this comparison: She loved Pachmann, then she loved Labori, and to the memory of both she remained devoted after their deaths. Nonetheless, her good fortune in having been loved by such men seems to have galled a French actress—and eventual suicide—named Hyacinthe Goujon, who felt obliged to give vent to her rage in some letters from which the American novelist Elliot Paul quoted in *The Last Time I Saw Paris.*

These letters are full of revealing inaccuracies. To begin with, Goujon writes that in 1928, Maggie attended Pachmann's farewell recital in Paris in the company of Labori. (In fact, Labori had died in 1917, and Maggie was escorted by Lionel, who reported that his mother wept—and not because of his father's playing.) Goujon gives Pachmann a program to play that does not correspond with the printed program; the Chopin piano sonata in "E minor," which brought her such pleasure, is nonexistent. She writes that "de Pachmann in all his long career had had only one pupil, a French girl [*sic*], now living in Paris (as an aged woman) and who had such pianistic genius and such an appeal to the master that he took time from his own practice and performance to develop her" (249).

> He would entrust her to no one else. Of course he was in love with her. No one can ever convince me that a man and a woman can share, day by day, what is magic and the breath of life to them, without the kind of harmony that would create a deep and fervent love. Sometimes the art would outlast the passion, and occasionally the respect. Of what importance is duration?
>
> De Pachmann and the pupil were married, and then began to lose the harmony and counterpoint in that ghastly endurance contest which must be, at once, a rivalry and a hash made from the remnants of initial raptures. One reads of men who love once, and never afterward. Apparently de Pachmann was one of those phenomena. They parted; de Pachmann swore he would never again set foot in Paris, and after a couple of years the pupil married a respectable lawyer (who later became famous), gave up the piano, and plowed through heavier courses after having eaten her dessert and sipped her liqueur.
>
> I began to hate that woman. (249–50)

"Elliot!" Goujon ejaculates at this point. "You will understand! I cannot even try to write how I felt in the Salle Gaveau" (250).

> Mama and I were among the first to enter, and I examined breathlessly each woman's face who came in afterward. At last I saw *her* and her lawyer

husband, distinguished in appearance I must confess, and looking uneasy and protective as men do when they know they are in the presence of something more important to a woman than they could ever be. She was small, chicly dressed, if a woman of seventy [*sic*] can be so described. . . .

. . . What died when de Pachmann ceased breathing? Not that smug detestable woman who had been inadequate, doubtless ranting about her own career, as if a woman could have a more sacred career than to sustain a genius. (250–51)

After the recital, another instance in which Mama did not dare refuse me, I went *alone*—that is without Mama—and stood in the line before his dressing room and inch by inch moved nearer. I have forgotten to tell you the most touching incident. My heart is thumping as I write and the blood is rushing to the front of my brain to confuse me. After the nocturne, not hearing the applause, de Pachmann stood looking at his hands as if they were miracles that did not belong to him.

"You've done well tonight, my hands," he said, and waited as if he expected them to answer. (251–52)

Goujon's by now positively surreal fantasy concludes with a visit to Pachmann backstage.

When I came face to face with him, in the dressing room, and extended my hand, my eyes on his, he must have felt what the moment was meaning to me. I am sure that he must always have been kind as well as difficult, and I am thankful that in a lifetime of tribute and gratitude and appreciation he realized what my silence and vertigo meant. What he did was take my hand, and to the consternation of his manager, an offensive little man, and the throng of admirers, he led me into a small room near by and locked the door. There was a piano, a bench and one piano chair. Through the door and the walls I could hear mild clamoring outside. He paid no attention. With amazing vigor, considering that he was eighty years old, he pushed the bench away from the piano and indicated with a gesture of that inspired left hand that I was to sit there. The piano chair he placed in front of the keyboard.

"Which?—For you?" he asked.

"The nocturne," I said, surprised that my voice was audible.

He played three nocturnes that evening [*sic*; unless two of them were encores], but he knew which one I meant, and he rose from his chair to clasp me in his arms and kiss me on the cheek. Then he played the F minor, as exquisitely as before and even more personally. He had forgotten his former wife and pupil and her stuffed shirt of a husband (*vieux fumiste*). (252–53)

Pachmann had always been an object of fascination for his women admirers; one of them had even dared to hope that he might injure his thumb "like darling Paderewski. I'd give him twenty-five dollars if he'd wrap it in my handkerchief." Nowhere, however, is the degree of devotion that he could inspire more evident than in Goujon's letters, in which she assigns to herself the role that she accuses Maggie of having abandoned: sustainer of genius, the pianist's adored and adoring muse. That the reality of Maggie's marriage to and divorce from Pachmann bears not the slightest resemblance to Goujon's delusional melodrama does not detain her, however; nor did it detain Elliot Paul, whose decision to publish the letters without any correction or clarification only served to give his correspondent a wider audience for her slander.

That summer, according to Cesco, Pachmann played a number of concerts in cities along the Adriatic coast of Italy, Ancona and Venice among them. (Pachmann became an Italian subject in 1928.) Then he was allowed to rest before returning to England. On 21 October 1928, he played at the Royal Albert Hall, and on 18 November at the London Coliseum, where he gave the final concert of his jubilee tour. By now he had become an anachronism, as had part of his audience. Gaisberg described some members of the "loyal coterie of ladies" who had long attended Pachmann's London concerts as "genuine survivors from the Victorian Age" (192). The pianist cherished them because they had grown old with him and shared his memories. "Anyone is young once," he said. "Genius is eternal. That is why women, who always know the meaning of eternity, prefer genius to youth."

As one generation was approaching its end, another was in full cry. At the end of 1928 Dagmar Godowsky was with Adrian in Paris. She wrote in *First Person Plural:*

> I knew him casually, and we met and had lunch. He was such a correct Frenchman. Once, at Longchamps, someone greeted him while his wife was powdering her nose. He and I were standing together. His introduction went, "And may I introduce Mademoiselle Godowsky, a friend of my wife's."
>
> So correct. *Quel gentilhomme!* After our business, he asked if I would like to stop off at a typically French club, a club of aristocrats. No American ever saw them. He would love to show me one. I was delighted. We stopped at a house and went through a labyrinth of corridors until we reached a door. Adrian knocked on the door oddly. It was a signal of some sort. Then—as in our speak-easies—a little opening revealed an eye. The door was opened for us.
>
> There was an enormous room with no furniture—only a long table with some Dubonnet and vermouth on it. Everyone stood about, heads high and voices low.
>
> It looked like a very dull party, and then I saw more of these aristocrats than I had expected. As if on cue, they all quietly removed their clothes. I couldn't believe my eyes. All I wanted was to get out quickly. I raced to the

door. As I reached the exit, I came face to face with the police. All the women were herded in black Marias—comtesses, marquises, me and my claustrophobia. The men were ignored. We ladies landed in the Bastille! My wicked barrister came along for the ride.

Innocent again! Well! One didn't know Paris until one knew her jails. Now my sightseeing exceeded [my father's]. But this was one time when I didn't have to call my lawyer—there he was, with me! He didn't leave me for a moment. He managed to free me long before the others. I should think so! (184)

TWELVE

The Vanishing Years

The last four years of his life Pachmann essentially divided between Rome and Fabriano. If Olin Downes is to be trusted (and he should be), the pianist played in Vienna again in 1929, however. On that occasion, Downes wrote in 1930, "He stopped in the middle of a work, got up with that air of engaging frankness, and said, 'You must excuse me. It's a very long piece and I am a little'—tapping his head—'tired.'" Thus his career ended where it had begun, in the city of Mozart, Beethoven, and Schubert.

Pachmann projected tours of England and America that never materialized. When he was in Rome, more from a sense of duty than of pleasure, he often auditioned the young pianists who sought him out or who had been sent to him armed with a letter of introduction. These auditions were not necessarily pleasant for the pianists. In an article titled "Little Stories of Big Men" (*Good Housekeeping,* January 1934), the writer Konrad Berkovici recalled a hapless protégé of Godowsky arriving at the villa with a letter of introduction to Pachmann at the bottom of which Godowsky had written, "The young man is very modest."

> De Pachmann hit the ceiling. He jumped up and threw his hands in the air, twirled his arms as if they were wings of a windmill, and danced like a dervish the while he cursed himself and the world in the choicest curses of a half-dozen languages.
>
> The antics of the aged master were amusing, but my heart bled for the poor young victim standing there, pale as a ghost, kneading his hat and not knowing what to do next. He looked at me, looked at the door, and was about to bolt when I said,
>
> "Master, that postscript merely said that the young man is very modest."
>
> "Shut up!" De Pachmann yelled, and buttonholing the fellow, he grinned into his face and demanded:
>
> "What have you already accomplished to be modest about? Ha, tell me! Sit down at the piano and show me what you are so modest about."

Whether it was due to the reception De Pachmann had given him or to the fact that Godowsky, who is the kindest of all men, had overpraised him, the young man showed less than mediocre talent. When he had gone, De Pachmann drank four glasses of water in succession and said to me:

"I am not modest *yet,* and he is *already* very modest! The impudence!"

In 1930, Pachmann was diagnosed with prostate cancer. His doctor's prognosis was optimistic: He assured the pianist that if he submitted to surgery, he would live to a great age. Fearing that this surgery would not only render him impotent but affect his hands and his ability to play the piano, however, he refused treatment. In addition, while in America, he had developed a strabismus in his right eye (it would not focus in line with his left eye). "I don't see so well with this eye," he told his audiences, "but the other one's all right. I don't have to see."

From time to time, Cesco would organize musical parties to which he would invite musicians, famous and obscure alike, who happened to be in Rome. At some point the assembled would adjourn to Pachmann's music room for an impromptu concert by one or more of the musicians present. An element of sadism undercut this seemingly benevolent interest on Cesco's part in keeping Pachmann involved with the musical world, since Pachmann, who had never enjoyed sharing the spotlight, hated these occasions, during which he felt at best patronized and at worst ignored. In the past, he had only enjoyed those parties at which he was the star and which took place in the homes of other people—for example, violinist Efrem Zimbalist. In truth, the Roman parties benefited only Cesco's career as an impresario.

Whenever Pachmann expressed his anguish, Cesco tried to reassure him by telling him that he would live to be a hundred. Yes, Pachmann would reply, he did think that he would live to be a hundred—and that he would play many concerts still. Tomorrow, he promised, he would write to Lionel Powell to make arrangements. But the tomorrows passed in quick succession, the years vanishing in this sad ceremony of postponement.

On 5 February 1930, Pachmann wrote to T. O. Williams at the Gramophone Company in Hayes in answer to a letter of 15 January requesting a testimonial.

> I have heard by friends that your machine are wonderful, and my records are reproduced most beautifully. It would be great pleasure and joy for me to have one of this machine and to hear my play as I was used to hear it in the pass.
>
> As I have heard that this machine are rather expensive, will you please be very kind and help me if I can get one of this machine in a reasonable price?

This letter reveals the degree to which Cesco had forsaken him. For a man who had once bought diamonds, the price of a Gramophone should have been as nothing. In earlier years, Cesco had corrected Pachmann's letters in English, since his own command of the language was greater. Now, as the grammatical errors indicate, he was leaving Pachmann almost entirely to his own devices. The image of the pianist—old, ill, poor (notwithstanding living in a villa), and struggling in a language not his own—is a woeful one.

A male nurse, a relative of Cesco's, was now hired to take care of Pachmann. If the intention of this plan was to free Cesco from some of his duties, however, it backfired, for Pachmann soon developed an intense attachment to the nurse, to whom he gave his jewels. Cesco is supposed to have chased down his relative in order to retrieve the jewels; if he succeeded, it is unclear what he did with them, since no trace of the jewels remains. (A century ago they were valued at between $1 million and $1.5 million. Their present value would be in the tens of millions.)

In 1932, Pachmann made his last journey, to Siena, for the inauguration of Count Guido Chigi Saraceni's Accademia Musicale Chigiana, which continues to present concerts and master classes. On Christmas Day, Alice gave birth to another son, Duilio. Paul Landormy (*Le Figaro,* January 1933) described Pachmann's last performance, at home, on New Year's Day.

> He begged of his secretary and the nurse watching over him to allow him to get up. They did not oppose this last desire. He drags himself into the adjoining room, opens the piano, and his trembling fingers touch the keys. He begins Chopin's F minor nocturne [opus 55], one of his triumphs of olden times. He feels he has not the strength to play it through. He improvises a cut—leaving out the middle part—and arrives at the celebrated "envolée" at the end, which soars into the air like a bird, and he executes it with all the grace, all the finesse, all the prodigious delicacy of the days gone by. A supreme effort and a supreme rendering, a supreme joy for himself—which leaves him so profoundly moved that he regains his bed with difficulty and closes his eyes. He has bade farewell to his piano, to Chopin, to music.

On 6 January 1933, Pachmann lapsed into unconsciousness and died. He was buried in Rome on 8 January. The *New York Times* (9 January 1933) noted:

> A hearse with only three wreaths, followed by an automobile bearing his two sons, both of Paris, and his impresario, Francesco Pallottelli-Corinaldesi, carried the body to Campo Verano Cemetery without a preliminary ceremony.

There a Capuchin monk read the last prayers. The coffin was opened, disclosing the pianist in full-dress attire with a white tie which he always wore while playing at concerts.

The monk sprinkled holy water over the coffin, which then was closed and lowered into the grave.

Later a simple headstone will be placed.

The obituaries of Pachmann befitted his reputation as one of the great pianists of his, and indeed of all, time.

It was Pachmann's hope that his recordings would keep his memory alive. "I shall not be forgotten," he said not long before he died. "And when your children and grandchildren ask you, 'Who was this de Pachmann?' you will be able to show them how he played. . . . And though they cannot see me, they will hear my voice through my music and then they will know why all the world worshipped de Pachmann."

Cesco, however, had gotten closer to the essence of this man whom he had understood, if not always appreciated, when during the Great War he had written:

De Pachmann is a great success because he is an extraordinary personality, and because he possesses the art of impressing that personality on the public. In art, personality—individuality—is the only thing that tells. We may have the most wonderful finger technique, our memory may include a repertory of a thousand pieces and be infallibly correct, and we may possess all the artistic virtues under the sun; but unless we have personality, we will be as nothing. And it is just here that de Pachmann is supreme. (43–44)

The only personal possession Pachmann retained at the time of his death was a leather bag that had accompanied him on all his tours. It was found to contain a Byzantine icon of the Madonna and Child, given to him by his mother for his protection.

Epilogue: The Others

After Pachmann's death, Maggie continued to head the Pachmann School of Pianoforte Playing in Paris, where diplomas were awarded to qualified pupils by a jury composed of members of an illustrious committee.[1] She also inherited Pachmann's music library, from which she "transcribed," for Augener, an edition of Chopin's works based on Pachmann's fingerings and phrasings. Her prefatory note to this edition reads, in part: "His fingering once mastered, the most intricate passages will be exempt from any blur or unevenness, and the hands will retain the position in which they seem to move effortlessly"—the fruit of his new method.

On 1 April 1935, the *Australian Musical News* published an article by her, entitled "Pachmann's Sincerity." It was a refutation of remarks about Pachmann that had stung her and proved how little known and understood he had been. "Pachmann, with all his originalities, which so often disconcerted his friends and his public, was always sincere," she wrote.

> I trust my protest will not be thought out of place. I feel it a duty towards a departed one, recognised the world over as a great pianist, to say what— coming from me—may be taken as the expression of the strictest verity. Felix Remo says, "He stares at the nearest member of the audience—stares with effrontery and insolence, thus giving the impression of a man who would be quite capable of turning the handle of a barrel-organ. He has studied all the tricks of the charlatan." If Pachmann "stared at a member of the audience," he was simply seeking to know if the person he gazed on was appreciating with him the beauty of what he was playing. But no one could ever have made him understand that he was allowing himself to be misjudged! He was happy when at his piano, and he wanted to know that others were happy with him.

Marguerite Fernand Labori died 3 July 1952 and was buried with her husband in the Montparnasse cemetery. She was eighty-seven.

In January 1933, Cesco published a long and much-illustrated piece on Pachmann in *La Nuova Italia Musicale*. In essence, it was a repetition of information from the booklet about the pianist that he had written almost two decades earlier—with one addition: "To the end he nurtured a great love for Italy and for *il Duce,* of whom he was an enthusiastic admirer." This ludicrous and self-serving claim was Cesco's final betrayal of Pachmann, whose very individualism put him at odds with all forms of totalitarianism. In fact, he had left Russia not simply because he had achieved his first fame in the West; he could, if he had wanted, have remained there—at least until 1917—as a professor of piano (the conservatory in St. Petersburg, the first in Russia, had opened in 1862; the conservatory in Moscow in 1866) and, through his brother's influence, possibly even as a court pianist. Yet for all his aesthetic appreciation of its splendor, Pachmann saw czarist Russia for what it was: a totalitarian state. To him this was unacceptable—as was fascism, by which, as a foreigner in Italy who was sexually heterodox and possibly Jewish besides, he stood to gain nothing; indeed, stood to lose everything.

During the Fascist era, Cesco became the *podestà* of Fabriano—in effect, the mayor. The word *podestà* was used in the Middle Ages, and for this reason it was preferred by the Fascists. Not all the Fabrianesi were loyal to Mussolini, however, and when, in anticipation of a visit by Hitler, the town merchants were ordered to display his photograph in their windows, the proprietor of the Caffè Storelli stacked boxes of Lazzaroni cookies underneath his photograph. *Lazzarone* is more or less synonymous with *birbante,* which means a scoundrel, a rogue. The irony of Cesco's life was that the resources that had permitted his ascent in Fascist Italy owed ultimately to a fortunate assignation made when he was working, in essence, as a homosexual prostitute. The myth of his own career he cultivated with lies.

Pallottelli proved to be an irresponsible steward of Pachmann's legacy: Scores, photographs, letters, test pressings, and so on were sold at the Porta Portese flea market in Rome. Items of incalculable value thus lost included copies of Muzio Clementi's *Gradus ad Parnassum* and the first book of Bach's *Well-Tempered Clavier,* both containing penciled annotations by Chopin. (Pachmann had bought the former at an auction in London.) Pallottelli continued to represent a number of musicians, among them Pachmann's former pupil Allan Bier.

Cesco died on 9 January 1965, at the age of eighty.

Just up the hill from Campodonico, against a backdrop of oppressive mountains, is the small cemetery containing the Pallottelli family mausoleum. The walls of the cemetery are stacked with graves, most of them marked with photographs of the deceased and decorated with paper flowers, toys, even, in one case, a snow-filled paperweight. Yet from all this life and color (rural Italian cemeteries can be amazingly lively) the Pallottelli mausoleum sits a bit remote, a bit aloof. Its structure is that of a second-class couchette car—three bunks on either side. On the left, from top to bottom, lie Alice (died 11 September 1973), Cesco, and Cesco's parents (buried together). On the right lies Virgilio (died 30 July 1986). The other tombs are empty. The white marble gravestones are unadorned. To the left of the doors is a majolica plaque on which are written the words to Saint Francis of Assisi's *Canto delle Creature,* accompanied by a tiny reproduction of Giotto's fresco of the Saint preaching to the birds.

Cesco and Alice's second son, Duilio, became a photographer[2] and writer whose books include the memoir *Voglia di famiglia.* Neither his mother nor his father has much of a role in the story—he judged them to have been undependable parents—even as their spiritual presence is strongly felt.

Alice was hypercritical and demanding and withal nervous. (She had the habit of folding and refolding pieces of paper until they formed a packet in the shape of a coffin.) Although he was in America when she died, her death had been described to him:

> At the end, poor Mamma had lived in an almost vegetative state. Moments of lucidity were ever more rare and the will to pull through had completely abandoned her. The night she died, she recovered for an instant a glimmer of consciousness. Looking around, the poor thing did not find my face among the many that surrounded her.
> "And where is he?" she asked.
> "He's gone to work in America, *Nonna,* you know that."
> "That one. Considering how he started, he's done almost too much."
> Then she said nothing more. She closed her eyes, and passed away. (164–65)

When Cesco died, Duilio was in New York. After receiving the telephone call from Rome, during which his mother assured him that his father's had been "a beautiful death, serene, as was his life" (193), he thought back to the day he had left his father's house:

> A friend of mine had come to take me to the airport, and my father was there to say good-bye to me, in the doorway. I had hugged him. Clasping him to me proved to be a strange sensation, indefinable. Like hugging a cloud. I looked at him again, from the car. He was looking at me, too. He was there on the sidewalk, beside a tree, in the clear air of January. It seemed to me that his soft body mingled, almost too much, almost to the point of vanishing, with the bright air of that winter day. Now I know why: he was already leaving. (193)

Duilio Cambellotti's work formed the basis of an exhibition at the Galleria Comunale d'Arte Moderna e Contemporanea, Rome, that ran from 24 September 1999 through 23 January 2000. In the catalog for this exhibition, his contributions to the Villino Pallottelli are traced in detail. Even in connection with the music room, however, Pachmann's name is not given once. Instead, the music room is described simply as having been built for auditions in connection with Pallottelli's work as an impresario. It is with real indignation that one reads in *Duilio Cambellotti: Arredi e decorazioni* that the piano in the music room was used by

> celebrated pianists such as Alfred Cortot, Wilhelm Backhaus, Vladimir de Pachmann. The last of these, famous for his Chopin interpretations, emigrated to Paris after the Russian Revolution and there met Pallottelli, who became his agent and invited him to stay, as a permanent guest, in his recently completed villa. Pachmann resided there until his death. (59)

To the end, Cesco unrepentantly betrayed his friend's memory for the sake of an appearance.

Adrian de Pachmann died in December 1937. The *New York Times* (23 December) published only a short obituary.

History has obscured Adrian. In the few works in which it is given, the year of his birth is approximate—even though it is known: 1886. Moreover, he is sometimes described as having been a musician. The entry on him in Wilson Lyle's *Dictionary of Pianists* reads:

> Pachmann, Adrian de (*c.* 1893–1937)
>
> b. . Son of Vladimir and Marguerite de P. Became a concert pianist and pursued own career. Did not, however, appear to receive any tuition from father, and their careers were unconnected. Domiciled in Paris most of his life.

Lyle had clearly confused him with his brother Lionel.

There is little else to relate. A small cache of postcards to Adrian trace him, at various times, in care of Madame F. Labori, La Bourboule, Puy-de-Dôme (a spa town in the Auvergne); Les Marguerites, Samois, Seine et Marne; and Chez Monsieur le docteur Sauvage, Villa Garnier Pagés, Cannet, Alpes Maritimes.

The most complete reference to Lionel de Pachmann is to be found in connection with the biographies of his father and mother in the Fasquelle *Encyclopédie de la Musique:*

> Léonide, dit. *Lionel de P.* (Hampton, Angleterre, 28.8.1887–), de nat. franç., élève de ses parents, de G. Caussade et de X. Leroux, est également pian.,

prof., critique (*Courrier mus.*, 1920–30), dir.-fondateur de l'école (1947) et de l'acad. (1956) Frédéric Chopin; il a composé 1 quatuor à cordes (1929–1936), *Triptyque anti-sériel* (p., 1948–49), *Hommage à Gabriel Fauré* (p. [1950]), de la mus. de scène, de chambre.

Although this entry gives his place of birth (like Adrian's) as Hampton, there is no record at the General Register Office of his having been born in England. (His biography in the 1938 *Macmillan Encyclopedia of Music and Musicians* likewise gives Hampton as his place of birth, but errs on the date by a decade: 1877.) As for "dit. *Lionel* . . .": According to Evans, Leonide preferred to be called Lionel (pronounced in the English way) because he disliked the redundancy of Leon*ide de* Pachmann. (It is amusing that Leonide did not consider dropping the particule from his surname as a remedy to this infelicity.) On the other hand, Lionel told Robert Dumm that he preferred the Russian form of his Christian name (but pronounced like Brezhnev's).

In the early 1940s, in Lyons, Lionel de Pachmann taught Pierre Boulez piano and harmony. (Boulez had been introduced to Lionel by Ninon Vallin, a French soprano, whose *répétiteur* was Violette Lubail, Lionel's half-sister.) He did not impress the young Boulez, who presently moved to Paris in order to continue his studies at the Paris Conservatory. In 1947, in Paris, Lionel founded and headed the École Frédéric Chopin; in 1956, the Académie Frédéric Chopin (located in his apartment at 199 bis Boulevard St. Germain, at the corner of rue de Luynes). He composed his *Triptyque anti-sériel* for piano in 1948 and 1949; a title, as the musicologist Jean Lambert noted, that showed the composer's aversion to Serialism. Lambert's remarks, which were delivered in an homage to Lionel from the Académie Frédéric Chopin, of which he was a member, imply that Lionel, in rejecting dodecaphonic writing, de facto expressed sentiments and soul states in his music: a somewhat ironic homage, since the most distinguishing feature of Lionel's music appears to have been its failure to leave any enduring impression.

In his manuscript, Blickstein wrote that Lionel de Pachmann's studio "breathed the atmosphere of the turn of the century, of Massenet and Saint-Saëns."

> All around was beautiful disorder. Scores were piled on a piano whose top was partially covered with some velvet material, and on the walls were many pictures. Among those I recognized were pictures of his father, his mother, and his stepfather, Labori. . . . The effect of the studio was enhanced by the view from the balcony: a breathless [*sic;* breathtaking?] panorama of Paris.

As they warmed to each other, Lionel played for Blickstein, who remembered that Lionel also would make asides à la Pachmann. "Particularly vivid" to Blickstein, however, was Lionel's memory of his father's hands: "They were fleshy but quite firm and strong. He could move his fingers along the back of one's own hand with such power that it really hurt, and yet he could also caress the piano keys with a delicacy and lightness of touch that was absolutely unique. It was as if his fingers were made of both steel and Indian rubber."

The first festival of Lionel's works took place in Paris on 9 May 1926; another, again in Paris (Parthenon), took place on 21 November 1931. A third concert, in which the performers were the composer himself (piano), Jacqueline Barde (soprano), Isabelle Flory (violin), and Christian Petitjean (baritone), was given at the Salle Debussy-Pleyel on 13 December 1974. By then, Lionel was eighty-seven. At the time Evans and Dumm interviewed him, he still lived at 199 bis Boulevard St. Germain. Although he was a nonagenarian, in the recordings of Dumm's *entretiens* with him (conducted in French) there are flashes of ugliness that cannot be credited simply to a nonagenarian's irascibility. For instance, when he tells Dumm that he was interviewed years before by Blickstein, he adds that Blickstein was an "Israelite," as if this fact were relevant to the interview. One would not have expected this from the stepson of Labori, whose fame rested above all on his defense of Dreyfus. What is certain is that by identifying Blickstein as an "Israelite," Lionel made it clear that the revival of old questions about his father's racial origins would not be welcome.

The year after their meeting, Lionel wrote to Evans (letter of 1 October 1980), "My health is still sufficient enough for a moderate activity (just a few pupils and gramophone private performances of some of my best compositions). I am now 93 years old, and am taking care of myself and following strictly the doctor's prescriptions." Notwithstanding Lionel's "moderate activity," no one remembers the names of his pupils, his private audiences, or the engineer(s) who recorded his works. (His letter does, at the very least, confirm the year of his birth: 1887.) Neither the École nor the Académie Frédéric Chopin exists any longer. Nor is the disposition of Lionel's possessions, among them an album of photographs and a disc of his mother playing a Raff gavotte (as well as, presumably, his mother's music library), known at present.

Although a piece Lionel composed for guitarist Andres Segovia, *Exotismes,* has recently come to light in Spain, many of his works are yet to be rediscovered. He also produced a quantity of music for films and the music hall under a pseudonym, which is still not known.

The interviewers who went to Lionel questioned him mostly about his father and his father's playing, and this is regrettable. In the long run, it is not really important what Lionel had to say, for example, about his father's playing of a Chopin mazurka. On the other hand, knowledge could have been gained if Lionel had been asked more about his own life: Who did you feel was your real father, Pachmann or Labori? Did you consider your father a homosexual? Were you close to your mother? What is your attitude toward the Pallottelli family? What do you consider to be your nationality? What are your fondest memories of your childhood? Did your parents ever come to hear you play? What was the most important relationship in your life?

Pachmann's gravestone, made from travertine marble, has so worn over the years that today his name is barely legible. Moreover, in 1967 Pallottelli's family, which owned the grave, elected to deposit a second corpse into it; that of one Mario Casaccia. Today his name is so much more prominent—and legible—that one could easily pass by the grave without realizing that it was Vladimir de Pachmann's.

DISCOGRAPHY
by Allan Evans

Matrix	Composition	Catalog Number of Original Record

SESSION 1:
London, Gramophone & Typewriter, 1907

a. 6001e	Chopin: Étude 25/9; Valse 64/1	5566
b. 6003e	Chopin: Valse 64/2	5568
c. 6004e	Raff: *La Fileuse*	5567
d. 1850f	Chopin: *Barcarolle* (abridged)	05502
e. 1851f	Chopin: Nocturne 37/2	05501
f. 1856f	Chopin: Preludes nos. 22, 23; Mazurka 50/2	05500

SESSION 2:
London, Gramophone, 1909

a. 3136f	Chopin: Étude 10/12	05517, D 835
b. 3138f	Raff: *La Fileuse*	05518, D 835
c. 3139f	Mendelssohn: *Rondo capriccioso*	05519
d. 3154f	Verdi/Liszt: *Rigoletto* paraphrase	05516

SESSION 3:
Camden, N.J., Victor, 7 November 1911

a. C 11198-1	Chopin: Nocturne 15/1	72493, 6377, 05636, D 263
b. C 11199-1	Raff: *La Fileuse*	74301
c. C 11200-1	Chopin: Prelude no. 24; Étude 10/5	74260, 6363, 05593, D 264
d. C 11201-1	Chopin: Impromptu opus 29; Prelude no. 23	74284, 6363
e. C 11202-1	Verdi/Liszt: *Rigoletto* paraphrase	74261, 6083

SESSION 4:
Camden, N.J., Victor, 8 November 1911

a. C 11203-1	Weber/Pachmann: *Perpetuum mobile*	unissued

b. C 11204-1	Mendelssohn: SWW 67/4; Schumann: *Prophet Bird*	74285, 6082, 05594, D 265
c. C 11205-1	Liszt: *Mazurka brillante*	unissued (on tape at IPAM)*
d. C 11206-1	Chopin: Études 10/1, 25/2	unissued (on tape at IPAM)*
e. C 11207-1	Chopin: Mazurka 50/2	64224, 907, 5639, E 80
f. C 11208-1	Chopin: Mazurkas 67/4, 33/3	unissued (metal part extant)
g. C 11209-1	Chopin: Valse 64/2	unissued

SESSION 5:
Camden, N.J, Victor, 25 April 1912

a. C 11924-1	Chopin: Preludes no. 6, 7, 10	unissued (on tape at IPAM)*
b. C 11925-1	Chopin: Nocturne 55/1	unissued*, IPA LP
c. C 11926-1	Chopin: Valse 64/3; Mazurka 17/1	unissued
d. C 11927-1	Chopin: *Berceuse*	unissued*
e. C 11928-1	Mendelssohn: SWW	74315, 6377, 05596, D 265
f. C 11929-1	Schumann: *Ende vom Lied*	unissued
g. C 11930-1	Chopin: Polonaise 26/1	unissued (on tape at IPAM)*
h. B 11931-1	Chopin: Étude 10/3	unissued (metal part extant)
i. C 11932-1	Chopin: Ballade opus 47, part 1	unissued (on tape at IPAM)*

SESSION 6:
Camden, N.J., Victor, 26 April 1912

a. C 11933-1	Chopin: *Funeral March* from opus 35	unissued
b. C 11934-1	Chopin: Prelude no. 15	unissued
c. C 11935-1	Chopin: Mazurka 59/3	64263, 907, 5640, E 80
d. C 11936-1	Chopin: Nocturne 37/2	74313, 6082, 05635, D 263
e. C 11937-1	Chopin: Preludes nos. 20, 16	unissued (on tape at IPAM)*
f. C 11938-1	Chopin: Étude 25/5	74318, 05597, D 262
g. C 11939-1	Bach/Saint-Saëns: Gavotte	unissued

h. C 11940-1	Chopin: Ballade opus 47, part 2	74309, 05597, D 262
i. C 11941-1	Chopin: *Funeral March* from opus 35	74304, 6083, 05595, D 264
j. C 11942-1	Chopin/Godowsky: Étude 10/12 (l. hand)	74302

SESSION 7:
London (at Pachmann's home on his Baldwin piano), Columbia, December 1915

a. 6591	Chopin: Étude 25/3; Prelude 16	L 1010, A 5831
b. 6595	Liszt: Polonaise no. 2, part 2	L 1010, A 5831
c. 6596	Chopin: Prelude no. 24	L 1009
d. 6598	Chopin: Impromptu opus 29	L 1009
e. 6616	Chopin: Mazurka 67/4; Prelude no. 23	L 1014
f. 6619	Chopin: Nocturne 9/2	L 1014

SESSION 8:
London (at Pachmann's home on his Baldwin piano), Columbia, early 1916

a. 6968	Chopin: Nocturne 27/2	L 1124
b. 6969	Chopin: Valse 70/1; *Eccossaise* in D♭	L 1103
c. 6971	Schumann: *Grillen*	L 1131
d. 6972	Chopin: Scherzo from sonata opus 58	L 1131
e. 6973	Raff: *La Fileuse*	L 1112
f. 6974	Liszt: *Liebestraume* no. 3	L 1102
g. 6976	Chopin: Mazurka 33/4	L 1102
h. 6977	Verdi/Liszt: *Rigoletto* paraphrase	L 1103
i. 6978	Brahms: Capriccio 76/5	L 1124
j. 6979	Chopin: Mazurka 33/3; Étude 25/3	L 1112

SESSION 9:
Camden, N.J., Victor, 14 December 1923

a. C 29085-1	Chopin: Nocturne 55/2	unissued
b. C 29086-1	Chopin: Impromptu opus 36	74864, 6441
c. C 29088-1	Chopin: Étude 25/3; Mazurka 67/4	unissued
d. C 29090-1	Schumann: *Novelette* 21/1	HMV 05786, DB 858
e. C 11934-2	Chopin: Prelude no. 15	HMV 05824, DB 858
f. C 11934-3	Chopin: Prelude no. 15	unissued
g. C 29091-1	Chopin: Nocturne 32/1	74868, 6441
h. C 29092-1	Chopin: Valses in E (opus posth.), 64/1	unissued

SESSION 10:
Camden, N.J., Victor, 26 May 1924

a. C 11934-4 Chopin: Prelude no. 15   unissued
b. C 11934-5 Chopin: Prelude no. 15   6480
c. C 11934-6 Chopin: Prelude no. 15   unissued
d. C 29090-2 Schumann: *Novelette* 21/1   unissued
e. C 11204-1 Mendelssohn: SWW 67/4; Schumann: unissued
                 Prophet Bird
f. C 11202-2 Verdi/Liszt: *Rigoletto* paraphrase   unissued
g. C 11202-3 Verdi/Liszt: *Rigoletto* paraphrase   unissued

SESSION 11:
Camden, N.J., Victor, 23 September 1924

a. C 29090-3 Schumann: *Novelette* 21/1   unissued
b. C 29090-4 Schumann: *Novelette* 21/1   74865, 6480
c. B 30934-1 Mendelssohn: SWW   1110
d. B 30934-1 Mendelssohn: SWW   unissued
e. B 30935-1 Schumann: *Prophet Bird*   1110
f. B 30935-2 Schumann: *Prophet Bird*   unissued

SESSION 12:
Hayes [London], Studio B (Pachmann's Baldwin piano) HMV, 26 June 1925

a. Cc 6253-1 Chopin: Nocturne 27/2   DB 860
b. Cc 6254-1 Chopin: Nocturne 72/1   unissued
c. Cc 6255-1 Chopin: Mazurka 24/4   DB 861
d. Cc 6255-2 Chopin: Mazurka 24/4   unissued
e. Cc 6256-1 Chopin: Mazurka 50/2   DB 861
f. Bb 6257-1 Chopin: Mazurka in C# minor (with speech)   unissued
g. Bb 6258-1 Chopin: Prelude no. 6; Mazurka 67/1   DA 1302
h. Cc 6259-1 Chopin: Nocturne 32/1   unissued
i. Cc 6259-2 Chopin: Nocturne 32/1 (with speech)   DB 859
j. Cc 6260-1 Chopin: Valse 64/2; Étude 25/3   DB 860
k. Cc 6261-1 Chopin: Impromptu opus 36   DB 859

SESSION 13:
Hayes [London], Studio A (Pachmann's Baldwin piano) HMV, 15 December 1925

a. Cc 7529-1 Chopin: Polonaise 26/1   DB 931
b. Cc 7530-1 Chopin: Preludes nos. 2, 6, 7   unissued
c. Cc 7530-2 Chopin: Preludes nos. 2, 6, 7   unissued

d. Cc 7531-1   Chopin: Mazurka 33/4   unissued
e. Cc 7532-1   Chopin: Mazurka 56/2; Prelude no. 1   unissued
f. Cc 7533-1   Chopin: Nocturne 72/1   unissued
g. Cc 7533-2   Chopin: Nocturne 72/1   unissued
h. Cc 7534-1   Chopin: Nocturne 37/1   unissued
i. Bb 7535-1   Chopin: Valse 64/1   unissued
    (may survive)
j. Bb 7535-2   Chopin: Valse 64/1 (with speech)   DA 761
k. Cc 7536-1   Grieg: *Holberg* suite, 40/5   unissued
l. Bb 7537-1   Chopin: Valse 70/1   DA 761
m. Bb 7537-2   Chopin: Valse 70/1   DA 761
n. Cc 7538-1   Chopin: Valse 64/3   DB 931

SESSION 14:
Small Queen's Hall, London, Studio C (Pachmann's Baldwin piano)
HMV, 3 November 1927

a. Cc 11757-1   Chopin: Nocturne 72/1   unissued
b. Cc 11757-2   Chopin: Nocturne 72/1   DB 1106, 6879
c. Cc 11758-1   Chopin: Étude 10/7; Valse 34/3   unissued
d. Bb 11759-1   Chopin: Preludes nos. 3, 6   DA 927, 1459
e. Cc 11760-1   Chopin: Prelude no. 15   unissued
f. Bb 11761-1   Mendelssohn: Prelude 35/1   DA 927, 1459
g. Cc 11762-1   Chopin: Mazurkas 63/3, 67/4   DB 1106, 6879
h. Bb 11763-1   Chopin: Étude 10/5 (with speech)   DA 1302

Arbiter Records has embarked on a project to issue at least one recording of every work that Pachmann committed to disc. The first compact disc, *Vladimir de Pachmann: The Mythic Pianist,* was issued in 2001; the second is forthcoming. In addition to publishing several Pachmann recordings for the first time, Arbiter's project makes available again several out-of-print performances issued on other labels. More information may be obtained from www.arbiterrecords.com.

Although Pachmann recorded a number of piano rolls, I have chosen not to include a list of them here: The roll is an inferior, essentially non-musical medium and contributes nothing substantive to our understanding of how Pachmann—or any other pianist who made them—played the piano.

WORKS PLAYED
1882 (VIENNA)–1929 (VIENNA)

C. P. E. Bach
   Keyboard sonata (edited by Bülow)

J. S. Bach
   Chromatic Fantasie and Fugue
   English suites (movements)
   Italian concerto
   Well-Tempered Clavier (Tausig edition?)

John Francis Barnett
   Nocturne

Ludwig van Beethoven
   Bagatelle 126/4
   Fugue in D (two pianos)
   Piano concerto no. 3 (Liszt cadenzas)
   Piano concerto no. 4 (Bülow cadenzas?)
   Piano concerto no. 5
   Piano sonatas 2/2 and 3
   Piano sonata opus 13 (*Pathétique*)
   Piano sonata 14/1
   Piano sonata opus 22
   Piano sonata opus 26
   Piano sonata 27/2 ("Moonlight")
   Piano sonata 31/ 2 ("Tempest")
   Piano sonatas 49/1 and 2
   Piano sonata opus 53 ("Waldstein")
   Piano sonata opus 54
   Piano sonata opus 57 ("Appassionata")
   Piano sonata opus 78
   Piano sonata opus 90 (?)
   Piano sonata opus 101
   Piano sonata opus 110
   Piano sonata opus 111

Piano trio ("Archduke")
Piano and violin sonata 30/3
Piano and violin sonata opus 47 ("Kreutzer")
Rondo à capriccio, opus 129
32 Variations in C minor

Johannes Brahms
Ballade 10/2
Capricci 76/2 and 5
Rhapsody 79/1
Scherzo in E-flat minor
Waltzes

Hans von Bülow
Tarantella opus 21

Frédéric Chopin
Allegro de Concert
Andante spianato and *Grande Polonaise* (with orchestral accompaniment)
Four ballades
Barcarolle
Berceuse
Bolero
Études (except 10/2 and 25/11)
Fantasie
Four impromptus
Mazurkas 7/1, 2, 3 and 5, 17/1, 24/2 and 4, 30/2 and 3, 33/3 and 4,
    41/1 and 3, 50/1 and 2, 56/1 and 2, 59/2 and 3, 63/1 and 3, 67/1
    and 4, 68/3, and the one in A minor dedicated "à son ami Émile
    Gaillard"
Nocturnes 9/1, 2 and 3, 15/1, 27/1 and 2, 32/1, 37/1 and 2, 48/1, 55/1
    and 2, 62/1, and opus 72
Piano concerto in E minor
Piano concerto in F minor
Piano sonata in B minor, opus 58
Piano sonata in B-flat minor, opus 35
Piano trio
Polonaises 26/1 and 2, 40/1 and 2, opus 44, opus 53, opus 61, and 71/2
Preludes 28/1, 2, 3, 4, 6, 7, 8, 10, 11, 12, 15, 16, 17, 19, 20, 21, 22,
    23, and 24
Rondo opus 16
Rondo for two pianos, opus 73

Four scherzi
Tarantella
Trois Ecossaises
Waltzes 34/1, 2 and 3, opus 42, 64/1, 2 and 3, 69/1 and 2, 70/1, opus
     posthumous

Muzio Clementi
     Unspecified work(s)

Frederic Cowen
     Three Pieces (*Allegretto grazioso,* Romance, and Scherzo)

Johann Baptist Cramer
     Five studies

Antonin Dvořák
     Unspecified work(s)

John Field
     Rondo

Benjamin Godard
     Mazurka

Leopold Godowsky
     Concert Allegro (Scarlatti)
     Invitation to the Dance (Weber)
     Pastorale (Corelli)
     Study for the left hand on Chopin's étude 10/12
     Study on Chopin's *Grande Valse brillante,* opus 18
     Tambourin (Rameau)
     Tyll Eulenspiegel (from *Walzermasken*)

Edvard Grieg
     Ballade en forme de variations
     Holberg suite

Georg Friedrich Händel
     Aria con variazioni

Franz Josef Haydn
     Unspecified work(s)

Adolf von Henselt
Characteristic études 2/3, 6, 7, 8, 11, and 12
Danklied nach Sturm
Episodischer Gedanke (Weber)
La Fileuse (Raff)
Frühlingslied
Gondolieri
Invitation to the Dance (Weber)
Liebeslied
Piano concerto
Polacca brillante (Weber)
Rondo brillante (Weber)
Rondo capriccioso (Mendelssohn)
Toccatina, opus 25
Wiegenlied, opus 45

Tom Hood
Song of the Shirt

Johann Nepomuk Hummel
Piano concerto in B minor
Rondo opus 11

Walter Imboden
Berceuse
Hommage à Pachmann
Valsettes, opus 10 (dedicated to Pachmann)

Josef Lamberg
Unspecified work(s)

Leideritz
Nocturne (dedicated to Pachmann)

Franz Liszt
Après une lecture de Dante (*Années de Pélèrinage* II)
Au bord d'une source (*Années de Pélèrinage* I)
Ballade no. 2
Bénédiction de Dieu dans la solitude (*Harmonies poétiques et religieuses*)
Cantique d'amour (*Harmonies poétiques et religieuses*)
Chants polonais (Nocturne)
La danza (Rossini)
Eclogue (*Années de Pélèrinage* I)

Hungarian Rhapsodies nos. 6, 8, 9 (*Pesther Carneval*), 10, and 13
Introduction to Weber/Henselt *Polacca brillante*
Liebestraume no. 3
Die Loreley
Mazurka brillante
Mendelssohn Lieder transcription (*Auf Flügeln des Gesanges*)
Piano concerto no. 1
Piano sonata in B minor
Polonaises nos. 1 (*Polonaise mélancolique*) and 2
Rigoletto: paraphrase de concert (Verdi)
Schubert Lieder transcriptions (*Ave Maria, Du bist die Ruh, Gretchen am
    Spinnrade, Horch, horch! die Lerch!, Der Lindenbaum, Sei mir gegrüsst,*
    and *Trockne Blumen*)
Sonnetto del Petrarca 104
St. François de Paule marchant sur les flots (*Deux légendes,* no. 2)
Tarantella da Guillaume Louis Cottrau (*Venezia e Napoli*)
Transcendental Études (*Harmonies du soir*)
Trois études de concert (*La leggierezza* and *Un sospiro*)
Valse-caprice d'après Schubert no. 6
Valse-impromptu
Zwei Konzertetüden (*Gnomenreigen* and *Waldesrauschen*)

Felix Mendelssohn
    Caprice 16/2
    Fantasie in F-sharp minor ("Scottish")
    Piano concerto in D minor
    Piano concerto in G minor
    Prelude 35/1
    Prelude and fugue 35/5
    Rondo capriccioso
    Scherzo
    Scherzo à capriccio
    Songs without Words
        30/6 (*Venezianisches Gondellied*)
        53/2 (*Fleecy Cloud*) and 3
        62/1 (*May Breezes*), 2 (*The Departure*), and 6 (*Frühlingslied*)
        67/4 (*Spinnerlied*)
        102/4
    Variations sérieuses

Ignaz Moscheles
    Étude in G major, opus 70
    (and Mendelssohn) Variations on the Gypsy March from Weber's *Preciosa*

Moriz Moszkowski
 En automne
 Minuet opus 17

Wolfgang Amadeus Mozart
 Fantasie in C minor
 Piano concerto in A major, K. 488
 Piano concerto in C major, K. 467 or K. 503
 Piano concerto in D minor, K. 466 (Beethoven cadenzas)
 Piano quartet in G minor
 Piano sonata, K. 331
 Piano and violin sonata in E minor (Allegro. Adagio. Theme with
  variations.)
 Rondo in A minor, K. 511
 Rondo
 Trio for clarinet, viola and piano, K. 498 ("Kegelstatt")

Marguerite de Pachmann
 Rêverie du lac
 Thème et variations

Vladimir de Pachmann
 Fantasie
 The Maiden's Prayer (Badarzewska-Baranowska)
 Overture to *A Midsummer Night's Dream* (Mendelssohn)
 Perpetuum mobile (Weber)

Ede Poldini
 Unspecified work(s)

Joachim Raff
 La Fileuse (157/2)
 Giga con variazioni (from Suite opus 91)
 Prelude and fugue in E minor (from Suite opus 72)
 Rigaudon

Anton Rubinstein
 Air with variations
 Barcarolle no. 4
 Étude (On False Note)
 Mélancolie (51/1)
 Piano concerto in D minor

Camille Saint-Saëns
  Gavotte from violin sonata no. 6 (J. S. Bach)
  Scherzo for two pianos, opus 87

Domenico Scarlatti
  Cat's Fugue
  Sonata in A major (unspecified)

Franz Schubert
  Fantasie for piano and violin in C major, opus 159
  Impromptus 90/2 and 4
  Impromptus 142/2, 3, and 4
  Moment Musicaux 94/3 and 5
  Piano quintet ("Trout")

Robert Schumann
  Andante and variations in B-flat, opus 46 (two pianos)
  Carnaval
  Davidsbündlertänze
  Études symphoniques
  Fantasie
  Fantasiestücke (*Aufschwung, Warum?, Grillen, In der Nacht, Traumes Wirren,*
    Ende vom Lied)
  Faschingsschwank aus Wien
  Kreisleriana (three sections)
  Nachtstücke 23/3 and 4
  Novelletten 21/1, 4, 6 and 7
  Piano sonata in F-sharp minor
  Piano sonata in G minor
  Piano and violin sonata in D minor, opus 121
  Romanzen 28/2 and 32/3
  Toccata
  Waldszenen (*Vogel als Prophet, Jagdlied, Abschied*)

Giovanni Sgambati
  Gavotte opus 14

Karl Gottfried Wilhelm Taubert
  Waltz

Peter Ilyich Tchaikovsky
  In the Troika (37/11)

Polka (9/2)
Piano sonata in G major
Waltz (51/1)

Carl Maria von Weber
   Invitation to the Dance
   Perpetuum mobile (from piano sonata in C major)
   Piano sonata in A-flat major
   Piano sonata in D minor
   Piano sonata in E minor
   Polacca brillante ("L'hilarité")
   Rondo brillante ("La gaité")

Niccolò Van Westerhout
   Ma belle qui danse

NOTES

INTRODUCTION

1. Cf. chapter 11 of *The Posthumous Papers of the Pickwick Club* by Charles Dickens.

2. The height of his piano stool was also of considerable concern to Pachmann, leading him eventually to have one made to his specifications—an innovation later adopted by Paderewski, Horowitz, and Glenn Gould, among others. When he was without this stool, his jests highlighted the problems faced by the traveling virtuoso. Finding himself in New York with a stool that was too low, for instance, he requested that a phone directory be brought to him on stage. He placed the directory on the stool, but now it was too high. He then tore one page from the directory, and placed this on the stool. Now he could play.

3. In another version of the story, the concert takes place at Queen's Hall in London and Pachmann plays twenty-five encores.

4. Pachmann gave proof to Adorno's assertion that music reminds the dehumanized masses of their humanity.

5. The story "Bachmann" (1924).

6. The Swiss circus clown Grock (1880–1959) had made Pachmann's comedies part of his own act. For instance, he would push the piano toward the stool rather than the stool toward the piano if they were too far apart for him to play the instrument, or he might contrive to fall through the seat of his piano chair. James Francis Cooke described Grock's piano act in an editorial on musical showmanship for the *Etude* (May 1955):

> After playing many instruments with virtuosity he discovers the grand piano and is shocked by its size. When the audience joined him with shouts of laughter, he would "shush" them with his forefinger to his lips and horror in his eyes. Gradually he moves toward the piano on his hands and knees with fear and trepidation in his eyes. He lifts the cover and lets it fall with a bang, which throws him into a faint. When he recovers he begins to explore the piano and then starts to dissect it. Out comes the action and then the keyboard and soon the stage is littered with parts. Then with great effort he gets it together again. Finally he sits down to play, with extraordinary facility, a short program of which any concert pianist might be proud. This pantomime is carried out with great taste and naturalness and lack of exaggeration, that once seen could not be forgotten. It was not Grock's clowning that made him great, but rather his human appeal which gained him the sympathy and affections of his thousands of admirers. He represented the joie de vivre of France, the Weltschmerz of Germany, and the jolly merriment of old England.

7. Borge, who was born in 1909, never heard Pachmann in concert. He did, however, know about Pachmann. Indeed, he tells a couple of familiar anecdotes about him—one concerning adjustments to his stool, another Chopin's socks—in *Victor Borge's My Favorite Comedies in Music*.

8. From the *Chicago Evening Post* review (15 or 16 October 1923) of the Marx Brothers in *I'll Say She Is* at the Studebaker Theater: "[Chico] can get as much fun and melody out of a piano as Vladimir de Pachmann."

9. All is relative, however. What would critics of Pachmann—and of Pachmann's day—have made of Robert Wilson's Singapore Festival 2000 "staging" of Liszt's *Transcendental Études* in which the pianist, Tzimon Barto, played shirtless? Or of Margaret Leng

Tan's February 2001 performance at Carnegie Hall of John Cage's *Suite for Toy Piano,* which ended with the pianist carrying her instrument off the stage? (For sheer spectacle, of course, no one has trumped Simon Barere, who actually *died* on the stage of Carnegie Hall during a performance of the Grieg piano concerto.)

10. Carl Flesch wrote in his memoirs that when Schnabel was introduced to Pachmann, Pachmann "first of all pretended not to be able to catch his name: after it had been repeated thrice, he at last remembered: 'Yes, of course, Schnabel, the well-known flutist'" (202).

11. Glover found Pachmann's playing "wistful (but not frivolous) in its subtle variations of touch, tone, and spontaneous rubato," while Hopkins, for his part, responded to the "extraordinary elasticity of his melodic inflexion, out of which the ornamentation grows with such an inevitability that it assumes an almost organic, yet never obtrusive, significance."

12. In the *Saturday Review* (22 February 1908) Arthur Symons reviewed a recital by Emil von Sauer. "[His] might be called in the best sense elegant playing," Symons wrote, "a kind of tender elegance, in which feeling never ceases to be gracious. We are losing this sort of playing, in which the piano is coaxed, not bullied."

13. In addition to the *Walzermasken: Twenty-four Tone Fantasies in Three-Quarter Time* (1912), Pachmann learned several of the Chopin studies and the *Symphonic Metamorphoses on Weber's "Invitation to the Dance."* Pachmann was, indeed, the first pianist—apart from the composer himself—to program Godowsky's music.

14. The absence from Pachmann's repertoire of works by certain composers is nonetheless notable: Alkan, Chabrier, Debussy, Fauré, Ravel, and Satie; Griffes and MacDowell; Albéniz and Granados; Janáček; and—excepting Rubinstein and Tchaikovsky—all the Russians.

15. Among other performances in which he took part in the 1880s and 1890s were Chopin's piano trio, Mozart's G minor piano quartet (with Joachim, Ludwig Straus, and Piatti), and Schubert's "Trout" quintet.

16. In addition to Russian and possibly Ukrainian (a dialect rather than a remote Slavic tongue), he spoke French and German, including Viennese dialect; to these English and a few words of Italian would later be added. Pachmann did well when he said that he spoke "Universalese."

1. BECOMING DE PACHMANN

1. Several other celebrated musicians, pianists especially, were to come from Odessa, among them Barere, Cherkassy, Gilels, Tina Lerner, Moiseiwitsch, Pouishnov (in 1938, he became the first pianist to appear on television), and Sapellnikov. The year before Pachmann was born, Liszt himself was in Odessa, where he played ten recitals in July and August; on 14 September, in Elisabetgrad (now Kirovohrad), he gave his last recital for his own benefit.

2. Handel's only fugue in C minor is the sixth of the six fugues or voluntarys, opus 3 (London, 1735). It is not, however, a double fugue.

3. Although this fugue was published as the first movement of the E minor suite, it was originally an independent work. The American pianist William Mason studied it with both Dreyschock (who had, in turn, studied it with Tomaschek) and Liszt.

4. Halm (1789–1872) also taught Julius Epstein, J. Fischof, Stephen Heller, and Henselt. As a composer, he was appreciated for his piano études opp. 59, 60, 61, and 62, as well as for his piano transcription of the Grosses fugue from Beethoven's string quartet opus 133 (made at Beethoven's behest).

5. The pupils of Sechter (1788–1867) included Bruckner, Schubert, Thalberg, and Vieuxtemps.

6. Door (1833–1919) was professor at the Conservatory from 1869 until 1901.

7. Many years later, Pachmann went to a student recital at the Royal Academy of Music at which Irene Scharrer played a group of Chopin études. "After the recital," Marian C. McKenna writes, "he rushed backstage, grasped her hand, kissed it and exclaimed: 'I could not play them better myself,' and with a sly glance to either side, he added quietly, 'Certainly I could not play them faster'" (18).

8. Isabelle Vengerova was Dachs's *second* most famous pupil. Her biography, by Joseph Rezits, was published in 1995.

9. Pachmann went to hear Rubinstein whenever and wherever he could and played his music in many of his own concerts. He admonished his student Aldo Mantia to do so as well, especially the studies.

10. Wagner, too, was overwhelmed by Tausig: "I am astonished, alternately, by his highly developed intellect and his wild ways. He will become something extraordinary if he becomes anything at all. As a musician he is enormously gifted, and his furious piano playing makes me tremble."

11. Vera Kologrivoff Rubio taught Jane Stirling, a Scottish woman whose devotion to the dying composer was so complete that she was known after his death as "Chopin's Widow." Kologrivoff's husband, Luigi Rubio, was long thought to have painted the famous portrait of Chopin reproduced in Alfred Cortot's book *In Search of Chopin*. (In 1962, the portrait was proven to have been done by Teofil Kwiatkowski.)

2. BUILDING THE MYTH

1. The concert had been announced in the *Neue Freie Presse* on 14 January 1882.

2. A caricature of Blowitz, titled "'The Times' in Paris," was published in *Vanity Fair* (7 December 1889). He had become famous for reporting on the Congress of Berlin (1878) in unsigned articles for the *Times*, obtaining for that paper, to German chancellor Otto von Bismarck's profound consternation, a copy of the Treaty of Berlin before it was signed.

3. The father of Ford Madox Hueffer (Ford Madox Ford) and translator of the Wagner-Liszt correspondence.

4. Cadenzas for the first movement of this concerto were written by Anton Rubinstein and Liszt's pupil Richard Burmeister, but there is no indication that Pachmann interpolated either into his own performances of the work.

5. Pachmann spelled "Wilhelm" with two *l*'s but then, catching his mistake, drew a line through the second of them.

6. In an interview with A. M. Diehl published in the *Musician* (May 1908), Pachmann described his musical relationship with Edward's wife, Queen Alexandra:

> [The queen] and her daughters are extremely musical and play the piano much more skilfully than the average talented amateur. Professional violinists and 'cellists are often invited to Windsor and Buckingham for chamber music *soirées* at which the queen takes the piano part in an *ensemble* sonata or a trio or quartet. When I play for Her Majesty, she invariably selects the numbers she wishes to hear, and you may be sure that she never omits the names of Bach, Beethoven, Brahms, Schumann, and of course, Chopin.

7. A perception of Chopin as a decadent persisted into the twentieth century. A curious proof of this: In the 1945 film adaptation of *The Portrait of Dorian Gray*, the (anti-) hero plays, almost as his theme (or motto), Chopin's D minor prelude.

8. Variations on the march *Suoni la tromba* from Bellini's *I Puritani* composed by Liszt, Thalberg, Pixis, Herz, Czerny, and Chopin.

9. Liszt was ever mocking of Leipzig and its conservative pretensions. Even his old friend Mendelssohn, onetime director of the Leipzig Conservatory, had discouraged his pupils from studying the music of Chopin.

10. Wilhelm von Lenz: "Beethoven confided to [Holz] that he improvised the Adagio while sitting beside the corpse of a friend in a room hung with black" (81).

11. This *Duo concertant* is listed as opus 87b in the catalog of Moscheles's works; without opus number in Mendelssohn's catalog. The first performance was given in London, by the authors, on 1 May 1833.

12. Mantia, in his turn, taught at the Accademia di Santa Cecilia (Rome). Among *his* pupils were Riccardo Belpassi and Giovanni Velluti.

13. The spelling of Maggie's last name has occasioned much confusion, having been given as Okey, O'Key, and Oakey. On the grave of her sister Carrie—whose burial in 1911 Maggie oversaw—the spelling is Okey, while on her own grave Maggie's maiden name is given as O'Key. Her burial, however, was not overseen by anyone bearing the name; therefore, I have used Okey in this book.

14. Mudgee is 254 kilometers northwest of Sydney. During the 1850s and 1860s, the area became prosperous thanks to both the excellent wool produced by local sheep and the discovery of gold. (Lionel de Pachmann, in his interview with Robert Dumm, said that Maggie's father was a "gold digger"—by which, of course, he meant prospector.) Today, the area is renowned for its wines and honey. The name Mudgee is of Aboriginal origin and means "nest in the hills."

15. Although Australia has exported some notable pianists (Percy Grainger, Ernest Hutcheson, and Eileen Joyce among them), to Maggie goes the distinction of being the first to achieve international fame—a fact for which she is little appreciated.

16. Maggie herself at least verified that she was five years of age when she went to London, seven when she gave her first concert.

17. *Yato* (Monte Carlo, 1913). A second opera, *Sélènis*, was left incomplete.

18. Francesco Libetta: "The concerto is pleasing to read. It is obviously written for a woman's hands: never a passage where the arms are called for (not even a gesture to disturb her graceful pose on the bench), never excessive speed or sonority. It is not written to arouse the enthusiasm of the mob, but it would not cut a poor figure in the concert hall either."

19. Liszt had first asked Clara Schumann to play the concerto. Although the occasion called for the putting aside of musical and personal differences, she refused to have anything to do with it—or him. (Liszt had already dedicated to Clara his Paganini études.)

20. Pachmann deplored the fingerings that Bülow and Klindworth gave in their editions of Chopin. In fact, he himself edited the études 25/6 and 8 (Schott), and consented to the publication, in *Good Housekeeping* magazine (February 1925), of Godowsky's notation of the prelude 28/2 "As Played by Vladimir de Pachmann."

21. Although Pachmann was not the only pianist to write about the preludes, his poetic images do not sully the works the way those of Bülow or Raoul Koczalski (a pupil of Chopin's pupil Mikuli) tend to do. Pachmann did not confine himself to poetic images, however. His responses are always those of a pianist, ever concerned with interpretation, first and last. His call for the eleventh to be played allegro moderato instead of vivace, his idea that the eighteenth is really a cadenza (but for which work?), and his clarification of legato indications in Chopin apropos the twenty-third, are most sensitive to the music. (In the whole article, only one sentence—Pachmann's description of the fourteenth as "all fun from beginning to end"—seems wrong.)

22. The only substantive reference to Pachmann in Walker's *Liszt* is this:

> [Liszt] heard Rubinstein give a piano recital in the auditorium of the Hungária Hotel on February 16th [1884]; and the following month he attended a Philharmonic concert especially to hear Vladimir de Pachmann play Chopin's F minor piano concerto. Pachmann never knew that he was in the audience, since Liszt had hidden himself in a box at the back of the theatre; he had long since stopped making official appearances at the Philharmonic concerts, with which organization he was still in contention. Both Pachmann and Rubinstein paid tribute to Liszt by performing some of his solo pieces, including *Au bord d'une source,* which was in the repertoire of both men. (3:462–63)

Pachmann apparently gave another concert in Budapest on 17 March.

23. Colin Armfield has worked out from the 1884 Rate Book that 78 Hamilton Terrace was owned by the music publisher Eugene Ascherberg and learned from the 1884 Kelly's Directory that the occupant of the house was Alfred Beverly Collard, a "gentleman of means." Since Ascherberg was a friend of Wilhelm Ganz, and Ganz brought Pachmann to England, Pachmann's presence at 78 Hamilton Terrace is easily explained. Collard was possibly connected to the piano manufacturer Collard and Collard.

3. M. AND MME. DE PACHMANN

1. Paderewski later became Pachmann's—and Rosenthal's—bête noire. Most of the Liszt pupils had a low opinion of Paderewski: Giovanni Sgambati called him "Paperewski" (*pasticcio*), while Rosenthal opined, "Yes, he plays well, I suppose, but he's no Paderewski." Pachmann and Paderewski met publicly only once after Kraków, in Chicago.

2. Liszt referred to Sophie Menter as "my only legitimate daughter as a pianist." Claudio Arrau described her in her old age to Joseph Horowitz in *Conversations with Arrau:*

> She lived outside of Munich with fifty cats. She hated human beings, and she hated her daughter. I remember she had a huge garden surrounded by chicken wire, to keep the cats in. Anyway, she was a very impressive lady, still gorgeously beautiful. And still very elegant, with lots of marvelous jewelry. She told us that the jewels were given to her in Russia by royalty—while she was playing, people would rip off their jewels and throw them on the stage, at her feet.

3. Pachmann's edition of seven pieces by Henselt—2/6 (*Si oiseau j'étais*) and 11 (*Dors tu, ma vie*), *Poëme d'Amour* (from opus 3), *Eutschwundenes Glück* (from opus 5), *Toccatina* (opus 25), impromptu no. 4 (opus 37), and *Wiegenlied* (opus 45)—was published by Novello, Ewer and Co. (1888).

4. Robert Hardy Andrews recalled Pachmann tossing rubies and emeralds into the air "to make a rainbow" at a speakeasy in Minneapolis (ca. 1924): "He lost one, and insisted on having the floorboards torn up while we searched for it," Andrews continued. "This brought in what de Pachmann insisted on calling the Cossacks: a couple of Prohibition agents who didn't really want to close the joint, but had to under the circumstances. We found the missing ruby in de Pachmann's shoe, which he had taken off to swat a cockroach" (21).

5. Edward Howell (1846–98) was cellist to Queen Victoria. According to the pianist Adelina de Lara, who at one time lodged with Howell's family, his cello had belonged to Handel.

6. Schubert wrote this work in the key of G-flat major. It was put into G major by Carl Haslinger, in which version it was much played and recorded (e.g., by Horowitz and Sauer) at one time.

7. *Rêverie du lac* was in the repertoire of both Pachmann and Rubinstein.

8. The acoustic of St. James's Hall was not universally admired. Tchaikovsky, for one, thought it worse than the Châtelet's in Paris.

9. From the entry on Richard Gompertz (1859–1921) in Eric Blom, ed., *Grove's Dictionary of Music and Musicians* (5th ed.): "On the foundation of the [Royal College of Music] in London in 1883 he became a teacher of the violin, joining the staff as professor in 1895. . . . In later years he appeared almost exclusively in the valuable concerts given by his own quartet, in which H. Inwards, E. Kreuz, and C. Ould were his companions."

10. E. Carl Abbott, in an abstract presented in 1989 to the History of Medicine section of the Royal College of Physicians and Surgeons in Toronto, suggested that certain aspects of Pachmann's behavior—"he gestured, grimaced and frequently interrupted his playing with chatter and demonstrations"—might be consistent with Tourette syndrome. Dr. Ab-

bott later admitted, however, that the lack of evidence from Pachmann's childhood weakened his case, and he revised his diagnosis to one of obsessive-compulsive disorder with motor and vocal tics.

11. Maggie's repertoire frequented byways unexplored by Pachmann. For instance, he is not known to have ever played a Schubert piano sonata.

12. Queenstown Harbor (now known as Cobh) was on the south coast of Ireland. As the stopping point on the journey from Liverpool to New York, it would have been Pachmann's last chance to abandon ship before reaching open sea.

4. "MY WIFE, MADAME LABORI"

1. *Fantasie,* five preludes, two mazurkas, two waltzes, two polonaises, eight nocturnes, impromptu no. 1, *Berceuse, Tarantella,* one scherzo, three ballades, seven études, and piano sonata opus 35.

2. After Chopin dedicated this work to Friedericke Müller, Liszt gave her the nickname "Mademoiselle opus quarante-six."

3. Saint-Saëns wrote the work in Cadiz in 1889. It is interesting for its forward-looking use of the whole-tone scale and the tritone (*diabolus in musica*).

4. Schubert's Fantasie sonata opus 78, Mendelssohn's *Variations sérieuses,* a Rubinstein barcarolle, Henselt's *Si oiseau j'étais,* Chopin's études 25/6 and 8 and 10/5, and *Andante spianato* and *Grande Polonaise,* her own *Rêverie du lac,* Liszt's *Waldesrauschen,* and Saint-Saëns's *Étude en forme de valse.*

5. Beerbohm was to present the ghost of Chopin in *Zuleika Dobson* (1911), but he is not "B" and this "Fantasy" is not an anticipation of that novel: In 1890, Beerbohm was eighteen and about to go up to Merton College, Oxford.

6. The works on this program were *Old Hundred,* sung by the Oratorio Society; an oration by the Right Reverend Henry C. Potter; the hymn *America,* sung by the Oratorio Society; Beethoven's third *Lenore* overture, conducted by Walter Damrosch; Tchaikovsky's *Marche solennelle,* conducted by the composer; and the Berlioz *Te Deum.*

7. "Asked to refrain from kissing porters at English railway stations," pianist Ivor Newton remembered, "[Pachmann] declared that to tip them instead would be too expensive" (151).

5. COLLEAGUES

1. There is a sequel to this story, told by Heifetz: "At a concert in London, one warm summer night, a famous pianist was listening to Josef Hofmann play the piano. He started to take his handkerchief out of his pocket and mop his forehead—but he noticed that several of us, violinists, were looking at him, with the obvious remark of Godowsky on our lips, and he placed his handkerchief sheepishly back into his pocket and sweated it out!"

2. "Yes, it is beautiful; but I will not choose Chopin because it annoys me so that the public seems invariably to associate me with the music of that master, as though I could not play all masters."

3. According to William Mason, an early admirer of Godowsky's Chopin transcriptions, Anton Rubinstein also experimented with the Chopin études, in order to "exercise and strengthen the fingers." Rubinstein illustrated the nature of his experiments for Mason by playing the right hand of the étude 10/2 with the left hand.

4. A few years later, Heyman was immured in an asylum. (Ironically, Heyman taught Edward MacDowell—who also went insane.)

5. The line, from Milton's *Paradise Lost* (book 4), reads:

> Silence accompanied, for beast and bird,
> They to their grassy couch, these to their nests,
> Were slunk, all but the wakeful nightingale;
> She all night long her amorous descant sung.

6. After Pachmann played Hummel's B minor piano concerto [Carnegie Hall Archives list the A minor piano concerto] with the Symphony Society of New York on 8 and 9 December 1893, a critic wrote that "probably only one pianist alive to-day"—Heyman—"could have played the concerto as well as did Mr. de Pachmann."

7. Defined by E. Cobham Brewer in his 1898 *Dictionary of Phrase and Fable* as "A corruption of *palla-toque*, a cloak with a hood. Called by Piers Plowman a *paltock*. The hood or toque has disappeared, but the word remains the same."

6. THE DEMON

1. Wladyslaw Zelenski (1837–1921), composer, pianist, conductor, and music journalist.

2. Odette was to marry first Dino Ceretti—a marriage annulled in 1926—then, on 10 January 1927, Prince Philippe Marie Alphonse Antoine Ferdinand de Bourbon-Siciles, the son of Alphonse I de Bourbon-Siciles and Marie-Antoinette de Bourbon-Siciles. This marriage ended in divorce. Odette died 19 June 1968, at Le Kremlin-Bicêtre. Her older sister, Denise, married André Franck, with whom she had one child, Lilian. This marriage ended in divorce, whereupon Denise married Count Henri Du Castaing, with whom she had two children, Bruno and Marie Jose. Denise died in 1934.

3. From Dante Gabriel Rossetti's "Lilith," written to accompany his painting *Lady Lilith*.

4. Modjeska's son Ralph had ambitions to become a pianist. In fact, Florence Churchill Casebeer wrote a "Biographical Sonnet" on Helena Modjeska after hearing Ralph play Chopin's "Raindrop" prelude (www.sonnets.org/biographical.htm). He became an engineer whose projects included the Oakland Bay Bridge, the Benjamin Franklin Bridge between Philadelphia and Camden, New Jersey, and the Tacony-Palmyra Bridge in northeast Philadelphia.

5. Pachmann's contribution to the program was a Mozart rondo and Chopin's nocturne 27/2 and first impromptu. The other participants were the Hess String Quartet, playing Brahms and Schumann, and Plunket Greene, singing Bach and Brahms.

6. Here Symons writes of hearing Pachmann again at St. James's Hall, in a recital of "nothing but the best of Chopin":

> There was the Funeral March Sonata, the first Ballade, the Fantasia, the Berceuse, the most beautiful of the Nocturnes (Op. 37, No. 2), an exquisite Valse, there were three Mazurkas, three Preludes, and two Etudes. There were encores, interspersed with conversation, and there was the horrible tour de force of playing two pieces at the same time.

7. "THE FACE OF ONE'S FRIEND"

1. Pachmann, who was superstitious, also created problems for Cesco through his belief in the malevolent power of the number thirteen—even though he had been the thirteenth child born to his parents. On one occasion, he refused to sit down at a restaurant table at which twelve other people, including Cesco, were already seated. To placate him, Pallottelli asked the proprietor of the restaurant to take the fourteenth chair. Whenever the proprietor had to get up to attend to other customers, however, Pachmann would get up, too.

2. A look at the other "attractions" Neumann presented that season gives us a rich sense of the musical life enjoyed by Chicagoans at the turn of the century: Ernestine Schumann-Heink, Max Bendix (violinist), Marcella Sembrich, Emma Calvé and her company, Hugo Heermann Quartet (three concerts, in which the "assisting artists" were, in turn, pianists Ella Dahl Rich, Mrs. Edwin N. Lapham, and Mrs. Bruno Steindel—the last named the wife of the quartet's cellist), Charles W. Clark (baritone), Johanna Gadski (dramatic soprano), New York Artist Quartet (Corinne Rider-Kelsey, soprano, Janet Spencer, contralto, Edward Johnson, tenor, and Gwilym Miles, baritone), Josef Hofmann, Teresa Carreño, Rudolph Ganz, Walter Spry (pianist, assisted by Albert Boroff, bass), Herbert Witherspoon ("the great American basso"), Fritz Kreisler, Lawrence Rea (baritone), Glenn Dillard Gunn (pianist), Walter Damrosch (conducting the New York Symphony Orchestra), Francis Rogers (baritone), David Bispham (baritone), Kneisel Quartet (four concerts, in which Ganz was the assisting artist), Fanny Bloomfield-Zeisler, George Hamlin (tenor), Olga Samaroff, Hofmann and Kreisler (joint appearance), Harold Bauer, Emilio de Gogorza (baritone), and Mischa Elman ("assisted by an orchestra of 60 musicians"). (Mahler was announced as conductor of a program of his own works, but the details of this concert had not been finalized when the publicity booklet was published.)

What a line-up!—and not only qualitatively. The programs were substantial. Schumann-Heink, for instance, sang twenty-three arias and songs, then the "Prison scene" from Meyerbeer's *Le Prophète*. The programs were also more flexible than those one is accustomed to hearing now. Bendix played—in addition to nine solo works—the Mendelssohn concerto and the Vieuxtemps fourth concerto with piano accompaniment; such a tradition has, regrettably, gone out of fashion. (At this epoch, piano concertos, too, were often played with a second piano taking the orchestral part.)

8. THE BLACK HAND

1. Richter, during his final years, played with only a small lamp to illuminate the score.

2. "I have heard only one performance that stands on a par with that of Pachmann's playing of the slow movement from the B minor sonata in the year 1909," one English critic wrote, "and that is Schnabel's playing of the slow movement of Beethoven's 'Hammerklavier' sonata in the year 1933."

3. Liszt, too, once crawled under a piano. On this occasion, Henry Finck writes, Chopin had been asked to play at a soirée in Paris, and was "quite willing to do so," but found that the piano had no pedals; they had been sent away for repairs. "In this dilemma a happy thought occurred to Liszt, who happened to be present. He crawled under the piano, and, while Chopin was playing, worked the mechanism to which the pedals ought to have been attached so cleverly that they were not missed at all! He stooped that his friend might conquer" (28).

4. There was also a Serbian nationalist organization called the Black Hand, to which belonged Gavrilo Princip, who would assassinate the archduke Franz Ferdinand and his wife at Sarajevo.

5. It had been suggested that the author of the Black Hand letter sent to Paderewski was Jewish—the pianist having subsidized the leading anti-Semitic paper in Warsaw (see *The Paderewski Memoirs,* in which Paderewski's attempts to exonerate himself make his actions look more suspect). But Rabbi Tobias Schanfarber of Chicago denied the charge. "An enemy of the Jews in Poland is an enemy of the Jews anywhere," he told a journalist. "[Paderewski] has attacked our co-religionists by furnishing that newspaper with money with which to carry on the fight against Jews. But I say that no violence against Paderewski is contemplated or will be tolerated by the Jews. We will fight the fight along moral lines, with the power of intelligence. I do not believe the letter threatening Paderewski was written by a Jew."

6. It was not. Matthew Arnold's poem "Growing Old" tenders no such consolations.

9. "THE SKY IS CHANGED!"

1. In her 1948 memoirs, *Memory Makes Music,* Margaret Chanler, an American who had studied the piano with Sgambati in Rome, wrote that during the summer of 1898, "while my husband was fighting Spaniards in Cuba, I found myself in Geneva to be near his Aunt Laura, Mrs. Franklin Delano (her husband was the great-uncle of our late president)."

> The good aunt lived in the exalted seclusion of the royal suite at the Hotel Beau Rivage. When the Empress Elisabeth of Austria ["Sissi"] came to Geneva that summer, she had, to the old lady's secret satisfaction, to be lodged in the second best apartment. The poor Empress was murdered while stepping on to the gangplank of an excursion boat, in sight of the hotel. This brought the whole Viennese Court to Geneva for a couple of days. The hotel was crowded to capacity but Aunt Laura lived on undisturbed in her royal suite. (82–83)

2. Today Abbazia is much come down in the world, although on a beautiful warm May afternoon the blue sea and the green mountains behind the town are an enchantment. The Villa Angiolina and its gardens, and to a lesser extent the Kvarner and Imperial hotels, both of which have a down-at-heel aspect, hint at the elegance of former times—and the historical reality of former times. The principal thoroughfare, however, is now a motley of cafés, bars, and ice-cream stands, businesses catering to the young, even though the resident population seems mostly elderly There are no bookstores—nothing to suggest the life of the mind. Nor is there much in the way of chic. There is, however, a bazaar very much like (although smaller than) the Stanley Market in Hong Kong, where innumerable seashells are for sale. Apparently the town also has a reputation for its candles. In the park to the west of the Kvarner, lace makers display their work—antimacassars, tablecloths, handkerchiefs—on the shrubs. In this context, it looks only like laundry that has been put out to dry. On the Lungomare, the seaside promenade, the poor sell their earthly chattel from the pavement. Still, one has no trouble picturing Pachmann walking and sitting here, taking his coffee, reading his newspaper, being a part of Abbazia's life *à l'époque.*

3. The Gaieté Lyrique was located on rue Papin (between Boulevard de Sebastopol and rue St. Martin).

4. Byron, *Childe Harold's Pilgrimage,* canto 3, stanza 92.

5. Cesco sent a copy to Godowsky, who replied with gratitude and affectionate reminiscences of Pachmann. Godowsky went on to write that the war had affected him "to an extent which almost passes human endurance. It has shaken my belief in man's sanity—it has shattered completely my faith in present day civilization and culture" (letter of 10 June 1917).

6. Pachmann, who had been called "the Tetrazzini of the Piano," occasionally gave concerts with the famous Florentine soprano. In fact, they had shared the stage many years before in Blackburn, England. Ivor Newton, her accompanist on that occasion, recalled in *At the Piano* that "Tetrazzini was met at the railway station by Pachmann, who had been provided with a large and very expensive bunch of grapes to present to her. Inevitably, he succeeded in dropping them on to the grimy station platform." After the interval of the much-anticipated concert, Newton relates that Pachmann led Tetrazzini back on to the platform "and, not content with kissing her hand, kissed the entire length of her arm" (151–52).

10. TALKING TO THE MOON

1. Enrico Caruso also wore a red diamond ring on his little finger. Godowsky's daughter Dagmar recalled that when, as a girl, she spent time with the tenor, he would allow her to wear it on her second finger like Lucrezia Borgia.

2. In October 1922, Mussolini led a Fascist march on Rome, the effect of which was to force King Vittorio Emmanuele III to invite him to form a coalition government.

3. Pachmann was never one to encourage the pretensions of the illustrious. Meeting the famously conceited composer Karl Goldmark outside his house in Vienna, for instance, he remarked that it would certainly be decorated with a plaque after Goldmark's death. The delighted composer asked what the plaque would say. "To let," Pachmann replied.

4. In the 1947 film *Night Song,* Eugene Ormandy tells Rubinstein an anecdote about a pianist who could only have been Pachmann.

5. Leginska was described by Muriel Draper in *Music at Midnight:* "Her head, which was large in proportion to the tiny body that supported it, wore a face of furtive dissipations, pools of eyes lying shadowed under shags of hair."

6. Arrau described Pachmann's performance of this work as "quite beautiful—light, and all the passage-work somehow *beseelen* [soulful] also" (Horowitz 158).

EPILOGUE

1. This committee comprised Francis Plante (honorary president), Harold Bauer, Alfred Bruneau, Henri Dallier, Paul Dukas, Philippe Gaubert, Sir Hamilton Harty, D. E. Inghelbrecht, Pierre Monteux, Joaquin Nin, Paul Paray, Gabriel Pierne, Maurice Ravel, Rhene-Baton, Moriz Rosenthal, Albert Roussel, Emil von Sauer, Bruno Walter, Albert Wolf, and Sir Henry Wood.

2. Five pictures he took of Horowitz at Riverdale, New York, in June 1965 are among the papers of Vladimir Horowitz and Wanda Toscanini Horowitz at Yale University.

BIBLIOGRAPHY

Andrews, Robert Hardy. *A Corner of Chicago*. Boston: Little, Brown, 1963.

Annals of the Metropolitan Opera. Boston: G. K. Hall, 1883–1985.

Bache, Constance. *Brother Musicians: Reminiscences of Edward and Walter Bache*. London: Methuen, 1901.

Barbellion, W. N. P. [pseud. of Bruce Frederick Cummings]. *The Journal of a Disappointed Man and a Last Diary*. London: Hogarth Press, 1984.

Bauer, Harold. "Dinner with Pachmann." Manuscript, Library of Congress. New York, 17 June 1924 or 1925.

———. *His Book*. New York: Norton, 1948.

Beckson, Karl, ed. *The Memoirs of Arthur Symons: Life and Art in the 1890s*. University Park: Pennsylvania State University Press, 1977.

Beerbohm, Max. *Zuleika Dobson; or, An Oxford Love Story*. 1911, rpt., New York: Modern Library, 1998.

Blickstein, Edward, and Gregor Benko. Incomplete manuscript of a biography of Vladimir de Pachmann.

Blom, Eric, ed. *Grove's Dictionary of Music and Musicians*. 5th ed. London: Macmillan, 1954.

Bonasegale, Giovanna, Anna Maria Damigella, and Bruno Mantura. *Cambellotti (1876–1960)*. Catalog of an exhibition at the Galleria Comunale d'Arte Moderna e Contemporanea, Rome, 24 September 1999–23 January 2000. Rome: Edizioni De Luca, 1999.

Borge, Victor, and Robert Sherman. *Victor Borge's My Favorite Comedies in Music*. New York: Franklin Watts, 1980.

Brewer, E. Cobham. *A Dictionary of Phrase and Fable*. Philadelphia: Altemus, 1898.

Brower, Harriette. *Modern Masters of the Keyboard*. New York: Frederick A. Stokes, 1926.

Brown, James D., and Stephen S. Stratton. *British Musical Biography: A Dictionary of Musical Artists, Authors, and Composers Born in Britain and Its Colonies*. Birmingham: Chadfield, 1887.

Buffen, F. Forster. *Musical Celebrities*. 2d series. London: Chapman and Hall, 1893.

Capell, Richard. "Pachmann and Chopin: Some Secrets of a Past Master's Technique." *London Daily Telegraph*, 1 September 1934.

Cardus, Neville. *Talking of Music*. London: Collins, 1957.

Casella, Alfred. *Music in My Time*. Trans. and ed. Spencer Norton. Norman: University of Oklahoma Press, 1955.

Chanler, Margaret. *Memory Makes Music*. New York: Stephen-Paul, 1948.

Chasins, Abram. *Speaking of Pianists*. New York: Knopf, 1967.

Chopin, Frédéric. *Complete Works for the Pianoforte*. Book Eight. *Études*. Rev. and fingered by Arthur Friedheim, with a general prefatory note by James Huneker and introductory remarks by Arthur Friedheim. New York: G. Schirmer, 1916.

Colette. *Claudine in Paris.* Trans. from the French by Antonia White. London: Martin Secker and Warburg, 1958.

Cooke, James Francis. *Great Pianists on Piano Playing: Study Talks with Foremost Virtuosos.* Philadelphia: Presser, 1913.

Copeland, George. Manuscript of unpublished autobiography in the possession of David Dubal.

Cortot, Alfred. *In Search of Chopin.* Trans. Cyril and Rena Clarke. New York: Abelard, 1952.

Cowen, [Sir] Frederic H. *My Art and My Friends.* London: Edward Arnold, 1913.

Curtin, William M., ed. *The World and the Parish: Willa Cather's Articles and Reviews, 1893–1902.* Vol. 2. Lincoln: University of Nebraska Press, 1970.

Daudet, Alphonse. *Artists' Wives.* Trans. Laura Ensor. London: J. M. Dent, 1896.

Draper, Muriel. *Music at Midnight.* New York: Harper, 1929.

Downes, Irene, ed. *Olin Downes on Music; A Selection from His Writings during the Half Century 1906–1955.* New York: Simon and Schuster, 1957.

Dubal, David. *The Golden Age of the Piano.* Philips Classics, 1994. [Video.]

Dumm, Robert. Unpublished taped interviews with Lionel de Pachmann. Paris, 16 March 1979.

Elkin, Robert. *Royal Philharmonic: Annals of the Royal Philharmonic Society.* London: Rider, 1946.

———. *The Old Concert Rooms of London.* London: Edward Arnold, 1955.

Elson, Arthur. *Woman's Work in Music: Being an Account of Her Influence on the Art, in Ancient as Well as Modern Times; A Summary of Her Musical Compositions, in the Different Countries of the Civilized World; and an Estimate of Their Rank in Comparison with Those of Men.* Boston: L. C. Page, 1903.

Encyclopædia Britannica; or, Dictionary of Arts, Sciences, and General Literature. Vol. 16. 8th ed. Boston: Little, Brown, 1852–60.

Encyclopédie de la Musique. Paris: Fasquelle, 1961.

Evans, Allan. Interview with Lionel de Pachmann. Paris, September 1979.

———. Interview with Aldo Mantia. Rome, August 1980.

———. Interview with Erica Morini. New York, ca. 1992.

———. http://www.arbiterrecords.com/museum/pachmann.html

Ferrell, Robert H., ed. *Dear Bess: The Letters from Harry to Bess Truman, 1910–1959.* New York: Norton, 1983.

Finck, Henry T. *Chopin and Other Musical Essays.* Freeport, N.Y.: Books for Libraries Press, 1972.

Flesch, Carl. *The Memoirs of Carl Flesch.* Trans. from the German and ed. Hans Keller. London: Rockliff, 1957.

Forster, E. M. *Selected Letters.* Ed. Mary Lago and P. N. Furbank. 2 vols. Vol. 1: 1879–1920. Cambridge, Mass: Belknap Press, 1983.

Friedheim, Arthur. *Life and Liszt: The Recollections of a Concert Pianist.* Ed. Theodore L. Bullock. New York: Taplinger, 1961.

Fuller-Maitland, J. A. *A Door-Keeper of Music.* London: John Murray, 1929.

Fussell, Paul. *The Great War and Modern Memory.* London: Oxford University Press, 1975.

Gaisberg, Fred W. *The Music Goes Round.* New York: Macmillan, 1942.

———. "Notes from My Diary: Vladimir de Pachmann." *Gramophone,* October 1943, 73.

Ganz, Wilhelm. *Memories of a Musician.* London: John Murray, 1913.

Gide, André. *Notes on Chopin.* Trans. from the French by Bernard Frechtman. New York: Philosophical Library, 1949.

Gioia, Dana. *Daily Horoscope: Poems.* St. Paul, Minn.: Graywolf, 1986.

Godowsky, Dagmar. *First Person Plural: The Lives of Dagmar Godowsky.* New York: Viking, 1958.

Goethe, Johann Wolfgang von. *Elective Affinities.* Trans. R. J. Hollingdale. London: Penguin, 1971.

Grimal, Pierre. *Dictionnaire des Biographies: K à Z.* Paris: Presses Universitaires de France, 1958.

Guttry, Irene de, Maria Paola Maino, and Gloria Raimondi. *Duilio Cambellotti: Arredi e decorazioni.* 2d ed. Rome: Editori Laterza, 2000.

Hadden, J. Cuthbert. *Modern Musicians: A Book for Players and Singers.* London and Edinburgh: T. N. Foulis, 1914.

Hambourg, Mark. *From Piano to Forte: A Thousand and One Notes.* London: Cassell, 1931.

———. *The Eighth Octave: Tones and Semi-tones concerning Piano-playing, the Savage Club, and Myself.* London: Williams and Norgate, 1951.

Hamilton, Kenneth. "The Virtuoso Tradition." In *The Cambridge Companion to the Piano,* ed. David Rowland. Cambridge: Cambridge University Press, 1998.

Harasowski, Adam. *The Skein of Legends around Chopin.* 1967; rpt., New York: Da Capo, 1980.

Horowitz, Joseph. *Conversations with Arrau.* New York: Knopf, 1982.

Hughes, Adella Prentiss. *Music Is My Life.* Cleveland: World, 1947.

Huneker, James Gibbons. *Old Fogy: His Musical Opinions and Grotesques.* Philadelphia: Presser, 1913.

———. *Steeplejack.* New York: Scribner, 1920.

Huneker, Josephine, ed. *Letters of James Gibbons Huneker.* New York: Scribner, 1922.

Huysmans, J. K. [Joris-Karl]. *Against the Grain.* New York: Dover, 1969.

Israfel. *Musical Fantasies.* London: Simpkin, Marshall, Hamilton, Kent, 1903.

Jablonski, Edward. *Gershwin.* New York: Doubleday, 1987.

Jameux, Dominique. *Pierre Boulez.* Trans. from the French by Susan Bradshaw. Cambridge, Mass: Harvard University Press, 1990.

Jankélévitch, Vladimir. *Liszt: Rhapsodie et Improvisation.* Paris: Flammarion, 1998.

Jerger, Wilhelm, ed. *The Piano Master Classes of Franz Liszt, 1884–1886: Diary Notes of August Göllerich.* Trans. and ed. Richard Louis Zimdars. Bloomington: Indiana University Press, 1996.

Johnstone, Arthur. *Musical Criticisms:* Manchester: Manchester University Press, 1905.

Kehler, George. *The Piano in Concert.* Metuchen, N.J.: Scarecrow, 1982.

Kolodin, Irving. *The Musical Life.* New York: Knopf, 1958.

Labori, Marguerite Fernand. *Labori, ses notes manuscrites, sa vie.* Éditions Victor Attinger. Paris: Neuchatel, 1947.

Laforgue, Jules. *Berlin: The City and the Court.* Trans. William J. Smith. New York: Turtle Point Press, 1996.

Lambert, Constant. *Music Ho! A Study of Music in Decline.* London: Faber, 1934.

Langford, Samuel. "Vladimir de Pachmann—an Appreciation." *Pianola Journal,* 1998, 73–75.

Lara, Adelina de, in collaboration with Clare H-Abrahall. *Finale.* London: Burke, 1955.

Large, David Clay. *Berlin.* New York: Basic Books, 2000.

Laurence, Anya. *Women of Notes: 1,000 Women Composers Born before 1900.* New York: R. Rosen Press, 1978.

Laurence, Dan H. *Shaw's Music: The Complete Musical Criticism.* 3 vols. London: Max Reinhardt/Bodley Head, 1981.

Lenz, Wilhelm von. *The Great Piano Virtuosos of Our Time from Personal Acquaintance: Liszt, Chopin, Tausig, Henselt.* Trans. from the German by Madeleine R. Baker. New York: Da Capo, 1973.

Loesser, Arthur. *Men, Women, and Pianos: A Social History.* New York: Dover, 1990.

Long, Marguerite. *At the Piano with Debussy.* London: Dent, 1972.

Lyle, Wilson. *A Dictionary of Pianists.* London: Robert Hale, 1985.

MacShane, Frank, ed. *Selected Letters of Raymond Chandler.* New York: Columbia University Press, 1981.

Maisel, Edward M. Charles T. Griffes. *The Life of an American Composer.* New York: Knopf, 1943.

Mason, William. *Memories of a Musical Life.* New York: Century, 1901.

Mayne, Xavier [pseud. of Edward Irenaeus Prime-Stevenson]. *Imre: A Memorandum.* Naples: privately printed, 1906; rpt., New York: Arno Press, 1975.

———. *The Intersexes: A History of Similisexualism as a Problem in Social Life.* Privately printed, 1908.

McKenna, Marian C. *Myra Hess: A Portrait.* London: Hamish Hamilton, 1976.

Mitchell, Mark. *Virtuosi: A Defense and a (Sometimes Erotic) Celebration of Great Pianists.* Bloomington: Indiana University Press, 2000.

Moldenhauer, Hans. *Duo-Pianism.* Chicago: Chicago Musical College Press, 1950.

Nabokov, Vladimir. *Collected Short Stories.* New York: Knopf, 1995.

Nash, Jay Robert. *Bloodletters and Badmen: A Narrative Encyclopedia of American Criminals from the Pilgrims to the Present.* New York: M. Evans, 1973.

Newton, Ivor. *At the Piano.* London: Hamish Hamilton, 1966.

New York Public Library (Music Division). Vladimir de Pachmann clipping file.

Nicholas, Jeremy. *Godowsky: The Pianists' Pianist.* Wark, Hexham, Northumberland: Appian, 1989.

Niecks, Frederick. *Frederick Chopin as a Man and Musician.* 2 vols. New York: Novello, Ewer, 1902.

Pachmann, Lionel de. Unpublished letter to Allan Evans.

Pachmann, Vladimir de. "How to Play Chopin." *Etude,* October 1908, 629. [Also published in *The Strand,* October 1908.]

———. "Originality in Pianoforte Playing." *Etude,* October 1911, 657.

———. "Work, the Secret of Pianistic Success." *Etude,* November 1911, 734.

———. "Should Piano Playing Undergo a Radical Reform?" *Etude,* December 1923, 819–20.

———. Unpublished letter to Harold Bauer. June 1, 1928. Library of Congress.

———. Unpublished letter to T. O. Williams. February 5, 1930.

Paderewski, Ignace Jan, and Mary Lawton. *The Paderewski Memoirs.* New York: Scribner, 1938.

Pallottelli, Duilio. *Voglia di famiglia.* Milan: Rusconi, 1995.

Pallottelli, F[rancesco]. *Vladimir de Pachmann.* Trans. W. G. Cook. Rome, n.d.

Pater, Walter. *The Renaissance.* London: Macmillan, 1922.

Paul, Elliot. *The Last Time I Saw Paris.* New York: Random House, 1942.

Piggott, Patrick. *Rachmaninov.* [The Great Composers.] London: Faber and Faber, 1978.

Praz, Mario. *La carne, la morte e il diavolo nella letteratura romantica.* Florence: Sansoni, 1966.

Prime-Stevenson, Edward. *Long-Haired Iopas: Old Chapters from Twenty-five Years of Music-Criticism.* Florence: Privately printed by the press of "The Italian Mail," 1928.

Refardt. *Historisches-biographisches Musikerlexikon der Schweiz.* 1928.

Rezits, Joseph. *Beloved Tyranna: The Legend and Legacy of Isabelle Vengerova.* Bloomington, Ind.: David Daniel, 1995.

Riemanns Musik Lexikon. Berlin: Max Hesses, 1929.

Roell, Craig H. *The Piano in America, 1890–1940.* Chapel Hill: University of North Carolina Press, 1989.

Roman, Zoltan. *Gustav Mahler's American Years, 1907–1911: A Documentary History.* Stuyvesant, N.Y.: Pendragon, 1989.

Rubinstein, Arthur. *My Many Years.* New York: Knopf, 1980.

Said, Edward W. *Musical Elaborations.* London: Vintage, 1992.

Saleski, Gdal. *Famous Musicians of a Wandering Race.* New York: Bloch, 1927.

———. *Famous Musicians of Jewish Origin.* New York: Bloch, 1949.

Schnabel, Artur. *My Life and Music.* New York: Dover; Gerrards Cross, England: Smythe, 1988.

Schonberg, Harold C. *The Great Pianists from Mozart to the Present.* New York: Simon and Schuster, 1963.

Schumann, Robert. *Schumann on Music: A Selection from the Writings.* Trans. and ed. Henry Pleasants. New York: Dover, 1988.

Sitwell, Sacheverell. *Liszt.* London: Faber and Faber, 1934.

Škvorecký, Josef. *Dvořák in Love: A Light-hearted Dream.* Trans. from the Czech by Paul Wilson. New York: Norton, 1986.

Sorabji, Kaikhosru Shapurji. *Around Music.* London: Unicorn Press, 1932.

———. *Mi Contra Fa.* London: Porcupine, 1947.

———. *Collected Published Writings.* Bath, England: Sorabji Archive, 1992.

Spurling, Hilary. *La Grande Thérèse.* New York: HarperCollins, 2000.

Stargardt-Woolf, Edith. *Wegbereiter grosser Musiker.* Berlin: E. Bote and G. Bock, 1954. [Quoted passages trans. from the German by Michael Hofmann (unpublished).]

[Steinway and Sons.] *Portraits of Musical Celebrities: A Book of Notable Testimonials.* New York: William Bradford Press, 1926.

Stern, Susan. *Women Composers: A Handbook.* Metuchen, N.J.: Scarecrow, 1978.

Steuermann, Edward. *The Not Quite Innocent Bystander.* Ed. Clara Steuermann, David Porter, and Gunther Schuller. Trans. Richard Cantwell and Charles Messner. Lincoln: University of Nebraska Press, 1989.

Steiger, Franz. *Opernlexikon. Teil 2: Komponisten.* Tutzing: Verlegt bei Hans Schneider, 1977.

Stones of the Months: Giving the Legend, Lore, and Virtues of the Correct Birthday Stones for Each Month of the Year. London, n.d.

Swafford, Jan. *Johannes Brahms: A Biography.* New York: Knopf, 1998.

Sweet, Matthew. *Inventing the Victorians.* London: Faber and Faber, 2001.

Symons, Arthur. *Plays, Acting, and Music.* London: Duckworth, 1903.

———. *Fool of the World.* London: Heinemann, 1906.

———. *Spiritual Adventures.* 2d ed. London: Constable, 1908.

————. *Plays, Acting, and Music: A Book of Theory.* London: Constable, 1909.

————. *Collected Works,* vol. 2: *Poems.* London: Martin Secker, 1924.

Tchaikovsky, Pyotr Ilich. *The Diaries of Tchaikovsky.* Trans. from the Russian, with notes, by Wladimir Lakond. New York: Norton, 1945.

————. *Letters to His Family.* Trans. from the Russian by Galina von Meck. New York: Stein and Day, 1981.

Teleny. London: Gay Men's Press, 1986.

Toklas, Alice B. *The Alice B. Toklas Cookbook.* New York: Harper, 1954.

Tomaszewski, Mieczyslaw. *Fryderyk Chopin: A Diary in Images.* Trans. Rosemary Hunt. Arkady: Polskie Wydawnictwo Muzyczne, 1990.

Universal-Handbuch der Musikliteratur. Franz Padírek. Vienna, 1904–10.

Valperga, [Conte] Enrico di San Martino. *Regia Accademia di Santa Cecilia: I Concerto dal 1895 al 1933. Parte I. Ricordi del Presidente.* 1933.

Verne, Mathilde. *Chords of Remembrance.* London: Hutchinson, 1936.

Walker, Alan. *Franz Liszt: Volume Three, The Final Years, 1861–1886.* New York: Knopf, 1996.

Weir, Albert E., ed. *Macmillan Encyclopedia of Music and Musicians.* New York: Macmillan, 1938.

Wilde, Oscar. *Complete Works.* New York: Perennial Library, 1989.

Woollcott, Alexander. *Enchanted Aisles.* 2d ed. New York: Putnam, 1924.

INDEX

Page numbers in italics refer to illustrations.

MARK MITCHELL is the author of *Virtuosi: A Defense and a (Sometimes Erotic) Celebration of Great Pianists* (Indiana University Press). With David Leavitt, he edited E. M. Forster's *Selected Stories* for Penguin Twentieth-Century Classics as well as two anthologies, and wrote *Italian Pleasures* and *In Maremma: Life and a House in Southern Tuscany.* He now divides his time between Gainesville, Florida, and Vienna.